FORE!

F O R E !

THE BEST OF WODEHOUSE ON GOLF

P. G. Wodehouse

Edited and with a Preface by
D. R. Bensen

Ticknor & Fields
New York

Preface copyright © 1983 by D. R. Bensen

"The Coming of Gowf," "The Salvation of George Mackintosh," "The
Heel of Achilles," "A Mixed Threesome," and "The Long Hole" were
originally collected in *Golf Without Tears*, copyright 1919, 1920, 1921,
1922, and 1924 by P. G. Wodehouse; renewed 1947, 1948,
1949, 1950, and 1952.

"High Stakes," "Chester Forgets Himself," "The Awakening of Rollo
Podmarsh," "Rodney Fails to Qualify," and "The Heart of a Goof" were
originally collected in *Divots*, copyright 1923, 1924, 1925, 1926, and 1927
by P. G. Wodehouse; renewed 1951, 1952, 1953, 1954, and 1955.

"Tangled Hearts" and "Excelsior" were originally collected in *Nothing
Serious*, copyright 1939, 1947, 1948, 1949, 1950, and 1951 by P. G.
Wodehouse; renewed 1967.

Library of Congress Cataloging in Publication Data

Wodehouse, P. G. (Pelham Grenville), 1881–1975.
Fore! : the best of Wodehouse on golf.

Contents: The coming of gowf — The salvation of George
Mackintosh — High stakes — [etc.]
1. Golf — Fiction. I. Bensen, D. R. (Donald R.),
1927–   . II. Title.
PR6045.O53A6 1983   823'.912   83–5097
ISBN 0–89919–212–2
ISBN 0–89919–358–7 (pbk.)

Printed in the United States of America

S 10 9 8 7 6 5 4 3 2 1

This collection of slices (and hooks) of life
is affectionately dedicated to
Jimmy Heineman
Wodehouseian extraordinary
and golfer (emeritus) ordinary
in observance of whose performance on the links
the term "tee and sympathy"
was coined

Contents

Preface

O

P. G. Wodehouse was perhaps the most amiable of modern writers, his work reflecting little of the conflict, stress and tragic sense so present in that of such contemporaries as Thomas Hardy, Leo Tolstoy, Ernest Hemingway, William Faulkner, Norman Mailer and Robert Ludlum. (Any man who chooses to have a writing career beginning in 1901 and going on to 1975 has to expect to accumulate a mixed bag of contemporaries.) One topic only aroused the Wodehouse passions and stirred him to depict scenes of tormented emotions and violent action: golf.

He said of his first collection of golf stories, *Golf without Tears*, "This book marks an epoch of my literary life. It is written in blood." Bitten by the golf bug in what he then saw as middle age — but, as it took him nearly sixty more years to play out the course, he must at that point be considered actually to have been teeing up on the seventh hole — he was instantly and permanently infected, producing in the next half-century-plus some three dozen stories dealing with his obsession.

Obsession! There, perhaps, is the key to Wodehouse's work which so many have vainly sought. In fact, nobody may have been looking for it, but that need not deter us. Take Bertie Wooster, that Mayfair mayfly. The casual reader will see Bertram Wilberforce Wooster as the most idle of *flâneurs*, yet any constancy of attention will reveal his passion for being dressed in a way which combines the aspirations of the avant-garde with the surety of accepted tradition. That is living on the knife's edge, and no mistake about it. The moral rigor Bertie brings to his decisions about socks, or cummerbunds *v.* waistcoats would have done credit to Camus or Heidegger.

And take Clarence, Ninth Earl of Emsworth. Jeeves characterized Bertie as "mentally negligible," and one wonders what he would have made of Lord Emsworth, beside whom Wooster looms as a mental giant. Yet this walking vacuum is capable of action, interest, and something approaching thought, when in the grip of an obsession. At an early period it was scarabs; for a brief time later, pumpkins; but in his riper years it found full flower in his devotion to the growth and nurture of his black Berkshire sow, Empress of Blandings. Many, perhaps most, of his family and acquaintances find Emsworth irritating *à l'outrance,* but the reader will see him as ennobled by his ruling passion for the prodigious porker.

Stanley Ukridge and his enduring quest for his personal grail, the foolproof con game; Bingo Little's undying faith in a sure thing at the races; Gussie Fink-Nottle's preoccupation with newts — all show Wodehouse's keen appreciation of the story value of the driving force of obsession.

Nowhere is this seen more strongly than in the golf stories. Mortimer Sturgis, deeply in love though he was, abandoned romance to remain true to the links. When Rollo Bingham and Otis Jukes found themselves rivals for the same girl, it was to the most peculiar golf match ever played that they resorted to settle the matter. Bradbury Fisher, gripped by his mania for the memorabilia of the sport, risked the direst fate conceivable for a prize collectible. Rather than lose to a customer, Horace Bewstridge threw away his business future. Even that unplayable-through foursome, the Wrecking Crew, though certifiably subhuman, is (partly) redeemed by the fervor of its members for golf.

And, of course, the Oldest Member, recipient of a thousand confidences (and dispenser of all of them to any potential auditor not very fast on his feet), is the Spirit of Golf itself, though he is never shown with a club in his hands.* Like the Ancient Mariner, to whom he is often fondly compared by those compelled to hear his stories, the O.M. is so imbued with his obsession that its actual practice is no longer required. He is forever at the nineteenth hole, in no danger of being caught in a rough lie.

Choosing the stories for this volume has been a pleasurable agony. The professional obligation to reread Wodehouse cannot but be a pleasure; the need to pick a mere handful of jewels from the treasure-chest cannot but be painful. Where, knowledgeable readers will ask, is Vladimir Brusiloff, the Bolshevist golfer? Why are the sagas of Rodney Spelvin (torn between golf and that baser side of his nature which calls him to poetry) and of Agnes Flack and Sidney McMurdo (perpetually engaged and disengaged) incomplete? Have I really left Wallace Chesney and his magic plus-fours in the tee-box? these readers will mournfully demand. On this matter I must be firm. If you are doing a "Best of . . ." collection, something has got to go (unless you follow the example of a writer I know, who shoehorned forty-five stories into his own best-of book, which I think amounted to about ninety-eight per cent of his production to date), and the decisions of the handicapping committee must prevail.

Wodehouse once wrote, "Whenever you see me with a furrowed brow you can be sure that what is on my mind is the thought that if only I had taken up golf earlier and devoted my whole time to it instead of fooling about writing stories and things, I might have got my handicap down to under eighteen." It is our good fortune that he took that

*Except in "The Salvation of George Mackintosh," but it is clear from the circumstances that this is not a serious match but what might be termed a mercy round.

wrong turning; no scratch man could have brought to these stories the poignant insight that pervades them, as their author put it, "like the scent of muddy shoes in a locker-room."

D. R. Bensen
Croton-on-Hudson
August 1983

The Coming of Gowf

O

Prologue

After we had sent in our card and waited for a few hours in the marbled ante-room, a bell rang and the major-domo, parting the priceless curtains, ushered us in to where the editor sat writing at his desk. We advanced on all fours, knocking our head reverently on the Aubusson carpet.

"Well?" he said at length, laying down his jewelled pen.

"We just looked in," we said, humbly, "to ask if it would be all right if we sent you an historical story."

"The public does not want historical stories," he said, frowning coldly.

"Ah, but the public hasn't seen one of ours!" we replied.

The editor placed a cigarette in a holder presented to him by a reigning monarch, and lit it with a match from a golden box, the gift of the millionaire president of the Amalgamated League of Working Plumbers.

"What this magazine requires," he said, "is red-blooded, one-hundred-per-cent dynamic stuff, palpitating with warm human interest and containing a strong, poignant love-motive."

"That," we replied, "is us all over, Mabel."

"What I need at the moment, however, is a golf story."

"By a singular coincidence, ours is a golf story."

"Ha! say you so?" said the editor, a flicker of interest passing over his finely-chiselled features. "Then you may let me see it."

He kicked us in the face, and we withdrew.

The Story

On the broad terrace outside his palace, overlooking the fair expanse of the Royal gardens, King Merolchazzar of Oom stood leaning on the low parapet, his chin in his hand and a frown on his noble face. The day was fine, and a light breeze bore up to him from the garden below a fragrant scent of flowers. But, for all the pleasure it seemed to give him, it might have been bone-fertilizer.

The fact is, King Merolchazzar was in love, and his suit was not prospering. Enough to upset any man.

Royal love affairs in those days were conducted on the correspondence system. A monarch, hearing good reports of a neighbouring princess, would despatch messengers with gifts to her Court, beseeching an interview. The Princess would name a date, and a formal meeting would take place; after which everything usually buzzed along pretty smoothly. But in the case of King Merolchazzar's courtship of the Princess of the Outer Isles there had been a regrettable hitch. She had acknowledged the gifts, saying that they were just what she had wanted and how had he guessed, and had added that, as regarded a meeting, she would let him know later. Since that day no word had come from her, and a gloomy spirit prevailed in the capital. At the Courtiers' Club, the meeting-place of the aristocracy of Oom, five to one in *pazazas* was freely offered against Merolchazzar's chances, but found no takers; while in the taverns of the common people, where less conservative odds were always to be had, you could get a snappy hundred to eight. "For in good sooth," writes a chronicler of the time on a half-brick and a couple of paving-stones which have survived to this day, "it did indeed begin to appear as though our beloved monarch, the son of the sun and the nephew of the moon, had been handed the bitter fruit of the citron."

The quaint old idiom is almost untranslatable, but one sees what he means.

As the King stood sombrely surveying the garden, his attention was attracted by a small, bearded man with bushy eyebrows and a face like a walnut, who stood not far away on a gravelled path flanked by rose bushes. For some minutes he eyed this man in silence, then he called to the Grand Vizier, who was standing in the little group of courtiers and officials at the other end of the terrace. The bearded man, apparently unconscious of the Royal scrutiny, had placed a rounded stone on the gravel, and was standing beside it making curious passes over it with his hoe. It was this singular behaviour that had attracted the King's attention. Superficially it seemed silly, and yet Merolchazzar had a curious feeling that there was a deep, even a holy, meaning behind the action.

"Who," he inquired, "is that?"

"He is one of your Majesty's gardeners," replied the Vizier.

"I don't remember seeing him before. Who is he?"

The Vizier was a kind-hearted man, and he hesitated for a moment.

"It seems a hard thing to say of anyone, your Majesty," he replied, "but he is a Scotsman. One of your Majesty's invincible admirals recently made a raid on the inhospitable coast of that country at a spot known to the natives as S'nandrews and brought away this man."

"What does he think he's doing?" asked the King, as the bearded one slowly raised the hoe above his right shoulder, slightly bending the left knee as he did so.

"It is some species of savage religious ceremony, your Majesty. According to the admiral, the dunes by the seashore where he landed were covered with a multitude of men behaving just as this man is doing. They had sticks in their hands, and they struck with these at small round objects. And every now and again — "

"Fo-o-ore!" called a gruff voice from below.

"And every now and again," went on the Vizier, "they would utter the strange melancholy cry which you have just heard. It is a species of chant."

The Vizier broke off. The hoe had descended on the stone, and the stone, rising in a graceful arc, had sailed through the air and fallen within a foot of where the King stood.

"Hi!" exclaimed the Vizier.

The man looked up.

"You mustn't do that! You nearly hit his serene graciousness the King!"

"Mphm!" said the bearded man, nonchalantly, and began to wave his hoe mystically over another stone.

Into the King's careworn face there had crept a look of interest, almost of excitement.

"What god does he hope to propitiate by these rites?" he asked.

"The deity, I learn from your Majesty's admiral, is called Gowf."

"Gowf? Gowf?" King Merolchazzar ran over in his mind the muster-roll of the gods of Oom. There were sixty-seven of them, but Gowf was not of their number. "It is a strange religion," he murmured. "A strange religion, indeed. But, by Belus, distinctly attractive. I have an idea that Oom could do with a religion like that. It has a zip to it. A sort of fascination, if you know what I mean. It looks to me extraordinarily like what the Court physician ordered. I will talk to this fellow and learn more of these holy ceremonies."

And, followed by the Vizier, the King made his way into the garden. The Vizier was now in a state of some apprehension. He was exercised in his mind as to the effect which the embracing of a new religion by the King might have on the formidable Church party. It would be certain to cause displeasure among the priesthood; and in those days it was a ticklish business to offend the priesthood, even for a monarch. And, if Merolchazzar had a fault, it was a tendency to be a little tactless in his dealings with that powerful body. Only a few mornings back the High Priest of Hec had taken the Vizier aside to complain about the quality of the meat which the King had been using lately for his sacrifices. He might be a child in worldly matters, said the High Priest, but if the King supposed that he did not know the difference between home-grown domestic and frozen imported foreign, it was time his Majesty was disabused of the idea. If, on top of this little unpleasantness, King Merolchazzar were to become an adherent of this new Gowf, the Vizier did not know what might not happen.

The King stood beside the bearded foreigner, watching him closely. The second stone soared neatly on to the terrace. Merolchazzar uttered an excited cry. His eyes were glowing, and he breathed quickly.

"It doesn't look difficult," he muttered.

"Hoots!" said the bearded man.

"I believe I could do it," went on the King, feverishly. "By the eight green gods of the mountain, I believe I could! By the holy fire that burns night and day before the altar of Belus, I'm *sure* I could! By Hec, I'm going to do it now! Gimme that hoe!"

"Toots!" said the bearded man.

It seemed to the King that the fellow spoke derisively, and his blood boiled angrily. He seized the hoe and raised it above his shoulder, bracing himself solidly on widely-parted feet. His pose was an exact reproduction of the one in which the Court sculptor had depicted him when working on the life-size statue ("Our Athletic King") which stood in the principal square of the city; but it did not impress the stranger. He uttered a discordant laugh.

"Ye puir gonuph!" he cried, "whit kin' o' a staunce is that?"
The King was hurt. Hitherto the attitude had been generally admired.

"It's the way I always stand when killing lions," he said.
" 'In killing lions,' " he added, quoting from the well-known treatise of Nimrod, the recognised text-book on the sport, " 'the weight at the top of the swing should be evenly balanced on both feet.' "

"Ah, weel, ye're no' killing lions the noo. Ye're gowfing."

A sudden humility descended upon the King. He felt, as so many men were to feel in similar circumstances in ages to come, as though he were a child looking eagerly for guidance to an all-wise master — a child, moreover, handicapped by water on the brain, feet three sizes too large for him, and hands consisting mainly of thumbs.

"O thou of noble ancestors and agreeable disposition!" he said, humbly. "Teach me the true way."

"Use the interlocking grip and keep the staunce a wee bit open and slow back, and dinna press or sway the heid and keep yer e'e on the ba'."

"My which on the what?" said the King, bewildered.

"I fancy, your Majesty," hazarded the Vizier, "that he is respectfully suggesting that your serene graciousness should deign to keep your eye on the ball."

"Oh, ah!" said the King.

The first golf lesson ever seen in the kingdom of Oom had begun.

Up on the terrace, meanwhile, in the little group of courtiers and officials, a whispered consultation was in progress. Officially, the King's unfortunate love affair was supposed to be a strict secret. But you know how it is. These things get about. The Grand Vizier tells the Lord High Chamberlain; the Lord High Chamberlain whispers it in confidence to the Supreme Hereditary Custodian of the Royal Pet Dog; the Supreme

The Coming of Gowf

Hereditary Custodian hands it on to the Exalted Overseer of the King's Wardrobe on the understanding that it is to go no farther; and, before you know where you are, the varlets and scurvy knaves are gossiping about it in the kitchens, and the Society journalists have started to carve it out on bricks for the next issue of *Palace Prattlings*.

"The long and short of it is," said the Exalted Overseer of the King's Wardrobe, "we must cheer him up."

There was a murmur of approval. In those days of easy executions it was no light matter that a monarch should be a prey to gloom.

"But how?" queried the Lord High Chamberlain.

"I know," said the Supreme Hereditary Custodian of the Royal Pet Dog. "Try him with the minstrels."

"Here! Why us!" protested the leader of the minstrels.

"Don't be silly!" said the Lord High Chamberlain. "It's for your good just as much as ours. He was asking only last night why he never got any music nowadays. He told me to find out whether you supposed he paid you simply to eat and sleep, because if so he knew what to do about it."

"Oh, in that case!" The leader of the minstrels started nervously. Collecting his assistants and tip-toeing down the garden, he took up his stand a few feet in Merolchazzar's rear, just as that much-enduring monarch, after twenty-five futile attempts, was once more addressing his stone.

Lyric writers in those days had not reached the supreme pitch of excellence which has been produced by modern musical comedy. The art was in its infancy then, and the best the minstrels could do was this — and they did it just as Merolchazzar, raising the hoe with painful care, reached the top of his swing and started down:

> "Oh, tune the string and let us sing
> Our godlike, great, and glorious King!
> He's a bear! He's a bear! He's a bear!"

There were sixteen more verses, touching on their ruler's prowess in the realms of sport and war, but they were not destined to be sung on that circuit. King Merolchazzar jumped like a stung bullock, lifted his head, and missed the globe for the twenty-sixth time. He spun round on the minstrels, who were working pluckily through their song of praise:

> "Oh, may his triumphs never cease!
> He has the strength of ten!
> First in war, first in peace,
> First in the hearts of his countrymen."

"Get out!" roared the King.

"Your Majesty?" quavered the leader of the minstrels.

"Make a noise like an egg and beat it!" (Again one finds the chronicler's idiom impossible to reproduce in modern speech, and must be content with a literal translation.) "By the bones of my ancestors, it's a little hard! By the beard of the sacred goat, it's tough! What in the name of Belus and Hec do you mean, you yowling misfits, by starting that sort of stuff when a man's swinging? I was just shaping to hit it right that time when you butted in, you — "

The minstrels melted away. The bearded man patted the fermenting monarch paternally on the shoulder.

"Ma mannie," he said, "ye may no' be a gowfer yet, but hoots! ye're learning the language fine!"

King Merolchazzar's fury died away. He simpered modestly at these words of commendation, the first his bearded preceptor had uttered. With exemplary patience he turned to address the stone for the twenty-seventh time.

That night it was all over the city that the King had gone crazy over a new religion, and the orthodox shook their heads.

*

The Coming of Gowf

We of the present day, living in the midst of a million marvels of a complex civilisation, have learned to adjust ourselves to conditions and to take for granted phenomena which in an earlier and less advanced age would have caused the profoundest excitement and even alarm. We accept without comment the telephone, the automobile, and the wireless telegraph, and we are unmoved by the spectacle of our fellow human beings in the grip of the first stages of golf fever. Far otherwise was it with the courtiers and officials about the Palace of Oom. The obsession of the King was the sole topic of conversation.

Every day now, starting forth at dawn and returning only with the falling of darkness, Merolchazzar was out on the Linx, as the outdoor temple of the new god was called. In a luxurious house adjoining this expanse the bearded Scotsman had been installed, and there he could be found at almost any hour of the day fashioning out of holy wood the weird implements indispensable to the new religion. As a recognition of his services, the King had bestowed upon him a large pension, innumerable *kaddiz* or slaves, and the title of Promoter of the King's Happiness, which for the sake of convenience was generally shortened to The Pro.

At present, Oom being a conservative country, the worship of the new god had not attracted the public in great numbers. In fact, except for the Grand Vizier, who, always a faithful follower of his sovereign's fortunes, had taken to Gowf from the start, the courtiers held aloof to a man. But the Vizier had thrown himself into the new worship with such vigour and earnestness that it was not long before he won from the King the title of Supreme Splendiferous Maintainer of the Twenty-Four Handicap Except on Windy Days when It Goes Up to Thirty — a title which in ordinary conversation was usually abbreviated to The Dub.

All these new titles, it should be said, were, so far as the

courtiers were concerned, a fruitful source of discontent.
There were black looks and mutinous whispers. The laws of
precedence were being disturbed, and the courtiers did not
like it. It jars a man who for years has had his social position
all cut and dried — a man, to take an instance at random,
who, as Second Deputy Shiner of the Royal Hunting Boots,
knows that his place is just below the Keeper of the Eel-
Hounds and just above the Second Tenor of the Corps of
Minstrels — it jars him, we say, to find suddenly that he has
got to go down a step into favour of the Hereditary Bearer
of the King's Baffy.

But it was from the priesthood that the real, serious opposition was to be expected. And the priests of the sixty-seven
gods of Oom were up in arms. As the white-bearded High
Priest of Hec, who, by virtue of his office was generally regarded as leader of the guild, remarked in a glowing speech
at an extraordinary meeting of the Priests' Equity Associa-
tion, he had always set his face against the principle of the
Closed Shop hitherto, but there were moments when every
thinking man had to admit that enough was sufficient, and it
was his opinion that such a moment had now arrived. The
cheers which greeted the words showed how correctly he
had voiced popular sentiment.

Of all those who had listened to the High Priest's speech,
none had listened more intently than the King's half-brother,
Ascobaruch. A sinister, disappointed man, this Ascobaruch,
with mean eyes and a crafty smile. All his life he had been
consumed with ambition, and until now it had looked as
though he must go to his grave with this ambition unfulfilled.
All his life he had wanted to be King of Oom, and now he
began to see daylight. He was sufficiently versed in Court
intrigues to be aware that the priests were the party that
really counted, the source from which all successful revolu-

tions sprang. And of all the priests the one that mattered most was the venerable High Priest of Hec.

It was to this prelate, therefore, that Ascobaruch made his way at the close of the proceedings. The meeting had dispersed after passing a unanimous vote of censure on King Merolchazzar, and the High Priest was refreshing himself in the vestry — for the meeting had taken place in the Temple of Hec — with a small milk and honey.

"Some speech!" began Ascobaruch in his unpleasant, crafty way. None knew better than he the art of appealing to human vanity.

The High Priest was plainly gratified.

"Oh, I don't know," he said, modestly.

"Yessir!" said Ascobaruch. "Considerable oration! What I can never understand is how you think up all these things to say. I couldn't do it if you paid me. The other night I had to propose the Visitors at the Old Alumni dinner of Oom University, and my mind seemed to go all blank. But you just stand up and the words come fluttering out of you like bees out of a barn. I simply cannot understand it. The thing gets past me."

"Oh, it's just a knack."

"A divine gift, I should call it."

"Perhaps you're right," said the High Priest, finishing his milk and honey. He was wondering why he had never realised before what a capital fellow Ascobaruch was.

"Of course," went on Ascobaruch, "you had an excellent subject. I mean to say, inspiring and all that. Why, by Hec, even I — though, of course, I couldn't have approached your level — even I could have done something with a subject like that. I mean, going off and worshipping a new god no one has ever heard of. I tell you, my blood fairly boiled. Nobody has a greater respect and esteem for Merolchazzar than I have, but I mean to say, what! Not right, I mean, going off worshipping gods no one has ever heard of! I'm a peaceable man, and I've made it a rule never to mix in politics, but if you happened to say to me as we were sitting here, just as one reasonable man to another — if you happened to say, 'Ascobaruch, I think it's time that definite steps were taken,' I should reply frankly, 'My dear old High Priest, I absolutely agree with you, and I'm with you all the way.' You might even go so far as to suggest that the only way out of the muddle was to assassinate Merolchazzar and start with a clean slate."

The High Priest stroked his beard thoughtfully.

"I am bound to say I never thought of going quite so far as that."

"Merely a suggestion, of course," said Ascobaruch. "Take it or leave it. I shan't be offended. If you know a superior excavation, go to it. But as a sensible man — and I've always maintained that you are the most sensible man in the country — you must see that it would be a solution. Merolchazzar has been a pretty good king, of course. No one denies that. A fair general, no doubt, and a plus-man at lion-hunting. But, after all — look at it fairly — is life all battles and lion-hunting? Isn't there a deeper side? Wouldn't it be better for the country to have some good orthodox fellow who has worshipped Hec all his life, and could be relied on to maintain the old beliefs — wouldn't the fact that a man like that was on the throne be likely to lead to more general prosperity? There are dozens of men of that kind simply waiting to be asked. Let us say, purely for purposes of argument, that you approached *me*. I should reply, 'Unworthy though I know myself to be of such an honour, I can tell you this. If you put me on the throne, you can bet your bottom *pazaza* that there's one thing that won't suffer, and that is the worship of Hec!' That's the way I feel about it."

The High Priest pondered.

"O thou of unshuffled features but amiable disposition!" he said, "thy discourse soundeth good to me. Could it be done?"

"Could it!" Ascobaruch uttered a hideous laugh. "Could it! Arouse me in the night-watches and ask me! Question me on the matter, having stopped me for that purpose on the public highway! What I would suggest — I'm not dictating, mind you; merely trying to help you out — what I would suggest is that you took that long, sharp knife of yours, the one you use for the sacrifices, and toddled out to the Linx — you're sure to find the King there; and just when he's raising that sacrilegious stick of his over his shoulder — "

"O man of infinite wisdom," cried the High Priest, warmly, "verily hast thou spoken a fullness of the mouth!"

"Is it a wager?" said Ascobaruch.

"It is a wager!" said the High Priest.

"That's that, then," said Ascobaruch. "Now, I don't want to be mixed up in any unpleasantness, so what I think I'll do while what you might call the preliminaries are being arranged is to go and take a little trip abroad somewhere. The Middle Lakes are pleasant at this time of year. When I come back, it's possible that all the formalities will have been completed, yes?"

"Rely on me, by Hec!" said the High Priest grimly, as he fingered his weapon.

The High Priest was as good as his word. Early on the morrow he made his way to the Linx, and found the King holing-out on the second green. Merolchazzar was in high good humour.

"Greetings, O venerable one!" he cried, jovially. "Hadst thou come a moment sooner, thou wouldst have seen me lay my ball dead — aye, dead as mutton, with the sweetest little half-mashie-niblick chip-shot ever seen outside the sacred domain of S'nandrew, on whom" — he bared his head reverently — "be peace! In one under bogey did I do the hole — yea, and that despite the fact that, slicing my drive, I became ensnared in yonder undergrowth."

FORE!

The High Priest had not the advantage of understanding one word of what the King was talking about, but he gathered with satisfaction that Merolchazzar was pleased and wholly without suspicion. He clasped an unseen hand more firmly about the handle of his knife, and accompanied the monarch to the next altar. Merolchazzar stooped, and placed a small round white object on a little mound of sand. In spite of his austere views, the High Priest, always a keen student of ritual, became interested.

"Why does your Majesty do that?"

"I tee it up that it may fly the fairer. If I did not, then would it be apt to run along the ground like a beetle instead of soaring like a bird, and mayhap, for thou seest how rough and tangled is the grass before us, I should have to use a niblick for my second."

The High Priest groped for his meaning.

"It is a ceremony to propitiate the god and bring good luck?"

"You might call it that."

The High Priest shook his head.

"I may be old-fashioned," he said, "but I should have thought that, to propitiate a god, it would have been better to have sacrificed one of these *kaddiz* on his altar."

"I confess," replied the King, thoughtfully, "that I have often felt that it would be a relief to one's feelings to sacrifice one or two *kaddiz*, but The Pro for some reason or other has set his face against it." He swung at the ball, and sent it forcefully down the fairway. "By Abe, the son of Mitchell," he cried, shading his eyes, "a bird of a drive! How truly is it written in the book of the prophet Vadun, 'The left hand applieth the force, the right doth but guide. Grip not, therefore, too closely with the right hand!' Yesterday I was pulling all the time."

The High Priest frowned.

"It is written in the sacred book of Hec, your Majesty, 'Thou shalt not follow after strange gods.'"

"Take thou this stick, O venerable one," said the King, paying no attention to the remark, "and have a shot thyself. True, thou are well stricken in years, but many a man has so wrought that he was able to give his grandchildren a stroke a hole. It is never too late to begin."

The High Priest shrank back, horrified. The King frowned.

"It is our Royal wish," he said, coldly.

The High Priest was forced to comply. Had they been alone, it is possible that he might have risked all on one swift stroke with his knife, but by this time a group of *kaddiz* had drifted up, and were watching the proceedings with that supercilious detachment so characteristic of them. He took the stick and arranged his limbs as the King directed.

"Now," said Merolchazzar, "slow back and keep your e'e on the ba'!"

A month later, Ascobaruch returned from his trip. He had received no word from the High Priest announcing the success of the revolution, but there might be many reasons for that. It was with unruffled contentment that he bade his charioteer drive him to the palace. He was glad to get back, for after all a holiday is hardly a holiday if you have left your business affairs unsettled.

As he drove, the chariot passed a fair open space, on the outskirts of the city. A sudden chill froze the serenity of Ascobaruch's mood. He prodded the charioteer sharply in the small of the back.

"What is that?" he demanded, catching his breath.

All over the green expanse could be seen men in strange robes, moving to and fro in couples and bearing in their hands mystic wands. Some searched restlessly in the bushes, others were walking briskly in the direction of small red flags.

FORE!

A sickening foreboding of disaster fell upon Ascobaruch.
The charioteer seemed surprised at the question.

"Yon's the muneecipal linx," he replied.

"The what?"

"The muneecipal linx."

"Tell me, fellow, why do you talk that way?"

"Whit way?"

"Why, like that. The way you're talking."

"Hoots, mon!" said the charioteer. "His Majesty King
Merolchazzar — may his handicap decrease! — hae passit a
law that a' his soobjects shall do it. Aiblims, 'tis the language
spoken by The Pro, on whom be peace! Mphm!"

Ascobaruch sat back limply, his head swimming. The chariot drove on, till now it took the road adjoining the royal Linx.
A wall lined a portion of this road, and suddenly, from behind
this wall, there rent the air a great shout of laughter.

"Pull up!" cried Ascobaruch to the charioteer.

He had recognised that laugh. It was the laugh of Merolchazzar.

Ascobaruch crept to the wall and cautiously poked his head
over it. The sight he saw drove the blood from his face and
left him white and haggard.

The King and the Grand Vizier were playing a foursome
against the Pro and the High Priest of Hec, and the Vizier
had just laid the High Priest a dead stymie.

Ascobaruch tottered to the chariot.

"Take me back," he muttered, pallidly. "I've forgotten
something!"

And so golf came to Oom, and with it prosperity unequalled
in the whole history of the land. Everybody was happy.
There was no more unemployment. Crime ceased. The
chronicler repeatedly refers to it in his memoirs as the
Golden Age. And yet there remained one man on whom
complete felicity had not descended. It was all right while

he was actually on the Linx, but there were blank, dreary stretches of the night when King Merolchazzar lay sleepless on his couch and mourned that he had nobody to love him.

Of course, his subjects loved him in a way. A new statue had been erected in the palace square, showing him in the act of getting out of casual water. The minstrels had composed a whole cycle of up-to-date songs, commemorating his prowess with the mashie. His handicap was down to twelve. But these things are not all. A golfer needs a loving wife, to whom he can describe the day's play through the long evenings. And this was just where Merolchazzar's life was empty. No word had come from the Princess of the Outer Isles, and, as he refused to be put off with just-as-good substitutes, he remained a lonely man.

But one morning, in the early hours of a summer day, as he lay sleeping after a disturbed night, Merolchazzar was awakened by the eager hand of the Lord High Chamberlain, shaking his shoulder.

"Now what?" said the King.

"Hoots, your Majesty! Glorious news! The Princess of the Outer Isles waits without — I mean wi'oot!"

The King sprang from his couch.

"A messenger from the Princess at last!"

"Nay, sire, the Princess herself — that is to say," said the Lord Chamberlain, who was an old man and had found it hard to accustom himself to the new tongue at his age, "her ain sel'! And believe me, or rather, mind ah'm telling ye," went on the honest man, joyfully, for he had been deeply exercised by his monarch's troubles, "her Highness is the easiest thing to look at these eyes hae ever seen. And you can say I said it!"

"She is beautiful?"

"Your majesty, she is, in the best and deepest sense of the word, a pippin!"

King Merolchazzar was groping wildly for his robes.

FORE!

"Tell her to wait!" he cried. "Go and amuse her. Ask her riddles! Tell her anecdotes! Don't let her go. Say I'll be down in a moment. Where in the name of Zoroaster is our imperial mesh-knit underwear?"

A fair and pleasing sight was the Princess of the Outer Isles as she stood on the terrace in the clear sunshine of the summer morning, looking over the King's gardens. With her delicate little nose she sniffed the fragrance of the flowers. Her blue eyes roamed over the rose bushes, and the breeze ruffled the golden curls about her temples. Presently a sound behind her caused her to turn, and she perceived a godlike man hurrying across the terrace pulling up a sock. And at the sight of him the Princess's heart sang within her like the birds down in the garden.

"Hope I haven't kept you waiting," said Merolchazzar, apologetically. He, too, was conscious of a strange, wild exhilaration. Truly was this maiden, as his Chamberlain had said, noticeably easy on the eyes. Her beauty was as water in the desert, as fire on a frosty night, as diamonds, rubies, pearls, sapphires, and amethysts.

"Oh, no!" said the princess, "I've been enjoying myself. How passing beautiful are thy gardens, O King!"

"My gardens may be passing beautiful," said Merolchazzar, earnestly, "but they aren't half so passing beautiful as thy eyes. I have dreamed of thee by night and by day, and I will tell the world I was nowhere near it! My sluggish fancy came not within a hundred and fifty-seven miles of the reality. Now let the sun dim his face and the moon hide herself abashed. Now let the flowers bend their heads and the gazelle of the mountains confess itself a cripple. Princess, your slave!"

And King Merolchazzar, with that easy grace so characteristic of Royalty, took her hand in his and kissed it.

As he did so, he gave a start of surprise.

"By Hec!" he exclaimed. "What hast thou been doing to

thyself? Thy hand is all over little rough places inside. Has some malignant wizard laid a spell upon thee, or what is it?"

The Princess blushed.

"If I make that clear to thee," she said, "I shall also make clear why it was that I sent thee no message all this long while. My time was so occupied, verily I did not seem to have a moment. The fact is, these sorenesses are due to a strange, new religion to which I and my subjects have but recently become converted. And O that I might make thee also of the true faith. 'Tis a wondrous tale, my lord. Some two moons back there was brought to my Court by wandering pirates a captive of an uncouth race who dwell in the north. And this man has taught us — "

King Merolchazzar uttered a loud cry.

"By Tom, the son of Morris! Can this truly be so? What is thy handicap?"

The Princess stared at him, wide-eyed.

"Truly this is a miracle! Art thou also a worshipper of the great Gowf?"

"Am I!" cried the King. "Am I!" He broke off. "Listen!"

From the minstrels' room high up in the palace there came the sound of singing. The minstrels were practising a new pæan of praise — words by the Grand Vizier, music by the High Priest of Hec — which they were to render at the next full moon at the banquet of the worshippers of Gowf. The words came clear and distinct through the still air:

"Oh, praises let us utter
    To our most glorious King!
It fairly makes you stutter
    To see him start his swing;
Success attend his putter!
    And luck be with his drive!
And may he do each hole in two,
    Although the bogey's five!"

The voices died away. There was a silence.

"If I hadn't missed a two-foot putt, I'd have done the long fifteenth in four yesterday," said the King.

"I won the Ladies' Open Championship of the Outer Isles last week," said the Princess.

They looked into each other's eyes for a long moment. And then, hand in hand, they walked slowly into the palace.

Epilogue

"Well?" we said, anxiously.

"I like it," said the editor.

"Good egg!" we murmured.

The editor pressed a bell, a single ruby set in a fold of the tapestry upon the wall. The major-domo appeared.

"Give this man a purse of gold," said the editor, "and throw him out."

The Salvation
of George Mackintosh

O

The young man came into the club-house. There was a frown on his usually cheerful face, and he ordered a ginger-ale in the sort of voice which an ancient Greek would have used when asking the executioner to bring on the hemlock.

Sunk in the recesses of his favourite settee the Oldest Member had watched him with silent sympathy.

"How did you get on?" he inquired.

"He beat me."

The Oldest Member nodded his venerable head.

"You have had a trying time, if I am not mistaken. I feared as much when I saw you go out with Pobsley. How many a young man have I seen go out with Herbert Pobsley exulting in his youth, and crawl back at eventide looking like a toad under the harrow! He talked?"

"All the time, confound it! Put me right off my stroke."

The Oldest Member sighed.

"The talking golfer is undeniably the most pronounced pest of our complex modern civilisation," he said, "and the most difficult to deal with. It is a melancholy thought that the noblest of games should have produced such a scourge. I have frequently marked Herbert Pobsley in action. As the crackling of thorns under a pot. . . . He is almost as bad as poor George Mackintosh in his worst period. Did I ever tell you about George Mackintosh?"

"I don't think so."

"His," said the Sage, "is the only case of golfing garrulity

I have ever known where a permanent cure was effected. If you would care to hear about it — ?"

George Mackintosh (said the Oldest Member), when I first knew him, was one of the most admirable young fellows I have ever met. A handsome, well-set-up man, with no vices except a tendency to use the mashie for shots which should have been made with the light iron. And as for his positive virtues, they were too numerous to mention. He never swayed his body, moved his head, or pressed. He was always ready to utter a tactful grunt when his opponent foozled. And when he himself achieved a glaring fluke, his self-reproachful click of the tongue was music to his adversary's bruised soul. But of all his virtues the one that most endeared him to me and to all thinking men was the fact that, from the start of a round to the finish, he never spoke a word except when absolutely compelled to do so by the exigencies of the game. And it was this man who subsequently, for a black period which lives in the memory of all his contemporaries, was known as Gabby George and became a shade less popular than the germ of Spanish Influenza. Truly, *corruptio optimi pessima!*

One of the things that sadden a man as he grows older and reviews his life is the reflection that his most devastating deeds were generally the ones which he did with the best motives. The thought is disheartening. I can honestly say that, when George Mackintosh came to me and told me his troubles, my sole desire was to ameliorate his lot. That I might be starting on the downward path a man whom I liked and respected never once occurred to me.

One night after dinner when George Mackintosh came in, I could see at once that there was something on his mind, but what this could be I was at a loss to imagine, for I had been playing with him myself all the afternoon, and he had done an eighty-one and a seventy-nine. And, as I had not left the links till dusk was beginning to fall, it was practically impossible that he could have gone out again and done badly. The idea of financial trouble seemed equally out of the question. George had a good job with the old-established legal firm of Peabody, Peabody, Peabody, Peabody, Cootes, Toots, and Peabody. The third alternative, that he might be in love, I rejected at once. In all the time I had known him I had never seen a sign that George Mackintosh gave a thought to the opposite sex.

Yet this, bizarre as it seemed, was the true solution. Scarcely had he seated himself and lit a cigar when he blurted out his confession.

"What would you do in a case like this?" he said.

"Like what?"

"Well — " He choked, and a rich blush permeated his surface. "Well, it seems a silly thing to say and all that, but I'm in love with Miss Tennant, you know!"

"You are in love with Celia Tennant?"

"Of course I am. I've got eyes, haven't I? Who else is there that any sane man could possibly be in love with? That," he went on, moodily, "is the whole trouble. There's a field of about twenty-nine, and I should think my place in the betting is about thirty-three to one."

"I cannot agree with you there," I said. "You have every advantage, it appears to me. You are young, amiable, good-looking, comfortably off, scratch — "

"But I can't talk, confound it!" he burst out. "And how is a man to get anywhere at this sort of game without talking?"

"You are talking perfectly fluently now."

"Yes, to you. But put me in front of Celia Tennant, and I simply make a sort of gurgling noise like a sheep with the botts. It kills my chances stone dead. You know these other men. I can give Claude Mainwaring a third and beat him. I can give Eustace Brinkley a stroke a hole and simply trample on his corpse. But when it comes to talking to a girl, I'm not in her class."

"You must not be diffident."

"But I *am* diffident. What's the good of saying I mustn't be diffident when I'm the man who wrote the words and music, when Diffidence is my middle name and my telegraphic address? I can't help being diffident."

"Surely you could overcome it?"

"But how? It was in the hope that you might be able to suggest something that I came round to-night."

And this was where I did the fatal thing. It happened that, just before I took up Braid on the Push-Shot, I had been dipping into the current number of a magazine, and one of the advertisements, I chanced to remember, might have been framed with a special eye to George's unfortunate case. It was that one, which I have no doubt you have seen, which treats of "How to Become a Convincing Talker." I picked up this magazine now and handed it to George.

He studied it for a few minutes in thoughtful silence. He looked at the picture of the Man who had taken the course being fawned upon by lovely women, while the man who had let this opportunity slip stood outside the group gazing with a wistful envy.

"They never do that to me," said George.

"Do what, my boy?"

"Cluster round, clinging cooingly."

"I gather from the letterpress that they will if you write for the booklet."

"You think there is really something in it?"

"I see no reason why eloquence should not be taught by mail. One seems to be able to acquire every other desirable quality in that manner nowadays."

"I might try it. After all, it's not expensive. There's no doubt about it," he murmured, returning to his perusal, "that fellow does look popular. Of course, the evening dress may have something to do with it."

"Not at all. The other man, you will notice, is also wearing evening dress, and yet he is merely among those on the outskirts. It is simply a question of writing for the booklet."

"Sent post free."

"Sent, as you say, post free."

"I've a good mind to try it."

"I see no reason why you should not."

"I will, by Duncan!" He tore the page out of the magazine and put it in his pocket. "I'll tell you what I'll do. I'll give this thing a trial for a week or two, and at the end of that time I'll go to the boss and see how he reacts when I ask for a rise of salary. If he crawls, it'll show there's something in this. If he flings me out, it will prove the thing's no good."

We left it at that, and I am bound to say — owing, no doubt, to my not having written for the booklet of the Memory Training Course advertised on the adjoining page of the magazine — the matter slipped from my mind. When, therefore, a few weeks later, I received a telegram from young Mackintosh which ran:

Worked like magic,

I confess I was intensely puzzled. It was only a quarter of an hour before George himself arrived that I solved the problem of its meaning.

"So the boss crawled?" I said, as he came in.

He gave a light, confident laugh. I had not seen him, as I say, for some time, and I was struck by the alteration in his appearance. In what exactly this alteration consisted I could not at first have said; but gradually it began to impress itself on me that his eye was brighter, his jaw squarer, his carriage a trifle more upright than it had been. But it was his eye that struck me most forcibly. The George Mackintosh I had known had had a pleasing gaze, but, though frank and agreeable, it had never been more dynamic than a fried egg. This new George had an eye that was a combination of a gimlet and a searchlight. Coleridge's Ancient Mariner, I imagine, must have been somewhat similarly equipped. The Ancient Mariner stopped a wedding guest on his way to a wedding; George Mackintosh gave me the impression that he could have stopped the Twentieth Century Limited on its way to Chicago. Self-confidence — aye, and more than self-confidence — a sort of sinful, overbearing swank seemed to exude from his very pores.

"Crawled?" he said. "Well, he didn't actually lick my boots, because I saw him coming and side-stepped; but he did everything short of that. I hadn't been talking an hour when — "

"An hour!" I gasped. "Did you talk for an hour?"

"Certainly. You wouldn't have had me be abrupt, would you? I went into his private office and found him alone. I think at first he would have been just as well pleased if I had retired. In fact, he said as much. But I soon adjusted that outlook. I took a seat and a cigarette, and then I started to sketch out for him the history of my connection with the firm. He began to wilt before the end of the first ten minutes. At the quarter of an hour mark he was looking at me like a lost dog that's just found its owner. By the half-hour he was making little bleating noises and massaging my coat-sleeve. And when, after perhaps an hour and a half, I came to my peroration and suggested a rise, he choked back a sob, gave me double what I had asked, and invited me to dine at his club next Tuesday. I'm a little sorry now I cut the thing so short. A few minutes more, and I fancy he would have given me his sock-suspenders and made over his life-insurance in my favour."

"Well," I said, as soon as I could speak, for I was finding my young friend a trifle overpowering, "this is most satisfactory."

"So-so," said George. "Not un-so-so. A man wants an addition to his income when he is going to get married."

"Ah!" I said. "That, of course, will be the real test."

"What do you mean?"

"Why, when you propose to Celia Tennant. You remember you were saying when we spoke of this before — "

"Oh, that!" said George, carelessly. "I've arranged all that."

"What!"

"Oh, yes. On my way up from the station. I looked in on Celia about an hour ago, and it's all settled."

"Amazing!"

"Well, I don't know. I just put the thing to her, and she seemed to see it."

"I congratulate you. So now, like Alexander, you have no more worlds to conquer."

"Well, I don't know so much about that," said George. "The way it looks to me is that I'm just starting. This eloquence is a thing that rather grows on one. You didn't hear about my after-dinner speech at the anniversary banquet of the firm, I suppose? My dear fellow, a riot! A positive stampede. Had 'em laughing and then crying and then laughing again and then crying once more till six of 'em had to be led out and the rest down with hiccoughs. Napkins waving . . . three tables broken . . . waiters in hysterics. I tell you, I played on them as on a stringed instrument. . . ."

"Can you play on a stringed instrument?"

"As it happens, no. But as I would have played on a stringed instrument if I could play on a stringed instrument. Wonderful sense of power it gives you. I mean to go in pretty largely for that sort of thing in future."

"You must not let it interfere with your golf."

He gave a laugh which turned my blood cold.

"Golf!" he said. "After all, what is golf? Just pushing a small ball into a hole. A child could do it. Indeed, children have done it with great success. I see an infant of fourteen has just won some sort of championship. Could that stripling convulse a roomful of banqueters? I think not! To sway your fellow-men with a word, to hold them with a gesture . . . that is the real salt of life. I don't suppose I shall play much more golf now. I'm making arrangements for a lecturing-tour, and I'm booked up for fifteen lunches already."

Those were his words. A man who had once done the lake-hole in one. A man whom the committee were grooming for the amateur championship. I am no weakling, but I confess they sent a chill shiver down my spine.

George Mackintosh did not, I am glad to say, carry out his mad project to the letter. He did not altogether sever himself from golf. He was still to be seen occasionally on the links. But now — and I know of nothing more tragic that can befall a man — he found himself gradually shunned, he who in the days of his sanity had been besieged with more offers of games than he could manage to accept. Men simply would not stand his incessant flow of talk. One by one they dropped off, until the only person he could find to go round with him was old Major Moseby, whose hearing completely petered out as long ago as the year '98. And, of course, Celia Tennant would play with him occasionally; but it seemed to me that even she, greatly as no doubt she loved him, was beginning to crack under the strain.

So surely had I read the pallor of her face and the wild look of dumb agony in her eyes that I was not surprised when, as I sat one morning in my garden reading Ray on Taking Turf, my man announced her name. I had been half expecting her to come to me for advice and consolation, for I had known her ever since she was a child. It was I who had given her her first driver and taught her infant lips to lisp "Fore!" It is not easy to lisp the word "Fore!" but I had taught her to do it, and this constituted a bond between us which had been strengthened rather than weakened by the passage of time.

She sat down on the grass beside my chair, and looked up at my face in silent pain. We had known each other so long that I know that it was not my face that pained her, but rather some unspoken *malaise* of the soul. I waited for her to speak, and suddenly she burst out impetuously as though she could hold back her sorrow no longer.

"Oh, I can't stand it! I can't stand it!"

"You mean . . . ?" I said, though I knew only too well.

"This horrible obsession of poor George's," she cried passionately. "I don't think he has stopped talking once since we have been engaged."

"He is chatty," I agreed. "Has he told you the story about the Irishman?"

"Half a dozen times. And the one about the Swede oftener than that. But I would not mind an occasional anecdote. Women have to learn to bear anecdotes from the men they love. It is the curse of Eve. It is his incessant easy flow of chatter on all topics that is undermining even my devotion."

"But surely, when he proposed to you, he must have given you an inkling of the truth. He only hinted at it when he spoke to me, but I gather that he was eloquent."

"When he proposed," said Celia dreamily, "he was wonderful. He spoke for twenty minutes without stopping. He said I was the essence of his every hope, the tree on which the fruit of his life grew; his Present, his Future, his Past . . . oh, and all that sort of thing. If he would only confine his conversation now to remarks of a similar nature, I could listen to him all day long. But he doesn't. He talks politics and statistics and philosophy and . . . oh, and everything. He makes my head ache."

"And your heart also, I fear," I said gravely.

"I love him!" she replied simply. "In spite of everything, I love him dearly. But what to do? What to do? I have an awful fear that when we are getting married instead of answering 'I will,' he will go into the pulpit and deliver an address on Marriage Ceremonies of All Ages. The world to him is a vast lecture-platform. He looks on life as one long after-dinner, with himself as the principal speaker of the evening. It is breaking my heart. I see him shunned by his former friends. Shunned! They run a mile when they see him coming. The mere sound of his voice outside the club-house is enough to send brave men diving for safety beneath the sofas. Can you wonder that I am in despair? What have I to live for?"

"There is always golf."

"Yes, there is always golf," she whispered bravely.

"Come and have a round this afternoon."

"I had promised to go for a walk. . . ." She shuddered, then pulled herself together. ". . . for a walk with George."

I hesitated for a moment.

"Bring him along," I said, and patted her hand. "It may be that together we shall find an opportunity of reasoning with him."

She shook her head.

"You can't reason with George. He never stops talking long enough to give you time."

"Nevertheless, there is no harm in trying. I have an idea that this malady of his is not permanent and incurable. The very violence with which the germ of loquacity has attacked him gives me hope. You must remember that before this seizure he was rather a noticeably silent man. Sometimes I think that it is just Nature's way of restoring the average, and that soon the fever may burn itself out. Or it may be that a sudden shock. . . . At any rate, have courage."

"I will try to be brave."

"Capital! At half-past two on the first tee, then."

"You will have to give me a stroke on the third, ninth, twelfth, fifteenth, sixteenth and eighteenth," she said, with a quaver in her voice. "My golf has fallen off rather lately."

I patted her hand again.

"I understand," I said gently. "I understand."

The steady drone of a baritone voice as I alighted from my car and approached the first tee told me that George had not forgotten the tryst. He was sitting on the stone seat under the chestnut-tree, speaking a few well-chosen words on the Labor Movement.

"To what conclusion, then, do we come?" he was saying. "We come to the foregone and inevitable conclusion that . . ."

"Good afternoon, George," I said.

He nodded briefly, but without verbal salutation. He seemed to regard my remark as he would have regarded the unmannerly heckling of some one at the back of the hall. He proceeded evenly with his speech, and was still talking when Celia addressed her ball and drove off. Her drive, coinciding with a sharp rhetorical question from George, wavered in mid-air, and the ball trickled off into the rough halfway down the hill. I can see the poor girl's tortured face even now. But she breathed no word of reproach. Such is the miracle of woman's love.

"Where you went wrong there," said George, breaking off his remarks on Labour, "was that you have not studied the dynamics of golf sufficiently. You did not pivot properly. You allowed your left heel to point down the course when you were at the top of your swing. This makes for instability and loss of distance. The fundamental law of the dynamics of golf is that the left foot shall be solidly on the ground at the moment of impact. If you allow your heel to point down the course, it is almost impossible to bring it back in time to make the foot a solid fulcrum."

I drove, and managed to clear the rough and reach the fairway. But it was not one of my best drives. George Mackintosh, I confess, had unnerved me. The feeling he gave me resembled the self-conscious panic which I used to experience in my childhood when informed that there was One Awful Eye that watched my every movement and saw my every act. It was only the fact that poor Celia appeared even more affected by his espionage that enabled me to win the first hole in seven.

On the way to the second tee George discoursed on the beauties of Nature, pointing out at considerable length how exquisitely the silver glitter of the lake harmonized with the vivid emerald turf near the hole and the duller green of the rough beyond it. As Celia teed up her ball, he directed her attention to the golden glory of the sand-pit to the left of the flag. It was not the spirit in which to approach the lake-hole, and I was not surprised when the unfortunate girl's ball fell with a sickening plop halfway across the water.

"Where you went wrong there," said George, "was that you made the stroke a sudden heave instead of a smooth, snappy flick of the wrists. Pressing is always bad, but with the mashie — "

"I think I will give you this hole," said Celia to me, for my shot had cleared the water and was lying on the edge of the green. "I wish I hadn't used a new ball."

"The price of golf-balls," said George, as we started to round the lake, "is a matter to which economists should give some attention. I am credibly informed that rubber at the present time is exceptionally cheap. Yet we see no decrease in the price of golf-balls, which, as I need scarcely inform you, are rubber-cored. Why should this be so? You will say that the wages of skilled labour have gone up. True. But — "

"One moment, George, while I drive," I said. For we had now arrived at the third tee.

"A curious thing, concentration," said George, "and why certain phenomena should prevent us from focussing our attention — This brings me to the vexed question of sleep. Why is it that we are able to sleep through some vast convulsion of Nature when a dripping tap is enough to keep us awake? I am told that there were people who slumbered peacefully through the San Francisco earthquake, merely stirring drowsily from time to time to tell an imaginary person to leave it on the mat. Yet these same people — "

Celia's drive bounded into the deep ravine which yawns some fifty yards from the tee. A low moan escaped her.

"Where you went wrong there . . ." said George.

"I know," said Celia. "I lifted my head."

I had never heard her speak so abruptly before. Her manner, in a girl less noticeably pretty, might almost have been called snappish. George, however, did not appear to have noticed anything amiss. He filled his pipe and followed her into the ravine.

"Remarkable," he said, "how fundamental a principle of golf is this keeping the head still. You will hear professionals tell their pupils to keep their eye on the ball. Keeping the eye on the ball is only a secondary matter. What they really mean is that the head should be kept rigid, as otherwise it is impossible to — "

His voice died away. I had sliced my drive into the woods on the right, and after playing another had gone off to try to find my ball, leaving Celia and George in the ravine behind me. My last glimpse of them showed me that her ball had fallen into a stone-studded cavity in the side of the hill, and she was drawing her niblick from her bag as I passed out of sight. George's voice, blurred by distance to a monotonous murmur, followed me until I was out of earshot.

I was just about to give up the hunt for my ball in despair, when I heard Celia's voice calling to me from the edge of the undergrowth. There was a sharp note in it which startled me.

I came out, trailing a portion of some unknown shrub which had twined itself about my ankle.

"Yes?" I said, picking twigs out of my hair.

"I want your advice," said Celia.

"Certainly. What is the trouble? By the way," I said, looking round, "where is your *fiancé*?"

"I have no *fiancé*," she said, in a dull, hard voice.

"You have broken off the engagement?"

"Not exactly. And yet — well, I suppose it amounts to that."

"I don't quite understand."

"Well, the fact is," said Celia, in a burst of girlish frankness, "I rather think I've killed George."

"Killed him, eh?"

It was a solution that had not occurred to me, but now that it was presented for my inspection I could see its merits. In these days of national effort, when we are all working together to try to make our beloved land fit for heroes to live in, it was astonishing that nobody before had thought of a simple, obvious thing like killing George Mackintosh. George Mackintosh was undoubtedly better dead, but it had taken a woman's intuition to see it.

"I killed him with my niblick," said Celia.

I nodded. If the thing was to be done at all, it was unquestionably a niblick shot.

"I had just made my eleventh attempt to get out of that ravine," the girl went on, "with George talking all the time about the recent excavations in Egypt, when suddenly — you know what it is when something seems to snap — "

"I had the experience with my shoe-lace only this morning."

"Yes, it was like that. Sharp — sudden — happening all in a moment. I suppose I must have said something, for George stopped talking about Egypt and said that he was reminded by a remark of the last speaker's of a certain Irishman — "

I pressed her hand.

"Don't go on if it hurts you," I said, gently.

"Well, there is very little more to tell. He bent his head to light his pipe, and well — the temptation was too much for me. That's all."

"You were quite right."

"You really think so?"

"I certainly do. A rather similar action, under far less provocation, once made Jael the wife of Heber the most popular woman in Israel."

"I wish I could think so too," she murmured. "At the moment, you know, I was conscious of nothing but an awful elation. But — but — oh, he was such a darling before he got this dreadful affliction. I can't help thinking of G-George as he used to be."

She burst into a torrent of sobs.

"Would you care for me to view the remains?" I said.

"Perhaps it would be as well."

She led me silently into the ravine. George Mackintosh was lying on his back where he had fallen.

"There!" said Celia.

And, as she spoke, George Mackintosh gave a kind of snorting groan and sat up. Celia uttered a sharp shriek and sank on her knees before him. George blinked once or twice and looked about him dazedly.

"Save the women and children!" he cried. "I can swim."

"Oh, George!" said Celia.

"Feeling a little better?" I asked.

"A little. How many people were hurt?"

"Hurt?"

"When the express ran into us." He cast another glance around him. "Why, how did I get here?"

"You were here all the time," I said.

"Do you mean after the roof fell in or before?"

Celia was crying quietly down the back of his neck.

"Oh, George!" she said, again.

He groped out feebly for her hand and patted it.

"Brave little woman!" he said. "Brave little woman! She stuck by me all through. Tell me — I am strong enough to bear it — what caused the explosion?"

It seemed to me a case where much unpleasant explanation might be avoided by the exercise of a little tact.

"Well, some say one thing and some another," I said. "Whether it was a spark from a cigarette . . ."

Celia interrupted me. The woman in her made her revolt against this well-intentioned subterfuge.

"I hit you, George!"

"Hit me?" he repeated, curiously. "What with? The Eiffel Tower?"

"With my niblick."

"You hit me with your niblick? But why?"

She hesitated. Then she faced him bravely.

"Because you wouldn't stop talking."

He gaped.

"Me!" he said. "*I* wouldn't stop talking! But I hardly talk at all. I'm noted for it."

Celia's eyes met mine in agonised inquiry. But I saw what had happened. The blow, the sudden shock, had operated on George's brain-cells in such a way as to effect a complete cure. I have not the technical knowledge to be able to explain it, but the facts were plain.

"Lately, my dear fellow," I assured him, "you have dropped into the habit of talking rather a good deal. Ever since we started out this afternoon you have kept up an incessant flow of conversation!"

"Me! On the links! It isn't possible."

"It is only too true, I fear. And that is why this brave girl hit you with her niblick. You started to tell her a funny story just as she was making her eleventh shot to get her ball out of this ravine, and she took what she considered the necessary steps."

"Can you ever forgive me, George?" cried Celia.

George Mackintosh stared at me. Then a crimson blush mantled his face.

"So I did! It's all beginning to come back to me. Oh, heavens!"

"*Can* you forgive me, George?" cried Celia again.

He took her hand in his.

"Forgive you?" he muttered. "Can *you* forgive *me*? Me — a tee-talker, a green-gabbler, a prattler on the links, the lowest form of life known to science! I am unclean, unclean!"

"It's only a little mud, dearest," said Celia, looking at the sleeve of his coat. "It will brush off when it's dry."

"How can you link your lot with a man who talks when people are making their shots?"

"You will never do it again."

"But I have done it. And you stuck to me all through! Oh, Celia!"

"I loved you, George!"

The man seemed to swell with a sudden emotion. His eyes lit up, and he thrust one hand into the breast of his coat while he raised the other in a sweeping gesture. For an instant he appeared on the verge of a flood of eloquence. And then, as if he had been made sharply aware of what it was that he intended to do, he suddenly sagged. The gleam died out of his eyes. He lowered his hand.

"Well, I must say that was rather decent of you," he said.

A lame speech, but one that brought an infinite joy to both his hearers. For it showed that George Mackintosh was cured beyond possibility of relapse.

"Yes, I must say you are rather a corker," he added.

"George!" cried Celia.

I said nothing, but I clasped his hand; and then, taking my clubs, I retired. When I looked round she was still in his arms. I left them there, alone together in the great silence.

And so (concluded the Oldest Member) you see that a cure is possible, though it needs a woman's gentle hand to bring it about. And how few women are capable of doing what Celia Tennant did. Apart from the difficulty of summoning up the necessary resolution, an act like hers requires a straight eye and a pair of strong and supple wrists. It seems to me that for the ordinary talking golfer there is no hope. And the race seems to be getting more numerous every day. Yet the finest golfers are always the least loquacious. It is related of the illustrious Sandy McHoots that when, on the occasion of his winning the British Open Championship, he was interviewed by reporters from the leading daily papers as to his views on Tariff Reform, Bimetallism, the Trial by Jury System, and the Modern Craze for Dancing, all they could extract from him was the single word "Mphm!" Having uttered which, he shouldered his bag and went home to tea. A great man. I wish there were more like him.

High Stakes

O

The summer day was drawing to a close. Over the terrace outside the club-house the chestnut trees threw long shadows, and such bees as still lingered in the flower-beds had the air of tired business men who are about ready to shut up the office and go off to dinner and a musical comedy. The Oldest Member, stirring in his favourite chair, glanced at his watch and yawned.

As he did so, from the neighbourhood of the eighteenth green, hidden from his view by the slope of the ground, there came suddenly a medley of shrill animal cries, and he deduced that some belated match must just have reached a finish. His surmise was correct. The babble of voices drew nearer, and over the brow of the hill came a little group of men. Two, who appeared to be the ringleaders in the affair, were short and stout. One was cheerful and the other dejected. The rest of the company consisted of friends and adherents; and one of these, a young man who seemed to be amused, strolled to where the Oldest Member sat.

"What," inquired the Sage, "was all the shouting for?"

The young man sank into a chair and lighted a cigarette.

"Perkins and Broster," he said, "were all square at the seventeenth, and they raised the stakes to fifty pounds. They were both on the green in seven, and Perkins had a two-foot putt to halve the match. He missed it by six inches. They play pretty high, those two."

"It is a curious thing," said the Oldest Member, "that men

whose golf is of a kind that makes hardened caddies wince always do. The more competent a player, the smaller the stake that contents him. It is only when you get down into the submerged tenth of the golfing world that you find the big gambling. However, I would not call fifty pounds anything sensational in the case of two men like Perkins and Broster. They are both well provided with the world's goods. If you would care to hear the story — "

The young man's jaw fell a couple of notches.

"I had no idea it was so late," he bleated. "I ought to be — "

" — of a man who played for really high stakes — "

"I promised to — "

" — I will tell it to you," said the Sage.

"Look here," said the young man, sullenly, "it isn't one of those stories about two men who fall in love with the same girl and play a match to decide which is to marry her, is it? Because if so — "

"The stake to which I allude," said the Oldest Member, "was something far higher and bigger than a woman's love. Shall I proceed?"

"All right," said the young man, resignedly. "Snap into it."

It has been well said — I think by the man who wrote the sub-titles for "Cage-Birds of Society" (began the Oldest Member) — that wealth does not always bring happiness. It was so with Bradbury Fisher, the hero of the story which I am about to relate. One of America's most prominent tainted millionaires, he had two sorrows in life — his handicap refused to stir from twenty-four and his wife disapproved of his collection of famous golf relics. Once, finding him crooning over the trousers in which Ouimet had won his historic replay against Vardon and Ray in the American Open, she had asked him why he did not collect something worth while, like Old Masters or first editions.

Worth while! Bradbury had forgiven, for he loved the woman, but he could not forget.

For Bradbury Fisher, like so many men who have taken to the game in middle age, after a youth misspent in the pursuits of commerce, was no half-hearted enthusiast. Although he still occasionally descended on Wall Street in order to pry the small investor loose from another couple of million, what he really lived for now was golf and his collection. He had begun the collection in his first year as a golfer, and he prized it dearly. And when he reflected that his wife had stopped him purchasing J. H. Taylor's shirt-stud, which he could have had for a few hundred pounds, the iron seemed to enter into his soul.

The distressing episode had occurred in London, and he was now on his way back to New York, having left his wife to continue her holiday in England. All through the voyage he remained moody and distrait; and at the ship's concert, at which he was forced to take the chair, he was heard to observe to the purser that if the alleged soprano who had just sung "My Little Grey Home in the West" had the immortal gall to take a second encore he hoped that she would trip over a high note and dislocate her neck.

Such was Bradbury Fisher's mood throughout the ocean journey, and it remained constant until he arrived at his palatial home at Goldenville, Long Island, where, as he sat smoking a moody after-dinner cigar in the Versailles drawing-room, Blizzard, his English butler, informed him that Mr. Gladstone Bott desired to speak to him on the telephone.

"Tell him to go and boil himself," said Bradbury.

"Very good, sir."

"No, I'll tell him myself," said Bradbury. He strode to the telephone. "Hullo!" he said curtly.

He was not fond of this Bott. There are certain men who seem fated to go through life as rivals. It was so with Bradbury Fisher and J. Gladstone Bott. Born in the same town within a few days of one another, they had come to New York in the same week; and from that moment their careers had run side by side. Fisher had made his first million two days before Bott, but Bott's first divorce had got half a column and two sticks more publicity than Fisher's.

At Sing-Sing, where each had spent several happy years of early manhood, they had run neck and neck for the prizes which that institution has to offer. Fisher secured the position of catcher on the baseball nine in preference to Bott, but Bott just nosed Fisher out when it came to the choice of a tenor for the glee club. Bott was selected for the debating contest against Auburn, but Fisher got the last place on the cross-word puzzle team, with Bott merely first reserve.

They had taken up golf simultaneously, and their handicaps had remained level ever since. Between such men it is not surprising that there was little love lost.

"Hullo!" said Gladstone Bott. "So you're back? Say, listen, Fisher. I think I've got something that'll interest you. Something you'll be glad to have in your golf collection."

Bradbury Fisher's mood softened. He disliked Bott, but that was no reason for not doing business with him. And though he had little faith in the man's judgment it might be that he had stumbled upon some valuable antique. There crossed his mind the comforting thought that his wife was three thousand miles away and that he was no longer under her penetrating eye — that eye which, so to speak, was always "about his bath and about his bed and spying out all his ways."

"I've just returned from a trip down South," proceeded Bott, "and I have secured the authentic baffy used by Bobby Jones in his first important contest — the Infants' All-In Championship of Atlanta, Georgia, open to those of both sexes not yet having finished teething."

Bradbury gasped. He had heard rumours that this treasure was in existence, but he had never credited them.

"You're sure?" he cried. "You're positive it's genuine?"

"I have a written guarantee from Mr. Jones, Mrs. Jones, and the nurse."

"How much, Bott, old man?" stammered Bradbury. "How much do you want for it, Gladstone, old top? I'll give you a hundred thousand dollars."

"Ha!"

"Five hundred thousand."

"Ha, ha!"

"A million."

"Ha, ha, ha!"

"Two million."

"Ha, ha, ha, ha!"

Bradbury Fisher's strong face twisted like that of a tortured fiend. He registered in quick succession rage, despair, hate, fury, anguish, pique, and resentment. But when he spoke again his voice was soft and gentle.

"Gladdy, old socks," he said, "we have been friends for years."

"No, we haven't," said Gladstone Bott.

"Yes, we have."

"No, we haven't."

"Well, anyway, what about two million five hundred?"

"Nothing doing. Say, listen. Do you really want that baffy?"

"I do, Botty, old egg, I do indeed."

"Then listen. I'll exchange it for Blizzard."

"For Blizzard?" quavered Fisher.

"For Blizzard."

It occurs to me that, when describing the closeness of the rivalry between these two men I may have conveyed the impression that in no department of life could either claim a definite advantage over the other. If that is so, I erred. It is true that in a general way, whatever one had, the other had something equally good to counterbalance it; but in just one matter Bradbury Fisher had triumphed completely over Gladstone Bott. Bradbury Fisher had the finest English butler on Long Island.

Blizzard stood alone. There is a regrettable tendency on the part of English butlers to-day to deviate more and more from the type which made their species famous. The modern butler has a nasty nack of being a lissom young man in perfect condition who looks like the son of the house. But Blizzard was of the fine old school. Before coming to the Fisher home he had been for fifteen years in the service of an earl, and his appearance suggested that throughout those fifteen years he had not let a day pass without its pint of port. He radiated port and pop-eyed dignity. He had splay feet and three chins, and when he walked his curving waistcoat preceded him like the advance guard of some royal procession.

From the first, Bradbury had been perfectly aware that Bott coveted Blizzard, and the knowledge had sweetened his life. But this was the first time he had come out into the open and admitted it.

"Blizzard?" whispered Fisher.

"Blizzard," said Bott firmly. "It's my wife's birthday next week, and I've been wondering what to give her."

Bradbury Fisher shuddered from head to foot, and his legs wobbled like asparagus stalks. Beads of perspiration stood out on his forehead. The serpent was tempting him — tempting him grievously.

"You're sure you won't take three million — or four — or something like that?"

"No; I want Blizzard."

Bradbury Fisher passed his handkerchief over his streaming brow.

"So be it," he said in a low voice.

The Jones baffy arrived that night, and for some hours Bradbury Fisher gloated over it with the unmixed joy of a collector who has secured the prize of a lifetime. Then, stealing gradually over him, came the realisation of what he had done.

He was thinking of his wife and what she would say when she heard of this. Blizzard was Mrs. Fisher's pride and joy. She had never, like the poet, nursed a dear gazelle, but, had she done so, her attitude towards it would have been identical with her attitude towards Blizzard. Although so far away, it was plain that her thoughts still lingered with the pleasure she had left at home, for on his arrival Bradbury had found three cables awaiting him.

The first ran:

How is Blizzard? Reply.

The second:

How is Blizzard's sciatica? Reply.

The third:

Blizzard's hiccups. How are they? Suggest Doctor Murphy's Tonic Swamp-Juice. Highly spoken of. Three times a day after meals. Try for week and cable result.

It did not require a clairvoyant to tell Bradbury that, if on her return she found that he had disposed of Blizzard in exchange for a child's cut-down baffy, she would certainly sue him for divorce. And there was not a jury in America that would not give their verdict in her favour without a dissentient voice. His first wife, he recalled, had divorced him on far flimsier grounds. So had his second, third, and fourth. And Bradbury loved his wife. There had been a time in his life when, if he lost a wife, he had felt philosophically that there would be another along in a minute; but, as a man grows older, he tends to become set in his habits, and he could not contemplate existence without the company of the present incumbent.

What, therefore, to do? What, when you came right down to it, to do?

There seemed no way out of the dilemma. If he kept the Jones baffy, no other price would satisfy Bott's jealous greed. And to part with the baffy, now that it was actually in his possession, was unthinkable.

And then, in the small hours of the morning, as he tossed sleeplessly on his Louis Quinze bed, his giant brain conceived a plan.

On the following afternoon he made his way to the clubhouse, and was informed that Bott was out playing a round with another millionaire of his acquaintance. Bradbury waited, and presently his rival appeared.

"Hey!" said Gladstone Bott, in his abrupt, uncouth way. "When are you going to deliver that butler?"

"I will make the shipment at the earliest date," said Bradbury.

"I was expecting him last night."

"You shall have him shortly."

"What do you feed him on?" asked Gladstone Bott.

"Oh, anything you have yourselves. Put sulphur in his port in the hot weather. Tell me, how did your match go?"

"He beat me. I had rotten luck."

Bradbury Fisher's eyes gleamed. His moment had come.

"Luck?" he said. "What do you mean, luck? Luck has nothing to do with it. You're always beefing about your luck. The trouble with you is that you play rottenly."

"What!"

"It is no use trying to play golf unless you learn the first principles and do it properly. Look at the way you drive."

"What's wrong with my driving?"

"Nothing, except that you don't do anything right. In driving, as the club comes back in the swing, the weight should be shifted by degrees, quietly and gradually, until, when the club has reached its top-most point, the whole weight of the body is supported by the right leg, the left foot being turned at the time and the left knee bent in toward the right leg. But, regardless of how much you perfect your style, you cannot develop any method which will not require you to keep your head still so that you can see your ball clearly."

"Hey!"

"It is obvious that it is impossible to introduce a jerk or a sudden violent effort into any part of the swing without disturbing the balance or moving the head. I want to drive home the fact that it is absolutely essential to — "

"Hey!" cried Gladstone Bott.

The man was shaken to the core. From the local pro, and from scratch men of his acquaintance, he would gladly have listened to this sort of thing by the hour, but to hear these words from Bradbury Fisher, whose handicap was the same as his own, and out of whom it was his unperishable conviction that he could hammer the tar any time he got him out on the links, was too much.

"Where do you get off," he demanded, heatedly, "trying to teach me golf?"

Bradbury Fisher chuckled to himself. Everything was working out as his subtle mind had foreseen.

"My dear fellow," he said, "I was only speaking for your good."

"I like your nerve! I can lick you any time we start."

"It's easy enough to talk."

"I trimmed you twice the week before you sailed to England."

"Naturally," said Bradbury Fisher, "in a friendly round, with only a few thousand dollars on the match, a man does not extend himself. You wouldn't dare to play me for anything that really mattered."

"I'll play you when you like for anything you like."

"Very well. I'll play you for Blizzard."

"Against what?"

"Oh, anything you please. How about a couple of rail-roads?"

"Make it three."

"Very well."

"Next Friday suit you?"

"Sure," said Bradbury Fisher.

It seemed to him that his troubles were over. Like all twenty-four handicap men, he had the most perfect confidence in his ability to beat all other twenty-four handicap men. As for Gladstone Bott, he knew that he could disembowel him any time he was able to lure him out of the clubhouse.

Nevertheless, as he breakfasted on the morning of the fateful match, Bradbury Fisher was conscious of an unwonted nervousness. He was no weakling. On Wall Street his phlegm in moments of stress was a by-word. On the famous occasion when the B. and G. crowd had attacked C. and D., and in order to keep control of L. and M. he had been compelled to buy so largely of S. and T., he had not turned a hair. And yet this morning, in endeavouring to prong up segments of bacon, he twice missed the plate altogether and on a third occasion speared himself in the cheek with his fork. The spectacle of Blizzard, so calm, so competent, so supremely the perfect butler, unnerved him.

"I am jumpy to-day, Blizzard," he said forcing a laugh.

"Yes, sir. You do, indeed, appear to have the willies."

"Yes. I am playing a very important golf-match this morning."

"Indeed, sir?"

"I must pull myself together, Blizzard."

"Yes, sir. And, if I may respectfully make the suggestion,

you should endeavour, when in action, to keep the head down and the eye rigidly upon the ball."

"I will, Blizzard, I will," said Bradbury Fisher, his keen eyes clouding under a sudden mist of tears. "Thank you, Blizzard, for the advice."

"Not at all, sir."

"How is your sciatica, Blizzard?"

"A trifle improved, I thank you, sir."

"And your hiccups?"

"I am conscious of a slight though possibly only a temporary relief, sir."

"Good," said Bradbury Fisher.

He left the room with a firm step; and proceeding to his library, read for a while portions of that grand chapter in James Braid's "Advanced Golf" which deals with driving into the wind. It was a fair and cloudless morning, but it was as well to be prepared for emergencies. Then, feeling that he had done all that could be done, he ordered the car and was taken to the links.

Gladstone Bott was awaiting him on the first tee, in company with two caddies. A curt greeting, a spin of the coin, and Gladstone Bott, securing the honour, stepped out to begin the contest.

Although there are, of course, endless sub-species in their ranks, not all of which have yet been classified by science, twenty-four handicap golfers may be stated broadly to fall into two classes, the dashing and the cautious — those, that is to say, who endeavour to do every hole in a brilliant one and those who are content to win with a steady nine. Gladstone Bott was one of the cautious brigade. He fussed about for a few moments like a hen scratching gravel, then with a stiff quarter-swing sent his ball straight down the fairway for a matter of seventy yards, and it was Bradbury Fisher's turn to drive.

Now, normally, Bradbury Fisher was essentially a dasher. It was his habit, as a rule, to raise his left foot some six inches from the ground, and having swayed forcefully back on to his right leg, to sway sharply forward again and lash out with sickening violence in the general direction of the ball. It was a method which at times produced excellent results, though it had the flaw that it was somewhat uncertain. Bradbury Fisher was the only member of the club, with the exception of the club champion, who had ever carried the second green with his drive; but, on the other hand, he was also the only member who had ever laid his drive on the eleventh dead to the pin of the sixteenth.

But to-day the magnitude of the issues at stake had wrought a change in him. Planted firmly on both feet, he fiddled at the ball in the manner of one playing spillikens. When he swung, it was with a swing resembling that of Gladstone Bott; and, like Bott, he achieved a nice, steady, rainbow-shaped drive of some seventy yards straight down the middle. Bott replied with an eighty-yard brassie shot. Bradbury held him with another. And so, working their way cautiously across the prairie, they came to the green, where Bradbury, laying his third putt dead, halved the hole.

The second was a repetition of the first, the third and fourth repetitions of the second. But on the fifth green the fortunes of the match began to change. Here Gladstone Bott, faced with a fifteen-foot putt to win, smote his ball firmly off the line, as had been his practice at each of the preceding holes, and the ball, hitting a worm-cast and bounding off to the left, ran on a couple of yards, hit another worm-cast, bounded to the right, and finally, bumping into a twig, leaped to the left again and clattered into the tin.

"One up," said Gladstone Bott. "Tricky, some of these greens are. You have to gauge the angles to a nicety."

At the sixth a donkey in an adjoining field uttered a raucous bray just as Bott was addressing his ball with a mashie-niblick on the edge of the green. He started violently and, jerking his club with a spasmodic reflex action of the forearm, holed out.

"Nice work," said Gladstone Bott.

The seventh was a short hole, guarded by two large bunkers between which ran a narrow footpath of turf. Gladstone Bott's mashie-shot, falling short, ran over the rough, peered for a moment into the depths to the left, then, winding up the path, trickled on to the green, struck a fortunate slope, acquired momentum, ran on, and dropped into the hole.

"Nearly missed it," said Gladstone Bott, drawing a deep breath.

Bradbury Fisher looked out upon a world that swam and danced before his eyes. He had not been prepared for this sort of thing. The way things were shaping, he felt that it would hardly surprise him now if the cups were to start jumping up and snapping at Bott's ball like starving dogs.

"Three up," said Gladstone Bott.

With a strong effort Bradbury Fisher mastered his feelings. His mouth set grimly. Matters, he perceived, had reached a crisis. He saw now that he had made a mistake in allowing himself to be intimidated by the importance of the occasion into being scientific. Nature had never intended him for a scientific golfer, and up till now he had been behaving like an animated illustration out of a book by Vardon. He had taken his club back along and near the turf, allowing it to trend around the legs as far as was permitted by the movement of the arms. He had kept his right elbow close to the side, this action coming into operation before the club was allowed to describe a section of a circle in an upward direction, whence it was carried by means of a slow, steady, swinging movement. He had pivoted, he had pronated the wrists, and he had been careful about the lateral hip-shift.

And it had been all wrong. That sort of stuff might suit

some people, but not him. He was a biffer, a swatter, and a slosher; and it flashed upon him now that only by biffing, swatting, and sloshing as he had never biffed, swatted, and sloshed before could he hope to recover the ground he had lost.

Gladstone Bott was not one of those players who grow careless with success. His drive at the eighth was just as steady and short as ever. But this time Bradbury Fisher made no attempt to imitate him. For seven holes he had been checking his natural instincts, and now he drove with all the banked-up fury that comes with release from long suppression.

For an instant he remained on one leg like a stork; then there was a whistle and a crack, and the ball, smitten squarely in the midriff, flew down the course and, soaring over the bunkers, hit the turf and gambolled to within twenty yards of the green.

He straightened out the kinks in his spine with a grim smile. Allowing himself the regulation three putts, he would be down in five, and only a miracle could give Gladstone Bott anything better than a seven. "Two down," he said some minutes later, and Gladstone Bott nodded sullenly.

It was not often that Bradbury Fisher kept on the fairway with two consecutive drives, but strange things were happening to-day. Not only was his drive at the ninth a full two hundred and forty yards, but it was also perfectly straight. "One down," said Bradbury Fisher, and Bott nodded even more sullenly than before.

There are few things more demoralising than to be consistently outdriven; and when he is outdriven by a hundred and seventy yards at two consecutive holes the bravest man is apt to be shaken. Gladstone Bott was only human. It was with a sinking heart that he watched his opponent heave and sway on the tenth tee; and when the ball once more flew straight and far down the course a strange weakness seemed to come over him. For the first time he lost his morale and topped. The ball trickled into the long grass, and after three fruitless stabs at it with a niblick he picked up, and the match was squared.

At the eleventh Bradbury Fisher also topped, and his tee-shot, though nice and straight, travelled only a couple of feet. He had to scramble to halve in eight.

The twelfth was another short hole; and Bradbury, unable to curb the fine, careless rapture which had crept into his game, had the misfortune to overshoot the green by some sixty yards, thus enabling his opponent to take the lead once more.

The thirteenth and fourteenth were halved, but Bradbury, driving another long ball, won the fifteenth, squaring the match.

It seemed to Bradbury Fisher, as he took his stand on the sixteenth tee, that he now had the situation well in hand. At the thirteenth and fourteenth his drive had flickered, but on the fifteenth it had come back in all its glorious vigour and there appeared to be no reason to suppose that it had not come to stay. He recollected exactly how he had done that last colossal slosh, and he now prepared to reproduce the movements precisely as before. The great thing to remember was to hold the breath on the back-swing and not to release it before the moment of impact. Also, the eyes should not be closed until late in the down-swing. All great golfers have their little secrets, and that was Bradbury's.

With these aids to success firmly fixed in his mind, Bradbury Fisher prepared to give the ball the nastiest bang that a golf-ball had ever had since Edward Blackwell was in his prime. He drew in his breath and, with lungs expanded to their fullest capacity, heaved back on to his large, flat right foot. Then, clenching his teeth, he lashed out.

When he opened his eyes, they fell upon a horrid spec-

tacle. Either he had closed those eyes too soon or else he had
breathed too precipitately — whatever the cause, the ball,
which should have gone due south, was travelling with great
speed sou'-sou'-east. And, even as he gazed, it curved to earth
and fell into as uninviting a bit of rough as he had ever
penetrated. And he was a man who had spent much time in
many roughs.

Leaving Gladstone Bott to continue his imitation of a spav-
ined octogenarian rolling peanuts with a toothpick, Bradbury Fisher, followed by his caddy, set out on the long trail
into the jungle.

Hope did not altogether desert him as he walked. In spite
of its erratic direction, the ball had been so shrewdly smitten
that it was not far from the green. Provided luck was with
him and the lie not too desperate, a mashie would put him
on the carpet. It was only when he reached the rough and
saw what had happened that his heart sank. There the ball
lay, half hidden in the grass, while above it waved the strag-
gling tentacle of some tough-looking shrub. Behind it was a
stone, and behind the stone, at just the elevation required to
catch the back-swing of the club, was a tree. And, by an
ironical stroke of fate which drew from Bradbury a hollow,
bitter laugh, only a few feet to the right was a beautiful
smooth piece of turf from which it would have been a pleasure to play one's second.

Dully, Bradbury looked round to see how Bott was getting
on. And then suddenly, as he found that Bott was completely
invisible behind the belt of bushes through which he had just
passed, a voice seemed to whisper to him, "Why not?"

Bradbury Fisher, remember, had spent thirty years on
Wall Street.

It was at this moment that he realised that he was not
alone. His caddy was standing at his side.

Bradbury Fisher gazed upon the caddy, whom until now he had not had any occasion to observe with any closeness. The caddy was not a boy. He was a man, apparently in the middle forties, with bushy eyebrows and a walrus moustache; and there was something about his appearance which suggested to Bradbury that here was a kindred spirit. He reminded Bradbury a little of Spike Huggins, the safe-blower, who had been a fresher with him at Sing-Sing. It seemed to him that this caddy could be trusted in a delicate matter involving secrecy and silence. Had he been some babbling urchin, the risk might have been too great.

"Caddy," said Bradbury.

"Sir?" said the caddy.

"Yours is an ill-paid job," said Bradbury.

"It is, indeed, sir," said the caddy.

"Would you like to earn fifty dollars?"

"I would prefer to earn a hundred."

"I meant a hundred," said Bradbury.

He produced a roll of bills from his pocket, and peeled off one of that value. Then, stooping, he picked up his ball and placed it on the little oasis of turf. The caddy bowed intelligently.

"You mean to say," cried Gladstone Bott, a few moments later, "that you were out with your second? With your second!"

"I had a stroke of luck."

"You're sure it wasn't about six strokes of luck?"

"My ball was right out in the open in an excellent lie."

"Oh!" said Gladstone Bott, shortly.

"I have four for it, I think."

"One down," said Gladstone Bott.

"And two to play," trilled Bradbury.

It was with a light heart that Bradbury Fisher teed up on the seventeenth. The match, he felt, was as good as over. The whole essence of golf is to discover a way of getting out of rough without losing strokes; and with this sensible, broad-minded man of the world caddying for him he seemed to have discovered the ideal way. It cost him scarcely a pang when he saw his drive slice away into a tangle of long grass, but for the sake of appearances he affected a little chagrin.

"Tut, tut!" he said.

"I shouldn't worry," said Gladstone Bott. "You will probably find it sitting upon an india-rubber tee which some one has dropped there."

He spoke sardonically, and Bradbury did not like his manner. But then he never had liked Gladstone Bott's manner, so what of that? He made his way to where the ball had fallen. It was lying under a bush.

"Caddy," said Bradbury.

"Sir?" said the caddy.

"A hundred?"

"And fifty."

"And fifty," said Bradbury Fisher.

Gladstone Bott was still toiling along the fairway when Bradbury reached the green.

"How many?" he asked, eventually winning to the goal.

"On in two," said Bradbury. "And you?"

"Playing seven."

"Then let me see. If you take two putts, which is most unlikely, I shall have six for the hole and match."

A minute later Bradbury had picked up his ball out of the cup. He stood there, basking in the sunshine, his heart glowing with quiet happiness. It seemed to him that he had never seen the countryside looking so beautiful. The birds appeared to be singing as they had never sung before. The trees and the rolling turf had taken on a charm beyond anything he had ever encountered. Even Gladstone Bott looked almost bearable.

"A very pleasant match," he said, cordially, "conducted throughout in the most sporting spirit. At one time I thought you were going to pull it off, old man, but there — class will tell."

"I will now make my report," said the caddy with the walrus moustache.

"Do so," said Gladstone Bott, briefly.

Bradbury Fisher stared at the man with blanched cheeks. The sun had ceased to shine, the birds had stopped singing. The trees and the rolling turf looked pretty rotten, and Gladstone Bott perfectly foul. His heart was leaden with a hideous dread.

"Your report? Your — your report? What do you mean?"

"You don't suppose," said Gladstone Bott, "that I would play you an important match unless I had detectives watching you, do you? This gentleman is from the Quick Results Agency. What have you to report?" he said, turning to the caddy.

The caddy removed his bushy eyebrows, and with a quick gesture swept off his moustache.

"On the twelfth inst.," he began in a monotonous, singsong voice, "acting upon instructions received, I made my way to the Goldenville Golf Links in order to observe the movements of the man Fisher. I had adopted for the occasion the Number Three disguise and — "

"All right, all right," said Gladstone Bott, impatiently. "You can skip all that. Come down to what happened at the sixteenth."

The caddy looked wounded, but he bowed deferentially.

"At the sixteenth hole the man Fisher moved his ball into what — from his actions and furtive manner — I deduced to be a more favourable position."

"Ah!" said Gladstone Bott.

"On the seventeenth the man Fisher picked up his ball and

threw it with a movement of the wrist on to the green."

"It's a lie. A foul and contemptible lie," shouted Bradbury Fisher.

"Realising that the man Fisher might adopt this attitude, sir," said the caddy, "I took the precaution of snapshotting him in the act with my miniature wrist-watch camera, the detective's best friend."

Bradbury Fisher covered his face with his hands and uttered a hollow groan.

"My match," said Gladstone Bott, with vindictive triumph. "I'll trouble you to deliver that butler to me f.o.b. at my residence not later than noon to-morrow. Oh yes, and I was forgetting. You owe me three railroads."

Blizzard, dignified but kindly, met Bradbury in the Byzantine hall on his return home.

"I trust your golf-match terminated satisfactorily, sir?" said the butler.

A pang, almost too poignant to be borne, shot through Bradbury.

"No, Blizzard," he said. "No. Thank you for your kind inquiry, but I was not in luck."

"Too bad, sir," said Blizzard, sympathetically. "I trust the prize at stake was not excessive?"

"Well — er — well, it was rather big. I should like to speak to you about that a little later, Blizzard."

"At any time that is suitable to you, sir. If you will ring for one of the assistant-underfootmen when you desire to see me, sir, he will find me in my pantry. Meanwhile, sir, this cable arrived for you a short while back."

Bradbury took the envelope listlessly. He had been expecting a communication from his London agents announcing that they had bought Kent and Sussex, for which he had instructed them to make a firm offer just before he left England. No doubt this was their cable.

He opened the envelope, and started as if it had contained a scorpion. It was from his wife.

Returning immediately "Aquitania" it ran. *Docking Friday night. Meet without fail.*

Bradbury stared at the words, frozen to the marrow. Although he had been in a sort of trance ever since that dreadful moment on the seventeenth green, his great brain had not altogether ceased to function; and, while driving home in the car, he had sketched out roughly a plan of action which, he felt, might meet the crisis. Assuming that Mrs. Fisher was to remain abroad for another month, he had practically decided to buy a daily paper, insert in it a front-page story announcing the death of Blizzard, forward the clipping to his wife, and then sell his house and move to another neighbourhood. In this way it might be that she would never learn of what had occurred.

But if she was due back next Friday, the scheme fell through and exposure was inevitable.

He wondered dully what had caused her change of plans, and came to the conclusion that some feminine sixth sense must have warned her of peril threatening Blizzard. With a good deal of peevishness he wished that Providence had never endowed women with this sixth sense. A woman with merely five took quite enough handling.

"Sweet suffering soup-spoons!" groaned Bradbury.

"Sir?" said Blizzard.

"Nothing," said Bradbury.

"Very good, sir," said Blizzard.

For a man with anything on his mind, any little trouble calculated to affect the *joie de vivre,* there are few spots less cheering than the Customs sheds of New York. Draughts whistle dismally there — now to, now fro. Strange noises are heard. Customs officials chew gum and lurk grimly in the shadows, like tigers awaiting the luncheon-gong. It is not surprising that Bradbury's spirits, low when he reached the place, should have sunk to zero long before the gangplank was lowered and the passengers began to stream down it.

His wife was among the first to land. How beautiful she looked, thought Bradbury, as he watched her. And, alas, how intimidating. His tastes had always lain in the direction of spirited women. His first wife had been spirited. So had his second, third and fourth. And the one at the moment holding office was perhaps the most spirited of the whole platoon. For one long instant, as he went to meet her, Bradbury Fisher was conscious of a regret that he had not married one of those meek, mild girls who suffer uncomplainingly at their husband's hands in the more hectic type of feminine novel. What he felt he could have done with at the moment was the sort of wife who thinks herself dashed lucky if the other half of the sketch does not drag her round the billiard-room by her hair, kicking her the while with spiked shoes.

Three conversational openings presented themselves to him as he approached her.

"Darling, there is something I want to tell you — "

"Dearest, I have a small confession to make — "

"Sweetheart, I don't know if by any chance you remember Blizzard, our butler. Well, it's like this — "

But, in the event, it was she who spoke first.

"Oh, Bradbury," she cried, rushing into his arms, "I've done the most awful thing, and you must try to forgive me!"

Bradbury blinked. He had never seen her in this strange mood before. As she clung to him, she seemed timid, fluttering, and — although a woman who weighed a full hundred and fifty-seven pounds — almost fragile.

"What is it?" he inquired, tenderly. "Has somebody stolen your jewels?"

"No, no."

"Have you been losing money at bridge?"

"No, no. Worse than that."

Bradbury started.

"You didn't sing 'My Little Grey Home in the West' at the ship's concert?" he demanded, eyeing her closely.

"No, no! Ah, how can I tell you? Bradbury, look! You see that man over there?"

Bradbury followed her pointing finger. Standing in an attitude of negligent dignity beside a pile of trunks under the letter V was a tall, stout, ambassadorial man, at the very sight of whom, even at this distance, Bradbury Fisher felt an odd sense of inferiority. His pendulous cheeks, his curving waist-coat, his protruding eyes, and the sequence of rolling chins combined to produce in Bradbury that instinctive feeling of being in the presence of a superior which we experience when meeting scratch golfers, head-waiters of fashionable restaurants, and traffic-policemen. A sudden pang of suspicion pierced him.

"Well?" he said, hoarsely. "What of him?"

"Bradbury, you must not judge me too harshly. We were thrown together and I was tempted — "

"Woman," thundered Bradbury Fisher, "who is this man?"

"His name is Vosper."

"And what is there between you and him, and when did it start, and why and how and where?"

Mrs. Fisher dabbed at her eyes with her handkerchief.

"It was at the Duke of Bootle's, Bradbury. I was invited there for the week-end."

"And this man was there?"

"Yes."

"Ha! Proceed!"

"The moment I set eyes on him, something seemed to go all over me."

"Indeed!"

"At first it was his mere appearance. I felt that I had dreamed of such a man all my life, and that for all these wasted years I had been putting up with the second-best."

"Oh, you did, eh? Really? Is that so? You did, did you?" snorted Bradbury Fisher.

"I couldn't help it, Bradbury. I know I have always seemed so devoted to Blizzard, and so I was. But, honestly, there is no comparison between them — really there isn't. You should see the way Vosper stood behind the Duke's chair. Like a high priest presiding over some mystic religious ceremony. And his voice when he asks you if you will have sherry or hock! Like the music of some wonderful organ. I couldn't resist him. I approached him delicately, and found that he was willing to come to America. He had been eighteen years with the Duke, and he told me he couldn't stand the sight of the back of his head any longer. So — "

Bradbury Fisher reeled.

"This man — this Vosper. Who is he?"

"Why, I'm telling you, honey. He was the Duke's butler, and now he's ours. Oh, you know how impulsive I am. Honestly, it wasn't till we were half-way across the Atlantic that I suddenly said to myself, 'What about Blizzard?' What am I to do, Bradbury? I simply haven't the nerve to fire Blizzard. And yet what will happen when he walks into his pantry and finds Vosper there? Oh, think, Bradbury, think!"

Bradbury Fisher was thinking — and for the first time in a week without agony.

"Evangeline," he said, gravely, "this is awkward."

"I know."

"Extremely awkward."

"I know, I know. But surely you can think of some way out of the muddle!"

"I may. I cannot promise, but I may." He pondered deeply. "Ha! I have it! It is just possible that I may be able to induce Gladstone Bott to take on Blizzard."

"Do you really think he would?"

"He may — if I play my cards carefully. At any rate, I will

try to persuade him. For the moment you and Vosper had better remain in New York, while I go home and put the negotiations in train. If I am successful, I will let you know."

"Do try your very hardest."

"I think I shall be able to manage it. Gladstone and I are old friends, and he would stretch a point to oblige me. But let this be a lesson to you, Evangeline."

"Oh, I will."

"By the way," said Bradbury Fisher, "I am cabling my London agents to-day to instruct them to buy J. H. Taylor's shirt-stud for my collection."

"Quite right, Bradbury darling. And anything else you want in that way you will get, won't you?"

"I will," said Bradbury Fisher.

Chester Forgets Himself

O

The afternoon was warm and heavy. Butterflies loafed languidly in the sunshine, birds panted in the shady recesses of the trees.

The Oldest Member, snug in his favourite chair, had long since succumbed to the drowsy influence of the weather. His eyes were closed, his chin sunk upon his breast. The pipe which he had been smoking lay beside him on the turf, and ever and anon there proceeded from him a muffled snore.

Suddenly the stillness was broken. There was a sharp, cracking sound as of splitting wood. The Oldest Member sat up, blinking. As soon as his eyes had become accustomed to the glare, he perceived that a foursome had holed out on the ninth and was disintegrating. Two of the players were moving with quick, purposeful steps in the direction of the side door which gave entrance to the bar; a third was making for the road that led to the village, bearing himself as one in profound dejection; the fourth came on to the terrace.

"Finished?" said the Oldest Member.

The other stopped, wiping a heated brow. He lowered himself into the adjoining chair and stretched his legs out.

"Yes. We started at the tenth. Golly, I'm tired. No joke playing in this weather."

"How did you come out?"

"We won on the last green. Jimmy Fothergill and I were playing the vicar and Rupert Blake."

"What was that sharp, cracking sound I heard?" asked the Oldest Member.

"That was the vicar smashing his putter. Poor old chap, he had rotten luck all the way round, and it didn't seem to make it any better for him that he wasn't able to relieve his feelings in the ordinary way."

"I suspected some such thing," said the Oldest Member, "from the look of his back as he was leaving the green. His walk was the walk of an overwrought soul."

His companion did not reply. He was breathing deeply and regularly.

"It is a moot question," proceeded the Oldest Member, thoughtfully, "whether the clergy, considering their peculiar position, should not be more liberally handicapped at golf than the laymen with whom they compete. I have made a close study of the game since the days of the feather ball, and I am firmly convinced that to refrain entirely from oaths during a round is almost equivalent to giving away three bisques. There are certain occasions when an oath seems to be so imperatively demanded that the strain of keeping it in must inevitably affect the ganglions or nerve-centres in such a manner as to diminish the steadiness of the swing."

The man beside him slipped lower down in his chair. His mouth had opened slightly.

"I am reminded in this connection," said the Oldest Member, "of the story of young Chester Meredith, a friend of mine whom you have not, I think, met. He moved from this neighbourhood shortly before you came. There was a case where a man's whole happiness was very nearly wrecked purely because he tried to curb his instincts and thwart nature in this very respect. Perhaps you would care to hear the story?"

A snore proceeded from the next chair.

"Very well, then," said the Oldest Member, "I will relate it."

Chester Meredith (said the Oldest Member) was one of the nicest young fellows of my acquaintance. We had been friends ever since he had come to live here as a small boy, and I had watched him with a fatherly eye through all the more important crises of a young man's life. It was I who taught him to drive, and when he had all that trouble in his twenty-first year with shanking his short approaches, it was to me that he came for sympathy and advice. It was an odd coincidence, therefore, that I should have been present when he fell in love.

I was smoking my evening cigar out here and watching the last couples finishing their rounds, when Chester came out of the club-house and sat by me. I could see that the boy was perturbed about something, and wondered why, for I knew that he had won his match.

"What," I inquired, "is on your mind?"

"Oh, nothing," said Chester. "I was only thinking that there are some human misfits who ought not be allowed on any decent links."

"You mean — ?"

"The Wrecking Crew," said Chester, bitterly. "They held us up all the way round, confound them. Wouldn't let us through. What can you do with people who don't know enough of the etiquette of the game to understand that a single has right of way over a four-ball foursome? We had to loaf about for hours on end while they scratched at the turf like a lot of crimson hens. Eventually all four of them lost their balls simultaneously at the eleventh and we managed to get by. I hope they choke."

I was not altogether surprised at his warmth. The Wrecking Crew consisted of four retired business men who had taken up the noble game late in life because their doctors had ordered them air and exercise. Every club, I suppose, has a cross of this kind to bear, and it was not often that our members rebelled; but there was undoubtedly something particularly irritating in the methods of the Wrecking Crew. They tried so hard that it seemed almost inconceivable that they should be so slow.

"They are all respectable men," I said, "and were, I believe, highly thought of in their respective businesses. But on the links I admit that they are a trial."

"They are the direct lineal descendants of the Gadarene swine," said Chester firmly. "Every time they come out I expect to see them rush down the hill from the first tee and hurl themselves into the lake at the second. Of all the — "

"Hush!" I said.

Out of the corner of my eye I had seen a girl approaching, and I was afraid lest Chester in his annoyance might use strong language. For he was one of those golfers who are apt to express themselves in moments of emotion with a good deal of generous warmth.

"Eh?" said Chester.

I jerked my head, and he looked round. And, as he did so, there came into his face an expression which I had seen there only once before, on the occasion when he won the President's Cup on the last green by holing a thirty-yard chip with his mashie. It was a look of ecstasy and awe. His mouth was open, his eyebrows raised, and he was breathing heavily through his nose.

"Golly!" I heard him mutter.

The girl passed by. I could not blame Chester for staring at her. She was a beautiful young thing, with a lissom figure and a perfect face. Her hair was a deep chestnut, her eyes blue, her nose small and laid back with about as much loft as a light iron. She disappeared, and Chester, after nearly dislocating his neck trying to see her round the corner of the club-house, emitted a deep, explosive sigh.

"Who is she?" he whispered.

I could tell him that. In one way and another I get to know most things around this locality.

"She is a Miss Blakeney. Felicia Blakeney. She has come to stay for a month with the Waterfields. I understand she was at school with Jane Waterfield. She is twenty-three, has a dog named Joseph, dances well, and dislikes parsnips. Her father is a distinguished writer on sociological subjects; her mother is Wilmot Royce, the well-known novelist, whose last work, *Sewers of the Soul,* was, you may recall, jerked before a tribunal by the Purity League. She has a brother, Crispin Blakeney, an eminent young reviewer and essayist, who is now in India studying local conditions with a view to a series of lectures. She only arrived here yesterday, so this is all I have been able to find out about her as yet."

Chester's mouth was still open when I began speaking. By the time I had finished it was open still wider. The ecstatic look in his eyes had changed to one of dull despair.

"My God!" he muttered. "If her family is like that, what chance is there for a rough-neck like me?"

"You admire her?"

"She is the alligator's Adam's apple," said Chester, simply.

I patted his shoulder.

"Have courage, my boy," I said. "Always remember that the love of a good man, to whom the pro can give only a couple of strokes in eighteen holes, is not to be despised."

"Yes, that's all very well. But this girl is probably one solid mass of brain. She will look on me as an uneducated wart-hog."

"Well, I will introduce you, and we will see. She looked a nice girl."

"You're a great describer, aren't you?" said Chester. "A wonderful flow of language you've got, I don't think! Nice girl! Why, she's the only girl in the world. She's a pearl among women. She's the most marvellous, astounding, beautiful, heavenly thing that ever drew perfumed breath." He paused, as if his train of thought had been interrupted by an idea. "Did you say that her brother's name was Crispin?"

"I did. Why?"

Chester gave vent to a few manly oaths.

"Doesn't that just show you how things go in this rotten world?"

"What do you mean?"

"I was at school with him."

"Surely that should form a solid basis for friendship?"

"Should it? Should it, by gad? Well, let me tell you that I probably kicked that blighted worm Crispin Blakeney a matter of seven hundred and forty-six times in the few years I knew him. He was the world's worst. He could have walked straight into the Wrecking Crew and no questions asked. Wouldn't it jar you? I have the luck to know her brother, and it turns out that we couldn't stand the sight of each other."

"Well, there is no need to tell her that."

"Do you mean — ?" He gazed at me wildly. "Do you mean that I might pretend we were pals?"

"Why not? Seeing that he is in India, he can hardly contradict you."

"My gosh!" He mused for a moment. I could see that the idea was beginning to sink in. It was always thus with Chester. You had to give him time. "By Jove, it mightn't be a bad scheme at that. I mean, it would start me off with a rush, like being one up on bogey in the first two. And there's nothing like a good start. By gad, I'll do it."

"I should."

"Reminiscences of the dear old days when we were lads together, and all that sort of thing."

"Precisely."

"It isn't going to be easy, mind you," said Chester, meditatively. "I'll do it because I love her, but nothing else in this world would make me say a civil word about the blister. Well, then, that's settled. Get on with the introduction stuff, will you? I'm in a hurry."

One of the privileges of age is that it enables a man to thrust his society on a beautiful girl without causing her to draw herself up and say "Sir!" It was not difficult for me to make the acquaintance of Miss Blakeney, and, this done, my first act was to unleash Chester on her.

"Chester," I said, summoning him as he loafed with an overdone carelessness on the horizon, one leg almost inextricably entwined about the other, "I want you to meet Miss Blakeney. Miss Blakeney, this is my young friend Chester Meredith. He was at school with your brother Crispin. You were great friends, were you not?"

"Bosom," said Chester, after a pause.

"Oh, really?" said the girl. There was a pause. "He is in India now."

"Yes," said Chester.

There was another pause.

"Great chap," said Chester, gruffly.

"Crispin is very popular," said the girl, "with some people."

"Always been my best pal," said Chester.

"Yes?"

I was not altogether satisfied with the way matters were developing. The girl seemed cold and unfriendly, and I was afraid that this was due to Chester's repellent manner. Shyness, especially when complicated by love at first sight, is apt to have strange effects on a man, and the way it had taken Chester was to make him abnormally stiff and dignified. One of the most charming things about him, as a rule, was his delightful boyish smile. Shyness had caused him to iron this out of his countenance till no trace of it remained. Not only did he not smile, he looked like a man who never had smiled and never would. His mouth was a thin, rigid line. His back was stiff with what appeared to be contemptuous aversion.

He looked down his nose at Miss Blakeney as if she were less than the dust beneath his chariot-wheels.

I thought the best thing to do was to leave them alone together to get acquainted. Perhaps, I thought, it was my presence that was cramping Chester's style. I excused myself and receded.

It was some days before I saw Chester again. He came round to my cottage one night after dinner and sank into a chair, where he remained silent for several minutes.

"Well?" I said at last.

"Eh?" said Chester, starting violently.

"Have you been seeing anything of Miss Blakeney lately?"

"You bet I have."

"And how do you feel about her on further acquaintance?"

"Eh?" said Chester, absently.

"Do you still love her?"

Chester came out of his trance.

"Love her?" he cried, his voice vibrating with emotion. "Of course I love her. Who wouldn't love her? I'd be a silly chump not loving her. Do you know," the boy went on, a look in his eyes like that of some young knight seeing the Holy Grail in a vision, "do you know, she is the only woman I ever met who didn't overswing. Just a nice, crisp, snappy, half-slosh, with a good full follow-through. And another thing. You'll hardly believe me, but she waggles almost as little as George Duncan. You know how women waggle as a rule, fiddling about for a minute and a half like kittens playing with a ball of wool. Well, she just makes one firm pass with the club and then *bing!* There is none like her, none."

"Then you have been playing golf with her?"

"Nearly every day."

"How is your game?"

"Rather spotty. I seem to be mistiming them."

I was concerned.

"I do hope, my dear boy," I said, earnestly, "that you are taking care to control your feelings when out on the links with Miss Blakeney. You know what you are like. I trust you have not been using the sort of language you generally employ on occasions when you are not timing them right?"

"Me?" said Chester, horrified. "Who, me? You don't imagine for a moment that I would dream of saying a thing that would bring a blush to her dear cheek, do you? Why, a bishop could have gone round with me and learned nothing new."

I was relieved.

"How do you find you manage the dialogue these days?" I asked. "When I introduced you, you behaved — you will forgive an old friend for criticising — you behaved a little like a stuffed frog with laryngitis. Have things got easier in that respect?"

"Oh yes. I'm quite the prattler now. I talk about her brother mostly. I put in the greater part of my time boosting the tick. It seems to be coming easier. Will-power, I suppose. And then, of course, I talk a good deal about her mother's novels."

"Have you read them?"

"Every damned one of them — for her sake. And if there's a greater proof of love than that, show me! My gosh, what muck that woman writes! That reminds me, I've got to send to the bookshop for her latest — out yesterday. It's called *The Stench of Life*. A sequel, I understand, to *Grey Mildew*."

"Brave lad," I said, pressing his hand. "Brave, devoted lad!"

"Oh, I'd do more than that for her." He smoked for a while in silence. "By the way, I'm going to propose to her tomorrow."

"Already?"

"Can't put it off a minute longer. It's been as much as I could manage, bottling it up till now. Where do you think would be the best place? I mean, it's not the sort of thing you can do while you're walking down the street or having a cup of tea. I thought of asking her to have a round with me and taking a stab at it on the links."

"You could not do better. The links — Nature's cathedral."

"Right-o, then! I'll let you know how I come out."

"I wish you luck, my boy," I said.

And what of Felicia, meanwhile? She was, alas, far from returning the devotion which scorched Chester's vital organs. He seemed to her precisely the sort of man she most disliked. From childhood up Felicia Blakeney had lived in an atmosphere of highbrowism, and the type of husband she had always seen in her daydreams was the man who was simple and straightforward and earthy and did not know whether Artbashiekeff was a suburb of Moscow or a new kind of Russian drink. A man like Chester, who on his own statement would rather read one of her mother's novels than eat, revolted her. And his warm affection for her brother Crispin set the seal on her distaste.

Felicia was a dutiful child, and she loved her parents. It took a bit of doing, but she did it. But at her brother Crispin she drew the line. He wouldn't do, and his friends were worse than he was. They were high-voiced, supercilious, pince-nezed young men who talked patronisingly of Life and Art, and Chester's unblushing confession that he was one of them had put him ten down and nine to play right away.

You may wonder why the boy's undeniable skill on the links had no power to soften the girl. The unfortunate fact was that all the good effects of his prowess were neutralised by his behaviour while playing. All her life she had treated golf with a proper reverence and awe, and in Chester's attitude towards the game she seemed to detect a horrible shallowness. The fact is, Chester, in his efforts to keep himself from using strong language, had found a sort of relief in a girlish giggle, and it made her shudder every time she heard it.

His deportment, therefore, in the space of time leading up to the proposal could not have been more injurious to his cause. They started out quite happily, Chester doing a nice two-hundred-yarder off the first tee, which for a moment awoke the girl's respect. But at the fourth, after a lovely brassie-shot, he found his ball deeply embedded in the print of a woman's high heel. It was just one of those rubs of the green which normally would have caused him to ease his bosom with a flood of sturdy protest, but now he was on his guard.

"Tee-hee!" simpered Chester, reaching for his niblick. "Too bad, too bad!" and the girl shuddered to the depths of her soul.

Having holed out, he proceeded to enliven the walk to the next tee with a few remarks on her mother's literary style, and it was while they were walking after their drives that he proposed.

His proposal, considering the circumstances, could hardly have been less happily worded. Little knowing that he was rushing upon his doom, Chester stressed the Crispin note. He gave Felicia the impression that he was suggesting this marriage more for Crispin's sake than anything else. He conveyed the idea that he thought how nice it would be for brother Crispin to have his old chum in the family. He drew a picture of their little home, with Crispin for ever popping in and out like a rabbit. It is not to be wondered at that, when at length he had finished and she had time to speak, the horrified girl turned him down with a thud.

It is at moments such as these that a man reaps the reward of a good upbringing.

In similar circumstances those who have not had the benefit of a sound training in golf are too apt to go wrong. Goaded by the sudden anguish, they take to drink, plunge into dissipation, and write *vers libre*. Chester was mercifully saved from this. I saw him the day after he had been handed the mitten, and was struck by the look of grim determination in his face. Deeply wounded though he was, I could see that he was the master of his fate and the captain of his soul.

"I am sorry, my boy," I said, sympathetically, when he had told me the painful news.

"It can't be helped," he replied, bravely.

"Her decision was final?"

"Quite."

"You do not contemplate having another pop at her?"

"No good. I know when I'm licked."

I patted him on the shoulder and said the only thing it seemed possible to say.

"After all, there is always golf."

He nodded.

"Yes. My game needs a lot of tuning up. Now is the time to do it. From now on I go at this pastime seriously. I make it my life-work. Who knows?" he murmured, with a sudden gleam in his eyes. "The Amateur Championship — "

"The Open!" I cried, falling gladly into his mood.

"The American Amateur," said Chester, flushing.

"The American Open," I chorused.

"No one has ever copped all four."

"No one."

"Watch me!" said Chester Meredith, simply.

It was about two weeks after this that I happened to look in on Chester at his house one morning. I found him about to start for the links. As he had foreshadowed in the conversation which I have just related, he now spent most of the daylight hours on the course. In these two weeks he had gone about his task of achieving perfection with a furious energy which made him the talk of the club. Always one of the best players in the place, he had developed an astounding brilliance. Men who had played him level were now obliged to receive two and even three strokes. The pro. himself conceding one, had only succeeded in halving their match. The struggle for the President's Cup came round once more, and

Chester won it for the second time with ridiculous ease.

When I arrived, he was practising chip-shots in his sitting-room. I noticed that he seemed to be labouring under some strong emotion, and his first words gave me the clue.

"She's going away to-morrow," he said, abruptly, lofting a ball over the whatnot on to the Chesterfield.

I was not sure whether I was sorry or relieved. Her absence would leave a terrible blank, of course, but it might be that it would help him to get over his infatuation.

"Ah!" I said, non-committally.

Chester addressed his ball with a well-assumed phlegm, but I could see by the way his ears wiggled that he was feeling deeply. I was not surprised when he topped his shot into the coal-scuttle.

"She has promised to play a last round with me this morning," he said.

Again I was doubtful what view to take. It was a pretty, poetic idea, not unlike Browning's "Last Ride Together," but I was not sure if it was altogether wise. However, it was none of my business, so I merely patted him on the shoulder and he gathered up his clubs and went off.

Owing to motives of delicacy I had not offered to accompany him on his round, and it was not till later that I learned the actual details of what occurred. At the start, it seems, the spiritual anguish which he was suffering had a depressing effect on his game. He hooked his drive off the first tee and was only enabled to get a five by means of a strong niblick shot out of the rough. At the second, the lake hole, he lost a ball in the water and got another five. It was only at the third that he began to pull himself together.

The test of a great golfer is his ability to recover from a bad start. Chester had this quality to a pre-eminent degree. A lesser man, conscious of being three over bogey for the first two holes, might have looked on his round as ruined. To

Chester it simply meant that he had to get a couple of "bird-ies" right speedily, and he set about it at once. Always a long driver, he excelled himself at the third. It is, as you know, an uphill hole all the way, but his drive could not have come far short of two hundred and fifty yards. A brassie-shot of equal strength and unerring direction put him on the edge of the green, and he holed out with a long putt two under bogey. He had hoped for a "birdie" and he had achieved an "eagle."

I think that this splendid feat must have softened Felicia's heart, had it not been for the fact that misery had by this time entirely robbed Chester of the ability to smile. Instead, therefore, of behaving in the wholesome, natural way of men who get threes at bogey five holes, he preserved a drawn, impassive countenance; and as she watched him tee up her ball, stiff, correct, polite, but to all outward appearance abso-lutely inhuman, the girl found herself stifling that thrill of what for a moment had been almost adoration. It was, she felt, exactly how her brother Crispin would have comported himself if he had done a hole in two under bogey.

And yet she could not altogether check a wistful sigh when, after a couple of fours at the next two holes, he picked up another stroke on the sixth and with an inspired spoon-shot brought his medal-score down to one better than bogey by getting a two at the hundred-and-seventy-yard seventh. But the brief spasm of tenderness passed, and when he finished the first nine with two more fours she refrained from anything warmer than a mere word of stereotyped congratulation.

"One under bogey for the first nine," she said. "Splendid!"

"One under bogey!" said Chester, woodenly.

"Out in thirty-four. What is the record for the course?"

Chester started. So great had been his preoccupation that he had not given a thought to the course record. He suddenly realised now that the pro., who had done the lowest medal-score to date — the other course record was held by Peter Willard with a hundred and sixty-one, achieved in his first season — had gone out in only one better than his own figures that day.

"Sixty-eight," he said.

"What a pity you lost those strokes at the beginning!"

"Yes," said Chester.

He spoke absently — and, as it seemed to her, primly and without enthusiasm — for the flaming idea of having a go at the course record had only just occurred to him. Once before he had done the first nine in thirty-four, but on that occasion he had not felt that curious feeling of irresistible force which comes to a golfer at the very top of his form. Then he had been aware all the time that he had been putting chancily. They had gone in, yes, but he had uttered a prayer per putt. To-day he was superior to any weak doubtings. When he tapped the ball on the green, he knew it was going to sink. The course record? Why not? What a last offering to lay at her feet! She would go away, out of his life for ever; she would marry some other bird; but the memory of that supreme round would remain with her as long as she breathed. When he won the Open and Amateur for the second — the third — the fourth time, she would say to herself, "I was with him when he dented the record for his home course!" And he had only to pick up a couple of strokes on the last nine, to do threes at holes where he was wont to be satisfied with fours. Yes, by Vardon, he would take a whirl at it.

You, who are acquainted with these links, will no doubt say that the task which Chester Meredith had sketched out for himself — cutting two strokes off thirty-five for the second nine — was one at which Humanity might well shudder. The pro. himself, who had finished sixth in the last Open Championship, had never done better than a thirty-five, playing perfect golf and being one under par. But such was Chester's mood that, as he teed up on the tenth, he did not even consider the possibility of failure. Every muscle in his body was working in perfect co-ordination with its fellows, his wrists felt as if they were made of tempered steel, and his eyes had just that hawk-like quality which enables a man to judge his short approaches to the inch. He swung forcefully, and the ball sailed so close to the direction-post that for a moment it seemed as if it had hit it.

"Oo!" cried Felicia.

Chester did not speak. He was following the flight of the ball. It sailed over the brow of the hill, and with his knowledge of the course he could tell almost the exact patch of turf on which it must have come to rest. An iron would do the business from there, and a single putt would give him the first of the "birdies" he required. Two minutes later he had holed out a six-foot putt for a three.

"Oo!" said Felicia again.

Chester walked to the eleventh tee in silence.

"No, never mind," she said, as he stooped to put her ball on the sand. "I don't think I'll play any more. I'd much rather just watch you."

"Oh, that you could watch me through life!" said Chester, but he said it to himself. His actual words were "Very well!" and he spoke them with a stiff coldness which chilled the girl.

The eleventh is one of the trickiest holes on the course, as no doubt you have found out for yourself. It looks absurdly simple, but that little patch of wood on the right that seems so harmless is placed just in the deadliest position to catch even the most slightly sliced drive. Chester's lacked the austere precision of his last. A hundred yards from the tee it swerved almost imperceptibly, and, striking a branch, fell in the tangled undergrowth. It took him two strokes to hack it out and put it on the green, and then his long putt, after quivering on the edge of the hole, stayed there. For a swift instant red-hot words rose to his lips, but he caught them just as they were coming out and crushed them back. He looked at his ball and he looked at the hole.

FORE!

"Tut!" said Chester.

Felicia uttered a deep sigh. The niblick-shot out of the rough had impressed her profoundly. If only, she felt, this superb golfer had been more human! If only she were able to be constantly in this man's society, to see exactly what it was that he did with his left wrist that gave that terrific snap to his drives, she might acquire the knack herself one of these days. For she was a clear-thinking, honest girl, and thoroughly realised that she did not get the distance she ought to with her wood. With a husband like Chester beside her to stimulate and advise, of what might she not be capable? If she got wrong in her stance, he could put her right with a word. If she had a bout of slicing, how quickly he would tell her what caused it. And she knew that she had only to speak the word to wipe out the effects of her refusal, to bring him to her side for ever.

But could a girl pay such a price? When he had got that "eagle" on the third, he had looked bored. When he had missed this last putt, he had not seemed to care. "Tut!" What a word to use at such a moment! No, she felt sadly, it could not be done. To marry Chester Meredith, she told herself, would be like marrying a composite of Soames Forsyte, Sir Willoughby Patterne, and all her brother Crispin's friends. She sighed and was silent.

Chester, standing on the twelfth tee, reviewed the situation swiftly, like a general before a battle. There were seven holes to play, and he had to do these in two better than bogey. The one that faced him now offered few opportunities. It was a long, slogging, dog-leg hole, and even Ray and Taylor, when they had played their exhibition game on the course, had taken fives. No opening there.

The thirteenth — up a steep hill with a long iron-shot for one's second and a blind green fringed with bunkers? Scarcely practicable to hope for better than a four. The fourteenth — into the valley with the ground sloping sharply down to the ravine? He had once done it in three, but it had been a fluke. No; on these three holes he must be content to play for a steady par and trust to picking up a stroke on the fifteenth.

The fifteenth, straightforward up to the plateau green with its circle of bunkers, presents few difficulties to the finished golfer who is on his game. A bunker meant nothing to Chester in his present conquering vein. His mashie-shot second soared almost contemptuously over the chasm and rolled to within a foot of the pin. He came to the sixteenth with the clear-cut problem before him of snipping two strokes off par on the last three holes.

To the unthinking man, not acquainted with the layout of our links, this would no doubt appear a tremendous feat. But the fact is, the Greens Committee, with perhaps an unduly sentimental bias towards the happy ending, have arranged a comparatively easy finish to the course. The sixteenth is a perfectly plain hole with broad fairway and a down-hill run; the seventeenth, a one-shot affair with no difficulties for the man who keeps them straight; and the eighteenth, though its up-hill run makes it deceptive to the stranger and leads the unwary to take a mashie instead of a light iron for his second, has no real venom in it. Even Peter Willard has occasionally come home in a canter with a six, five, and seven, conceding himself only two eight-foot putts. It is, I think, this mild conclusion to a tough course that makes the refreshment-room of our club so noticeable for its sea of happy faces. The bar every day is crowded with rejoicing men who, forgetting the agonies of the first fifteen, are babbling of what they did on the last three. The seventeenth, with its possibilities of holing out a topped second, is particularly soothing.

Chester Meredith was not the man to top his second on any hole, so this supreme bliss did not come his way; but he laid a beautiful mashie-shot dead and got a three; and when with his iron he put his first well on the green at the seventeenth and holed out for a two, life, for all his broken heart, seemed pretty tolerable. He now had the situation well in hand. He had only to play his usual game to get a four on the last and lower the course record by one stroke.

It was at this supreme moment of his life that he ran into the Wrecking Crew.

You doubtless find it difficult to understand how it came about that if the Wrecking Crew were on the course at all he had not run into them long before. The explanation is that, with a regard for the etiquette of the game unusual in these miserable men, they had for once obeyed the law that enacts that foursomes shall start at the tenth. They had begun their dark work on the second nine, accordingly, at almost the exact moment when Chester Meredith was driving off at the first, and this had enabled them to keep ahead until now. When Chester came to the eighteenth tee, they were just leaving it, moving up the fairway with their caddies in mass formation and looking to his exasperated eye like one of those great race-migrations of the Middle Ages. Wherever Chester looked he seemed to see human, so to speak, figures. One was doddering about in the long grass fifty yards from the tee, others debouched to left and right. The course was crawling with them.

Chester sat down on the bench with a weary sigh. He knew these men. Self-centred, remorseless, deaf to all the promptings of their better nature, they never let any one through. There was nothing to do but wait.

The Wrecking Crew scratched on. The man near the tee rolled his ball ten yards, then twenty, then thirty — he was improving. Ere long he would be out of range. Chester rose and swished his driver.

But the end was not yet. The individual operating in the rough on the left had been advancing in slow stages, and now, finding his ball teed up on a tuft of grass, he opened his shoulders and let himself go. There was a loud report, and the ball, hitting a tree squarely, bounded back almost to the tee, and all the weary work was to do again. By the time Chester was able to drive, he was reduced by impatience, and the necessity of refraining from commenting on the state of affairs as he would have wished to comment, to a frame of mind in which no man could have kept himself from pressing. He pressed, and topped. The ball skidded over the turf for a meagre hundred yards.

"D-d-d-dear me!" said Chester.

The next moment he uttered a bitter laugh. Too late a miracle had happened. One of the foul figures in front was waving its club. Other ghastly creatures were withdrawing to the side of the fairway. Now, when the harm had been done, these outcasts were signalling to him to go through. The hollow mockery of the thing swept over Chester like a wave. What was the use of going through now? He was a good three hundred yards from the green, and he needed bogey at this hole to break the record. Almost absently he drew his brassie from his bag; then, as the full sense of his wrongs bit into his soul, he swung viciously.

Golf is a strange game. Chester had pressed on the tee and foozled. He pressed now, and achieved the most perfect shot of his life. The ball shot from its place as if a charge of powerful explosive were behind it. Never deviating from a straight line, never more than six feet from the ground, it sailed up the hill, crossed the bunker, eluded the mounds beyond, struck the turf, rolled, and stopped fifty feet from the hole. It was a brassie-shot of a lifetime, and shrill senile yippings of excitement and congratulation floated down from the Wrecking Crew. For, degraded though they were, these men were not wholly devoid of human instincts.

Chester drew a deep breath. His ordeal was over. That third shot, which would lay the ball right up to the pin, was precisely the sort of thing he did best. Almost from boyhood he had been a wizard at the short approach. He could hole out in two now on his left ear. He strode up the hill to his ball. It could not have been lying better. Two inches away there was a nasty cup in the turf; but it had avoided this and was sitting nicely perched up, smiling an invitation to the mashie-niblick. Chester shuffled his feet and eyed the flag keenly. Then he stooped to play, and Felicia watched him breathlessly. Her whole being seemed to be concentrated on him. She had forgotten everything save that she was seeing a course record get broken. She could not have been more wrapped up in his success if she had had large sums of money on it.

The Wrecking Crew, meanwhile, had come to life again. They had stopped twittering about Chester's brassie-shot and were thinking of resuming their own game. Even in foursomes where fifty yards is reckoned a good shot somebody must be away, and the man whose turn it was to play was the one who had acquired from his brother-members of the club the nickname of the First Grave-Digger.

A word about this human wen. He was — if there can be said to be grades in such a sub-species — the star performer of the Wrecking Crew. The lunches of fifty-seven years had caused his chest to slip down into the mezzanine floor, but he was still a powerful man, and had in his youth been a hammer-thrower of some repute. He differed from his colleagues — the Man With the Hoe, Old Father Time, and Consul, the Almost Human — in that, while they were content to peck cautiously at the ball, he never spared himself in his efforts to do it a violent injury. Frequently he had cut a blue dot almost in half with his niblick. He was completely muscle-bound, so that he seldom achieved anything beyond a series of chasms in the turf, but he was always trying, and it was his secret belief that, given two or three miracles happening simultaneously, he would one of these days bring off a snifter. Years of disappointment had, however, reduced the flood of hope to a mere trickle, and when he took his brassie now and addressed the ball he had no immediate plans beyond a vague intention of rolling the thing a few yards farther up the hill.

The fact that he had no business to play at all till Chester had holed out did not occur to him; and even if it had occurred he would have dismissed the objection as finicking. Chester, bending over his ball, was nearly two hundred yards away — or the distance of three full brassie-shots. The First Grave-Digger did not hesitate. He whirled up his club as in distant days he had been wont to swing the hammer, and, with the grunt which this performance always wrung from him, brought it down.

Golfers — and I stretch this term to include the Wrecking Crew — are a highly imitative race. The spectacle of a flubber flubbing ahead of us on the fairway inclines to make us flub as well; and, conversely, it is immediately after we have seen a magnificent shot that we are apt to eclipse ourselves. Consciously the Grave-Digger had no notion how Chester had made that superb brassie-biff of his, but all the while I suppose his subconscious self had been taking notes. At any rate, on this one occasion he, too, did the shot of a lifetime. As he opened his eyes, which he always shut tightly at the moment of impact, and started to unravel himself from the complicated tangle in which his follow-through had left him, he perceived the ball breasting the hill like some untamed jack-rabbit of the Californian prairie.

For a moment his only emotion was one of dreamlike amazement. He stood looking at the ball with a wholly impersonal wonder, like a man suddenly confronted with some terrific work of Nature. Then, as a sleep-walker awakens, he came to himself with a start. Directly in front of the flying ball was a man bending to make an approach-shot.

Chester, always a concentrated golfer when there was a

man's work to do, had scarcely heard the crack of the brassie behind him. Certainly he had paid no attention to it. His whole mind was fixed on his stroke. He measured with his eye the distance to the pin, noted the down-slope of the green, and shifted his stance a little to allow for it. Then, with a final swift waggle, he laid his club-head behind the ball and slowly raised it. It was just coming down when the world became full of shouts of "Fore!" and something hard smote him violently on the seat of his plus-fours.

The supreme tragedies of life leave us momentarily stunned. For an instant which seemed an age Chester could not understand what had happened. True, he realised that there had been an earthquake, a cloud-burst, and a railway accident, and that a high building had fallen on him at the exact moment when somebody had shot him with a gun, but these happenings would account for only a small part of his sensations. He blinked several times, and rolled his eyes wildly. And it was while rolling them that he caught sight of the gesticulating Wrecking Crew on the lower slopes and found enlightenment. Simultaneously, he observed his ball only a yard and a half from where it had been when he addressed it.

Chester Meredith gave one look at his ball, one look at the flag, one look at the Wrecking Crew, one look at the sky. His lips writhed, his forehead turned vermilion. Beads of perspiration started out on his forehead. And then, with his whole soul seething like a cistern struck by a thunderbolt, he spoke.

"! ! ! ! ! ! ! ! ! ! ! ! ! ! !" cried Chester.

Dimly he was aware of a wordless exclamation from the girl beside him, but he was too distraught to think of her now. It was as if all the oaths pent up within his bosom for so many weary days were struggling and jostling to see which could get out first. They cannoned into each other, they linked hands and formed parties, they got themselves all mixed up in weird vowel-sounds, the second syllable of some red-hot verb forming a temporary union with the first syllable of some blistering noun.

" — ! — !! — !!! — !!!! — !!!!!" cried Chester.

Felicia stood staring at him. In her eyes was the look of one who sees visions.

"***!!!***!!!***!!!***!!!" roared Chester, in part.

A great wave of emotion flooded over the girl. How she had misjudged this silver-tongued man! She shivered as she thought that, had this not happened, in another five minutes they would have parted for ever, sundered by seas of misunderstanding, she cold and scornful, he with all his music still within him.

"Oh, Mr. Meredith!" she cried, faintly.

With a sickening abruptness Chester came to himself. It was as if somebody had poured a pint of ice-cold water down his back. He blushed vividly. He realised with horror and shame how grossly he had offended against all the canons of decency and good taste. He felt like the man in one of those "What Is Wrong With This Picture?" things in the advertisements of the etiquette-books.

"I beg — I beg your pardon!" he mumbled, humbly. "Please, please, forgive me. I should not have spoken like that."

"You should! You should!" cried the girl, passionately. "You should have said all that and a lot more. That awful man ruining your record round like that! Oh, why am I a poor weak woman with practically no vocabulary that's any use for anything!"

Quite suddenly, without knowing that she had moved, she found herself at his side, holding his hand.

"Oh, to think how I misjudged you!" she wailed. "I thought you cold, stiff, formal, precise. I hated the way you sniggered when you foozled a shot. I see it all now! You were keeping it in for my sake. Can you ever forgive me?"

Chester, as I have said, was not a very quick-minded young

man, but it would have taken a duller youth than he to fail to read the message in the girl's eyes, to miss the meaning of the pressure of her hand on his.

"My gosh!" he exclaimed wildly. "Do you mean — ? Do you think — ? Do you really — ? Honestly, has this made a difference? Is there any chance for a fellow, I mean?"

Her eyes helped him on. He felt suddenly confident and masterful.

"Look here — no kidding — will you marry me?" he said.

"I will! I will!"

"Darling!" cried Chester.

He would have said more, but at this point he was interrupted by the arrival of the Wrecking Crew, who panted up full of apologies; and Chester, as he eyed them, thought that he had never seen a nicer, cheerier, pleasanter lot of fellows in his life. His heart warmed to them. He made a mental resolve to hunt them up some time and have a good long talk. He waved the Grave-Digger's remorse airily aside.

"Don't mention it," he said. "Not at all. Faults on both sides. By the way, my *fiancée*, Miss Blakeney."

The Wrecking Crew puffed acknowledgment.

"But, my dear fellow," said the Grave-Digger, "it was — really it was — unforgivable. Spoiling your shot. Never dreamed I would send the ball that distance. Lucky you weren't playing an important match."

"But he was," moaned Felicia. "He was trying for the course record, and now he can't break it."

The Wrecking Crew paled behind their whiskers, aghast at this tragedy, but Chester, glowing with the yeasty intoxication of love, laughed lightly.

"What do you mean, can't break it?" he cried, cheerily. "I've one more shot."

And, carelessly addressing the ball, he holed out with a light flick of his mashie-niblick.

*

"Chester, darling!" said Felicia.

They were walking slowly through a secluded glade in the quiet evenfall.

"Yes, precious?"

Felicia hesitated. What she was going to say would hurt him, she knew, and her love was so great that to hurt him was agony.

"Do you think — " she began. "I wonder whether — It's about Crispin."

"Good old Crispin!"

Felicia sighed, but the matter was too vital to be shirked. Cost what it might, she must speak her mind.

"Chester, darling, when we are married, would you mind very, *very* much if we didn't have Crispin with us *all* the time?"

Chester started.

"Good Lord!" he exclaimed. "Don't you like him?"

"Not very much," confessed Felicia. "I don't think I'm clever enough for him. I've rather disliked him ever since we were children. But I know what a friend he is of yours — "

Chester uttered a joyous laugh.

"Friend of mine! Why, I can't stand the blighter! I loathe the worm! I abominate the excrescence! I only pretended we were friends because I thought it would put me in solid with you. The man is a pest and should have been strangled at birth. At school I used to kick him every time I saw him. If your brother Crispin tries so much as to set foot across the threshold of our little home, I'll set the dog on him."

"Darling!" whispered Felicia. "We shall be very, very happy." She drew her arm through his. "Tell me, dearest," she murmured, "all about how you used to kick Crispin at school."

And together they wandered off into the sunset.

Tangled Hearts

O

A marriage was being solemnized in the church that stands about a full spoon shot from the club-house. The ceremony had nearly reached its conclusion. As the officiating clergyman, coming to the nub of the thing, addressed the young man in the cutaway coat and spongebag trousers, there reigned throughout the sacred edifice a tense silence, such as prevails upon a racecourse just before the shout goes up, "They're off!"

"Wilt thou," he said, " — hup — Smallwood, take this — hup — Celia to be thy wedded wife?"

A sudden gleam came into the other's horn-rimmed spectacled eyes.

"Say, listen," he began. "Lemme tell you what to — "

He stopped, a blush mantling his face.

"I will," he said.

A few moments later, the organ was pealing forth "The Voice That Breathed O'er Eden." The happy couple entered the vestry. The Oldest Member, who had been among those in the ringside pews, walked back to the club-house with the friend who was spending the week-end with him.

The friend seemed puzzled.

"Tell me," he said. "Am I wrong, or did the bridegroom at one point in the proceedings start to *ad lib* with some stuff that was not on the routine?"

"He did, indeed," replied the Oldest Member. "He was

about to advise the minister what to do for his hiccoughs. I find the fact that he succeeded in checking himself very gratifying. It seems to show that his cure may be considered permanent."

"His cure?"

"Until very recently Smallwood Bessemer was a confirmed adviser."

"Bad, that."

"Yes. I always advise people never to give advice. Mind you, one can find excuses for the young fellow. For many years he had been a columnist on one of the morning papers, and to columnists, accustomed day after day to set the world right on every conceivable subject, the giving of advice becomes a habit. It is an occupational risk. But if I had known young Bessemer better, I would have warned him that he was in danger of alienating Celia Todd, his betrothed, who was a girl of proud and independent spirit.

"Unfortunately, he was not a member of our little community. He lived in the city, merely coming here for occasional week-ends. At the time when my story begins, I had met him only twice, when he arrived to spend his summer vacation. And it was not long before, as I had feared would be the case, I found that all was not well between him and Celia Todd."

The first intimation I had of this (the Sage proceeded) was when she called at my cottage accompanied by her Pekinese, Pirbright, to whom she was greatly attached, and unburdened her soul to me. Sinking listlessly into a chair, she sat silent for some moments. Then, as if waking from a reverie, she spoke abruptly.

"Do you think," she said, "that true love can exist between a woman and a man, if the woman feels more and more every day that she wants to hit the man over the head with a brick?"

I was disturbed. I like to see the young folks happy. And my hope that she might merely be stating a hypothetical case vanished as she continued.

"Take me and Smallwood, for instance. I have to clench my fists sometimes till the knuckles stand out white under the strain, in order to stop myself from beaning him. This habit of his of scattering advice on every side like a sower going forth sowing is getting me down. It has begun to sap my reason. Only this morning, to show you what I mean, we were walking along the road and we met that wolfhound of Agnes Flack's, and it said something to Pirbright about the situation in China that made him hot under the collar. The little angel was just rolling up his sleeves and starting in to mix it, when I snatched him away. And Smallwood said I shouldn't have done it. I should have let them fight it out, he said, so that they could get it out of their systems, after which a beautiful friendship would have resulted. I told him he was the sort of human fiend who ought to be eating peanuts in the front row at a bull fight, and we parted on rather distant terms."

"The clouds will clear away."

"I wonder," said Celia. "I have a feeling that one of these days he will go too far, and something will crack."

In the light of this conversation, what happened at the dance becomes intelligible. Every Saturday night we have a dance at the club-house, at which all the younger set assembles. Celia was there, escorted by Smallwood Bessemer, their differences having apparently been smoothed over, and for a while all seems to have gone well. Bessemer was an awkward and clumsy dancer, but the girl's love enabled her to endure the way in which he jumped on and off her feet. When the music stopped, she started straightening out her toes without the slightest doubt in her mind that he was a king among men.

And then suddenly he turned to her with a kindly smile.

"I'd like to give you a bit of advice," he said. "What's wrong with your dancing is that you give a sort of jump at the turn, like a trout leaping at a fly. Now, the way to cure this is very simple. Try to imagine that the ceiling is very low and made of very thin glass, and that your head just touches it and you mustn't break it. You've dropped your engagement ring," he said, as something small and hard struck him on the side of the face.

"No, I haven't," said Celia. "I threw it at you."

And she strode haughtily out on to the terrace. And Smallwood Bessemer, having watched her disappear, went to the bar to get a quick one.

There was only one man in the bar, and yet it looked well filled. This was because Sidney McMurdo, its occupant, is one of those vast, muscled individuals who bulge in every direction. He was sitting slumped in a chair, scowling beneath beetling brows, his whole aspect that of one whose soul has just got the sleeve across the windpipe.

Sidney was not in any sense an intimate of Smallwood Bessemer. They had met for the first time on the previous afternoon, when Bessemer had advised Sidney always to cool off slowly after playing golf, as otherwise he might contract pneumonia and cease to be with us, and Sidney, who is a second vice-president of a large insurance company, had taken advantage of this all-flesh-is-as-grass note which had been introduced into the conversation to try to sell Bessemer his firm's all-accident policy.

No business had resulted, but the episode had served to make them acquainted, and they now split a bottle. The influence of his share on Sidney McMurdo was mellowing enough to make him confidential.

"I've just had a hell of a row with my *fiancée*," he said.

"I've just had a hell of a row with *my fiancée*," said Smallwood Bessemer, struck by the coincidence.

"She told me I ought to putt off the right foot. I said I was darned well going to keep right along putting off the left foot, as I had been taught at my mother's knee. She then broke off the engagement."

Smallwood Bessemer was not a golfer, but manlike he sympathized with the male, and he was in a mood to be impatient of exhibitions of temperament in women.

"Women," he said, "are all alike. They need to be brought to heel. You have to teach them where they get off and show them that they can't go about the place casting away a good man's love as if it were a used tube of toothpaste. Let me give you a bit of advice. Don't sit brooding in bars. Do as I intend to do. Go out and start making vigorous passes at some other girl."

"To make her jealous?"

"Exactly."

"So that she will come legging it back, pleading to be forgiven?"

"Precisely."

Sidney brightened.

"That sounds pretty good to me. Because I mean to say there's always the chance that the other girl will let you kiss her, and then you're that much ahead of the game."

"Quite," said Smallwood Bessemer.

He returned to the dance room, glad to have been able to be of assistance to a fellow man in his hour of distress. Celia was nowhere to be seen, and he presumed that she was still cooling off on the terrace. He saw Sidney, who had stayed behind for a moment to finish the bottle, flash past in a purposeful way, and then he looked about him to decide who should be his assistant in the little psychological experiment which he proposed to undertake. His eyes fell on Agnes Flack, sitting in a corner, rapping her substantial foot on the floor.

Have you met Agnes Flack? You don't remember? Then you have not, for once seen she is not forgotten. She is our female club champion, a position which she owes not only to her skill at golf but to her remarkable physique. She is a fine, large, handsome girl, built rather on the lines of Popeye the sailor, and Smallwood Bessemer, who was on the slender side, had always admired her.

He caught her eye, and she smiled brightly. He went over to where she sat, and presently they were out on the floor.

He saw Celia appear at the french windows and stand looking in, and intensified the silent passion of his dancing, trying to convey the idea of being something South American which ought to be chained up and muzzled in the interests of pure womanhood. Celia sniffed with a violence that caused the lights to flicker, and an hour or so later Smallwood Bessemer went home, well pleased with the start he had made.

He was climbing into bed, feeling that all would soon be well once more, when the telephone rang and Sidney McMurdo's voice boomed over the wire.

"Hoy!" said Sidney.

"Yes?" said Bessemer.

"You know that advice you gave me?"

"You took it, I hope?"

"Yes," said Sidney. "And a rather unfortunate thing has occurred. How it happened, I can't say, but I've gone and got engaged."

"Too bad," said Bessemer sympathetically. "There was always that risk, of course. The danger on these occasions is that one may overdo the thing and become too fascinating. I ought to have warned you to hold yourself in. Who is the girl?"

"A frightful pie-faced little squirt named Celia Todd," said Sidney and hung up with a hollow groan.

To say that this information stunned Smallwood Bessemer would scarcely be to overstate the facts. For some moments after the line had gone dead, he sat motionless, his soul seething within him like a Welsh rabbit at the height of its fever.

He burned with rage and resentment, and all the manhood in him called to him to make a virile gesture and show Celia Todd who was who and what was what.

An idea struck him. He called up Agnes Flack.

"Miss Flack?"

"Hello?"

"Sorry to disturb you at this hour, but will you marry me?"

"Certainly. Who is that?"

"Smallwood Bessemer."

"I don't get the second name."

"Bessemer. B for banana, e for erysipelas — "

"Oh, Bessemer? Yes, delighted. Good night, Mr. Bessemer."

"Good night, Miss Flack."

Sometimes it happens that after a restorative sleep a man finds that his views on what seemed in the small hours a pretty good idea have undergone a change. It was so with Bessemer. He woke next morning oppressed by a nebulous feeling that in some way, which for the moment eluded his memory, he had made rather a chump of himself overnight. And then, as he was brushing his teeth, he was able to put his finger on the seat of the trouble. Like a tidal wave, the events of the previous evening came flooding back into his mind, and he groaned in spirit.

Why in this dark hour he should have thought of me, I cannot say, for we were the merest acquaintances. But he must have felt that I was the sort of man who would lend a sympathetic ear, for he called me up on the telephone and explained the situation, begging me to step round and see Agnes and sound her regarding her views on the matter. An hour later, I was able to put him abreast.

"She says she loves you devotedly."

"But how can she? I scarcely know the girl."

"That is what she says. No doubt you are one of those men

who give a woman a single glance and — bing! — all is over."

There was a silence at the other end of the wire. When he spoke again, there was an anxious tremor in his voice.

"What would you say chances were," he asked, "for explaining that it was all a little joke, at which I had expected that no one would laugh more heartily than herself?"

"Virtually nil. As a matter of fact, that point happened to come up, and she stated specifically that if there was any rannygazoo — if, in other words, it should prove that you had been pulling her leg and trying to make her the plaything of an idle moment — she would know what to do about it."

"Know what to do about it?"

"That was the expression she employed."

"Know what to do about it," repeated Smallwood Bessemer thoughtfully. "'Myes. I see what you mean. Know what to do about it. Yes. But why on earth does this ghastly girl love me? She must be cuckoo."

"For your intellect, she tells me. She says she finds you a refreshing change after her late *fiancé*, Sidney McMurdo."

"Was she engaged to Sidney McMurdo?"

"Yes."

"H'm!" said Bessemer.

He told me subsequently that his first action after he had hung up was to go to his cupboard and take from it a bottle of tonic port which he kept handy in case he required a restorative or stimulant. He had fallen into the habit of drinking a little of this whenever he felt low, and Reason told him that he was never going to feel lower than he did at that moment. To dash off a glass and fill another was with him the work of an instant.

Generally, the effect of this tonic port was to send the blood coursing through his veins like liquid fire and make him feel that he was walking on the tip of his toes with his hat on the side of his head. But now its magic seemed to have failed. Spiritually, he remained a total loss.

Nor, I think, can we be surprised at this. It is not every day that a young fellow loses the girl he worships and finds that he has accumulated another whom he not only does not love but knows that he can never love. Smallwood Bessemer respected Agnes Flack. He would always feel for her that impersonal admiration which is inspired by anything very large, like the Empire State Building or the Grand Canyon of Arizona. But the thought of being married to her frankly appalled him.

And in addition to this there was the Sidney McMurdo angle.

Smallwood Bessemer, as I say, did not know Sidney McMurdo well. But he knew him well enough to be aware that his reactions on finding that another man had become engaged to his temporarily ex-*fiancée* would be of a marked nature. And as the picture rose before his eyes of that vast frame of his and those almost varicose muscles that rippled like dangerous snakes beneath his sweater, his soul sickened and he had to have a third glass of tonic port.

It was while he was draining it that Sidney McMurdo came lumbering over the threshold, and so vivid was the impression he created of being eight foot high and broad in proportion that Smallwood Bessemer nearly swooned. Recovering himself, he greeted him with almost effusive cordiality.

"Come in, McMurdo, come in," he cried buoyantly. "Just the fellow I wanted to see. I wonder, McMurdo, if you remember what you were saying to me the other day about the advisability of my taking out an all-accident insurance with your firm? I have been thinking it over, and am strongly inclined to do so."

"It's the sensible thing," said Sidney McMurdo. "A man ought to look to the future."

"Precisely."

"You never know when you may not get badly smashed up."

"Never. Shall we go round to your place and get a form?"

"I have one with me."

"Then I will sign it at once," said Bessemer.

And he had just done so and had written out a check for the first year's premium, when the telephone bell rang.

"Yoo-hoo, darling," bellowed a voice genially, and he recognized it as Agnes Flack's. A quick glance out of the corner of his eye told him that his companion had recognized it, too. Sidney McMurdo had stiffened. His face was flushed. He sat clenching and unclenching his hands. When Agnes Flack spoke on the telephone, there was never any need for extensions to enable the bystander to follow her remarks.

Smallwood Bessemer swallowed once or twice.

"Oh, good morning, Miss Flack," he said formally.

"What do you mean — Miss Flack? Call me Aggie. Listen, I'm at the club-house. Come on out. I want to give you a golf lesson."

"Very well."

"You mean 'Very well, darling.'"

"Er — yes. Er — very well, darling."

"Right," said Agnes Flack.

Smallwood Bessemer hung up the receiver, and turned to find his companion scrutinizing him narrowly. Sidney McMurdo had turned a rather pretty mauve, and his eyes had an incandescent appearance. It seemed to Bessemer that with a few minor changes he could have stepped straight into the Book of Revelation and no questions asked.

"That was Agnes Flack!" said McMurdo hoarsely.

"Er — yes," said Bessemer. "Yes, I believe it was."

"You called her 'darling.'"

"Er — yes. That's right. She seemed to wish it."

"Why?" asked Sidney McMurdo, who was one of those simple, direct men who like to come straight to the point.

"I've been meaning to tell you about that," said Smallwood

Bessemer. "We're engaged. It happened last night after the dance."

Sidney McMurdo gave a hitch to his shoulder muscles, which were leaping about under his sweater like adagio dancers. His scrutiny, already narrow, became narrower.

"So it was all a vile plot, was it?"

"No, no."

"Of course it was a vile plot," said Sidney McMurdo petulantly, breaking off a corner of the mantelpiece and shredding it through his fingers. "You gave me that advice about going out and making passes purely in order that you should be left free to steal Agnes from me. If that wasn't a vile plot, then I don't know a vile plot when I see one. Well, well, we must see what we can do about it."

It was the fact that Smallwood Bessemer at this moment sprang nimbly behind the table that temporarily eased the strain of the situation. For as Sidney McMurdo started to remove the obstacle, his eye fell on the insurance policy. He stopped as if spellbound, staring at it, his lower jaw sagging.

Bessemer, scanning him anxiously, could read what was passing through his mind. Sidney McMurdo was a lover, but he was also a second vice-president of the Jersey City and All Points West Mutual and Co-operative Life and Accident Insurance Company, an organization which had an almost morbid distaste for parting with its money. If as the result of any impulsive action on his part the Co. were compelled to pay over a large sum to Smallwood Bessemer almost before they had trousered his first check, there would be harsh words and raised eyebrows. He might even be stripped of his second vice-president's desk in the middle of a hollow square. And next to Agnes Flack and his steel-shafted driver, he loved his second vice-presidency more than anything in the world.

For what seemed an eternity, Smallwood Bessemer gazed at a strong man wrestling with himself. Then the crisis passed. Sidney McMurdo flung himself into a chair, and sat moodily gnashing his teeth.

"Well," said Bessemer, feeling like Shadrach, Meshach and Abednego, "I suppose I must be leaving you. I am having my first golf lesson."

Sidney McMurdo started.

"Your *first* golf lesson? Haven't you ever played?"

"Not yet."

A hollow groan escaped Sidney McMurdo.

"To think of my Agnes marrying a man who doesn't know the difference between a brassie and a niblick!"

"Well, if it comes to that," retorted Bessemer, with some spirit, "what price my Celia marrying a man who doesn't know the difference between Edna St. Vincent Millay and Bugs Baer?"

Sidney McMurdo stared.

"Your Celia? You weren't engaged to that Todd pipsqueak?"

"She is not a pipsqueak."

"She is, too, a pipsqueak, and I can prove it. She reads poetry."

"Naturally. I have made it my loving task to train her eager mind to appreciate all that is best and most beautiful."

"She says I've got to do it, too."

"It will be the making of you. And now," said Smallwood Bessemer, "I really must be going."

"Just a moment," said Sidney McMurdo. He reached out and took the insurance policy, studying it intently for a while. But it was as he feared. It covered everything. "All right," he said sombrely, "pop off."

I suppose there is nothing (proceeded the Oldest Member) more painful to the man of sensibility than the spectacle of tangled hearts. Here were four hearts as tangled as spaghetti, and I grieved for them. The female members of the quartette did not confide in me, but I was in constant demand by both McMurdo and Bessemer, and it is not too much to say that these men were passing through the furnace. Indeed, I cannot say which moved me the more — Bessemer's analysis of his emotions when jerked out of bed at daybreak by a telephone call from Agnes, summoning him to the links before breakfast, or McMurdo's description of how it felt to read W. H. Auden. Suffice it that each wrung my heart to the uttermost.

And so the matter stood at the opening of the contest for the Ladies' Vase.

This was one of our handicap events, embracing in its comprehensive scope almost the entire female personnel of the club, from the fire-breathing tigresses to the rabbits who had taken up golf because it gave them an opportunity of appearing in sports clothes. It was expected to be a gift once more for Agnes Flack, though she would be playing from scratch and several of the contestants were receiving as much as forty-eight. She had won the Vase the last two years, and if she scooped it in again, it would become her permanent possession. I mention this to show you what the competition meant to her.

For a while, all proceeded according to the form book. Playing in her usual bold, resolute style, she blasted her opponents off the links one by one, and came safely through into the final without disarranging her hair.

But as the tournament progressed, it became evident that a platinum blonde of the name of Julia Prebble, receiving twenty-seven, had been grossly underhandicapped. Whether through some natural skill at concealing the merits of her game, or because she was engaged to a member of the handicapping committee, one cannot tell, but she had, as I say, contrived to scrounge a twenty-seven when ten would have been more suitable. The result was that she passed into the final bracket with consummate ease, and the betting among the wilder spirits was that for the first time in three years Agnes Flack's mantelpiece would have to be looking about it for some other ornament than the handsome silver vase presented by the club for annual competition among its female members.

And when at the end of the first half of the thirty-six hole final Agnes was two down after a gruelling struggle, it seemed as though their prognostications were about to be fulfilled.

It was in the cool of a lovely summer evening that play was resumed. I had been asked to referee the match, and I was crossing the terrace on my way to the first tee when I encountered Smallwood Bessemer. And we were pausing to exchange a word or two, when Sidney McMurdo came along.

To my surprise, for I had supposed relations between the two men to be strained, Bessemer waved a cordial hand.

"Hyah, Sidney," he called.

"Hyah, Smallwood," replied the other.

"Did you get that tonic?"

"Yes. Good stuff, you think?"

"You can't beat it," said Bessemer, and Sidney McMurdo passed along towards the first tee.

I was astonished.

"You seem on excellent terms with McMurdo," I said.

"Oh, yes," said Bessemer. "He drops in at my place a good deal. We smoke a pipe and roast each other's girls. It draws us very close together. I was able to do him a good turn this morning. He was very anxious to watch the match, and Celia wanted him to go into town to fetch a specialist for her Peke, who is off-colour to-day. I told him to give it a shot of that tonic port I drink. Put it right in no time. Well, I'll be seeing you."

"You are not coming round?"

"I may look in toward the finish. What do you think of Agnes's chances?"

"Well, she has been battling nobly against heavy odds, but — "

"The trouble with Agnes is that she believes all she reads in the golf books. If she would only listen to me . . . Ah, well," said Smallwood Bessemer, and moved off.

It did not take me long after I had reached the first tee to see that Agnes Flack was not blind to the possibility of being deprived of her Vase. Her lips were tight, and there was a furrow in her forehead. I endeavoured to ease her tension with a kindly word or two.

"Lovely evening," I said.

"It will be," she replied, directing a somewhat acid glance at her antagonist, who was straightening the tie of the member of the handicapping committee to whom she was betrothed, "if I can trim that ginger-headed Delilah and foil the criminal skull-duggery of a bunch of yeggmen who ought to be blushing themselves purple. Twenty-seven, forsooth!"

Her warmth was not unjustified. After watching the morning's round, I, too, felt that that twenty-seven handicap of Julia Prebble's had been dictated by the voice of love rather than by a rigid sense of justice. I changed the subject.

"Bessemer is not watching the match, he tells me."

"I wouldn't let him. He makes me nervous."

"Indeed?"

"Yes. I started teaching him golf a little while ago, and now he's started teaching *me*. He knows it all."

"He is a columnist," I reminded her.

"At lunch to-day he said he was going to skim through Alex Morrison's book again, because he had a feeling that Alex hadn't got the right angle on the game."

I shuddered strongly, and at this moment Julia Prebble detached herself from her loved one, and the contest began.

I confess that, as I watched the opening stages of the play, I found a change taking place in my attitude towards Agnes

Flack. I had always respected her, as one must respect any woman capable of pasting a ball two hundred and forty yards, but it was only now that respect burgeoned into something like affection. The way she hitched up her sleeves and started to wipe off her opponent's lead invited sympathy and support.

At the outset, she was assisted by the fact that success had rendered Julia Prebble a little overconfident. She did not concentrate. The eye which should have been riveted on her ball had a tendency to smirk sideways at her affianced, causing her to top, with the result that only three holes had been played before the match was all square again.

However, as was inevitable, these reverses had the effect of tightening up Julia Prebble's game. Her mouth hardened, and she showed a disposition to bite at the man she loved, whom she appeared to consider responsible. On the fifth, she told him not to stand in front of her, on the sixth not to stand behind her, on the seventh she asked him not to move while she was putting. On the eighth she suggested that if he had really got St. Vitus Dance he ought to go and put himself in the hands of some good doctor. On the ninth she formally broke off the engagement.

Naturally, all this helped her a good deal, and at the tenth she recovered the lead she had lost. Agnes drew level at the eleventh, and after that things settled down to the grim struggle which one generally sees in finals. A casual observer would have said that it was anybody's game.

But the strain of battling against that handicap was telling on Agnes Flack. Once or twice, her iron resolution seemed to waver. And on the seventeenth Nature took its toll. She missed a short putt for the half, and they came to the eighteenth tee with Julia Prebble dormy one.

The eighteenth hole takes you over the water. A sort of small lake lies just beyond that tee, spanned by a rustic bridge. Across the bridge I now beheld Smallwood Bessemer approaching.

"How's it going?" he asked, as he came to where I stood. I told him the state of the game, and he shook his head. "Looks bad," he said. "I'm sorry. I don't like Agnes Flack, and never shall, but one has one's human feelings. It will cut her to the heart to lose that Vase. And when you reflect that if she had only let me come along, she would have been all right, it all seems such a pity, doesn't it? I could have given her a pointer from time to time, which would have made all the difference. But she doesn't seem to want my advice. Prefers to trust to Alex Morrison. Sad. Very sad. Ah," said Smallwood Bessemer, "She didn't relax."

He was alluding to Julia Prebble, who had just driven off. Her ball had cleared the water nicely, but it was plain to the seeing eye that it had a nasty slice on it. It came to rest in a patch of rough at the side of the fairway, and I saw her look sharply round, as if instinctively about to tell her betrothed that she wished he wouldn't shuffle his feet just as she was shooting. But he was not there. He had withdrawn to the club-house, where, I was informed later, he drank six Scotches in quick succession, subsequently crying on the barman's shoulder and telling him what was wrong with women.

In the demeanour of Agnes Flack, as she teed up, there was something that reminded me of Boadicea about to get in amongst a Roman legion. She looked dominant and conquering. I knew what she was thinking. Even if her opponent recovered from the moral shock of a drive like that, she could scarcely be down in less than six, and this was a hole which she, Agnes, always did in four. This meant that the match would go to the thirty-seventh, in which case she was confident that her stamina and the will to win would see her through.

She measured her distance. She waggled. Slowly and forcefully she swung back. And her club was just descending in a perfect arc, when Smallwood Bessemer spoke.

"Hey!" he said.

In the tense silence the word rang out like the crack of a gun. It affected Agnes Flack visibly. For the first time since she had been a slip of a child, she lifted her head in the middle of a stroke, and the ball, badly topped, trickled over the turf, gathered momentum as it reached the edge of the tee, bounded towards the water, hesitated on the brink for an instant like a timid diver on a cold morning and then plunged in.

"Too bad," said Julia Prebble.

Agnes Flack did not reply. She was breathing heavily through her nostrils. She turned to Smallwood Bessemer.

"You were saying something?" she asked.

"I was only going to remind you to relax," said Smallwood Bessemer. "Alex Morrison lays great stress on the importance of pointing the chin and rolling the feet. To my mind, however, the whole secret of golf consists in relaxing. At the top of the swing the muscles should be — "

"My niblick, please," said Agnes Flack to her caddy.

She took the club, poised it for an instant as if judging its heft, then began to move forward swiftly and stealthily, like a tigress of the jungle.

Until that moment, I had always looked on Smallwood Bessemer as purely the man of intellect, what you would describe as the thoughtful, reflective type. But he now showed that he could, if the occasion demanded it, be the man of action. I do not think I have ever seen anything move quicker than the manner in which he dived head-foremost into the thick clump of bushes which borders the eighteenth tee. One moment, he was there; the next, he had vanished. Eels could have taken his correspondence course.

It was a move of the highest strategic quality. Strong woman though Agnes Flack was, she was afraid of spiders.

For an instant, she stood looking wistfully at the bushes: then, hurling her niblick into them, she burst into tears and tottered into the arms of Sidney McMurdo, who came up at this juncture. He had been following the match at a cautious distance.

"Oh, Sidney!" she sobbed.

"There, there," said Sidney McMurdo.

He folded her in his embrace, and they walked off together. From her passionate gestures, I could gather that she was explaining what had occurred and was urging him to plunge into the undergrowth and break Smallwood Bessemer's neck, and the apologetic way in which he waved his hands told me that he was making clear his obligations to the Jersey City and All Points West Mutual and Co-operative Life and Accident Insurance Co.

Presently, they were lost in the gathering dusk, and I called to Bessemer and informed him that the All Clear had been blown.

"She's gone?" he said.

"She has been gone some moments."

"Are you sure?"

"Quite sure."

There was a silence.

"No," said Bessemer. "It may be a trap. I think I'll stick on here a while."

I shrugged my shoulder and left him.

The shades of night were falling fast before Smallwood Bessemer, weighing the pro's and con's, felt justified in emerging from his lair. As he started to cross the bridge that spans the water, it was almost dark. He leaned on the rail, giving himself up to thought.

The sweet was mingled with the bitter in his meditations. He could see that the future held much that must inevitably be distasteful to a man who liked a quiet life. As long as he remained in the neighbourhood, he would be compelled to exercise ceaseless vigilance and would have to hold himself in readiness, should the occasion arise, to pick up his feet and run like a rabbit.

This was not so good. On the other hand, it seemed reasonable to infer from Agnes Flack's manner during the recent episode that their engagement was at an end. A substantial bit of velvet.

Against this, however, must be set the fact that he had lost Celia Todd. There was no getting away from that, and it was this thought that caused him to moan softly as he gazed at the dark water beneath him. And he was still moaning, when there came to his ears the sound of a footstep. A woman's form loomed up in the dusk. She was crossing the bridge towards him. And then suddenly a cry rent the air.

Smallwood Bessemer was to discover shortly that he had placed an erroneous interpretation upon this cry, which had really been one of agitation and alarm. To his sensitive ear it had sounded like the animal yowl of an angry woman sighting her prey, and he had concluded that this must be Agnes Flack, returned to the chase. Acting upon this assumption, he stood not on the order of going but immediately soared over the rail and plunged into the water below. Rising quickly to the surface and clutching out for support, he found himself grasping something wet and furry.

For an instant, he was at a loss to decide what this could be. It had some of the properties of a sponge and some of a damp hearthrug. Then it bit him in the fleshy part of the thumb and he identified it as Celia Todd's Pekinese, Pirbright. In happier days he had been bitten from once to three times a week by this animal, and he recognized its technique.

The discovery removed a great weight from his mind. If Pirbright came, he reasoned, could Celia Todd be far behind? He saw that must be she, and not Agnes Flack, who stood on the bridge. Greatly relieved, he sloshed to the shore, endeavouring as best he might to elude the creature's snapping jaws.

In this he was not wholly successful. Twice more he had to endure nips, and juicy ones. But the physical anguish soon passed away as he came to land and found himself gazing into Celia's eyes. They were large and round, and shone with an adoring light.

"Oh, Smallwood!" she cried. "Thank heaven you were there! If you had not acted so promptly, the poor little mite would have been drowned."

"It was nothing," protested Bessemer modestly.

"Nothing? To have the reckless courage to plunge in like that? It was the sort of thing people get expensive medals for."

"Just presence of mind," said Bessemer. "Some fellows have it, some haven't. How did it happen?"

She caught her breath.

"It was Sidney McMurdo's doing."

"Sidney McMurdo's?"

"Yes. Pirbright was not well to-day, and I told him to fetch the vet. And he talked me into trying some sort of tonic port, which he said was highly recommended. We gave Pirbright a saucer full, and he seemed to enjoy it. And then he suddenly uttered a piercing bark and ran up the side of the wall. Finally he dashed out of the house. When he returned, his manner was lethargic, and I thought a walk would do him good. And as he came on to the bridge, he staggered and fell. He must have had some form of vertigo."

Smallwood Bessemer scrutinized the animal. The visibility was not good, but he was able to discern in its bearing all the symptoms of an advanced hangover.

"Well, I broke off the engagement right away," proceeded Celia Todd. "I can respect a practical joker. I can admire a man who is cruel to animals. But I cannot pass as fit for human consumption a blend of the two. The mixture is too rich."

Bessemer started.

"You are not going to marry Sidney McMurdo?"

"I am not."

"What an extraordinary coincidence. I am not going to marry Agnes Flack."

"You aren't?"

"No. So it almost looks — "

"Yes, doesn't it?"

"I mean, both of us being at a loose end, as it were . . ."

"Exactly."

"Celia!"

"Smallwood!"

Hand in hand they made their way across the bridge. Celia uttered a sudden cry, causing the dog Pirbright to wince as if somebody had driven a red-hot spike into his head.

"I haven't told you the worst," she said. "He had the effrontery to assert that you had advised the tonic port."

"The low blister!"

"I knew it could not be true. Your advice is always so good. You remember telling me I ought to have let Pirbright fight Agnes Flack's wolfhound? Well, you were quite right. He met it when he dashed out of the house after drinking that tonic port, and cleaned it up in under a minute. They are now the best of friends. After this, I shall always take your advice and ask for more."

Smallwood Bessemer mused. Once again he was weighing the pro's and con's. It was his habit of giving advice that had freed him from Agnes Flack. On the other hand, if it had not been for his habit of giving advice, Agnes Flack would never, so to speak, have arisen.

"Do you know," he said, "I doubt if I shall be doing much advising from now on. I think I shall ask the paper to release me from my columnist contract. I have a feeling that I shall be happier doing something like the Society News or the Children's Corner."

The Awakening
of Rollo Podmarsh

O

Down on the new bowling-green behind the club-house some sort of competition was in progress. The seats about the smooth strip of turf were crowded, and the weak-minded yapping of the patients made itself plainly audible to the Oldest Member as he sat in his favourite chair in the smoking-room. He shifted restlessly, and a frown marred the placidity of his venerable brow. To the Oldest Member a golf-club was a golf-club, and he resented the introduction of any alien element. He had opposed the institution of tennis-courts; and the suggestion of a bowling-green had stirred him to his depths.

A young man in spectacles came into the smoking-room. His high forehead was aglow, and he lapped up a ginger-ale with the air of one who considers that he has earned it.

"Capital exercise!" he said, beaming upon the Oldest Member.

The Oldest Member laid down his *Vardon On Casual Water,* and peered suspiciously at his companion.

"What did you go round in?" he asked.

"Oh, I wasn't playing golf," said the young man. "Bowls."

"A nauseous pursuit!" said the Oldest Member, coldly, and resumed his reading.

The young man seemed nettled.

"I don't know why you should say that," he retorted. "It's a splendid game."

"I rank it," said the Oldest Member, "with the juvenile pastime of marbles."

The young man pondered for some moments.

"Well, anyway," he said at length, "it was good enough for Drake."

"As I have not the pleasure of the acquaintance of your friend Drake, I am unable to estimate the value of his endorsement."

"*The* Drake. The Spanish Armada Drake. He was playing bowls on Plymouth Hoe when they told him that the Armada was in sight. 'There is time to finish the game,' he replied. That's what Drake thought of bowls."

"If he had been a golfer he would have ignored the Armada altogether."

"It's easy enough to say that," said the young man, with spirit, "but can the history of golf show a parallel case?"

"A million, I should imagine."

"But you've forgotten them, eh?" said the young man, satirically.

"On the contrary," said the Oldest Member. "As a typical instance, neither more nor less remarkable than a hundred others, I will select the story of Rollo Podmarsh." He settled himself comfortably in his chair, and placed the tips of his fingers together. "This Rollo Podmarsh — "

"No, I say!" protested the young man, looking at his watch.

"This Rollo Podmarsh — "

"Yes, but — "

This Rollo Podmarsh (said the Oldest Member) was the only son of his mother, and she was a widow; and like other young men in that position he had rather allowed a mother's tender care to take the edge off what you might call his rugged manliness. Not to put too fine a point on it, he had permitted his parent to coddle him ever since he had been in the nursery; and now, in his twenty-eighth year, he invariably wore flannel next his skin, changed his shoes the moment they got wet, and — from September to May, inclusive — never went to bed without partaking of a bowl of hot arrowroot. Not, you would say, the stuff of which heroes are made. But you would be wrong. Rollo Podmarsh was a golfer, and consequently pure gold at heart; and in his hour of crisis all the good in him came to the surface.

In giving you this character-sketch of Rollo, I have been at pains to make it crisp, for I observe that you are wriggling in a restless manner and you persist in pulling out that watch of yours and gazing at it. Let me tell you that, if a mere skeleton outline of the man has this effect upon you, I am glad for your sake that you never met his mother. Mrs. Podmarsh could talk with enjoyment for hours on end about her son's character and habits. And, on the September evening on which I introduce her to you, though she had, as a fact, been speaking only for some ten minutes, it had seemed like hours to the girl, Mary Kent, who was the party of the second part to the conversation.

Mary Kent was the daughter of an old school-friend of Mrs. Podmarsh, and she had come to spend the autumn and winter with her while her parents were abroad. The scheme had never looked particularly good to Mary, and after ten minutes of her hostess on the subject of Rollo she was beginning to weave dreams of knotted sheets and a swift getaway through the bedroom window in the dark of the night.

"He is a strict teetotaller," said Mrs. Podmarsh.

"Really?"

"And has never smoked in his life."

"Fancy that!"

"But here is the dear boy now," said Mrs. Podmarsh, fondly.

*

The Awakening of Rollo Podmarsh

Down the road towards them was coming a tall, well-knit figure in a Norfolk coat and grey flannel trousers. Over his broad shoulders was suspended a bag of golf-clubs.

"Is *that* Mr. Podmarsh?" exclaimed Mary.

She was surprised. After all she had been listening to about the arrowroot and the flannel next the skin and the rest of it, she had pictured the son of the house as a far weedier specimen. She had been expecting to meet a small, slender young man with an eyebrow moustache, and pince-nez; and this person approaching might have stepped straight out of Jack Dempsey's training-camp.

"Does he play golf?" asked Mary, herself an enthusiast.

"Oh, yes," said Mrs. Podmarsh. "He makes a point of going out on the links once a day. He says the fresh air gives him such an appetite."

Mary, who had taken a violent dislike to Rollo on the evidence of his mother's description of his habits, had softened towards him on discovering that he was a golfer. She now reverted to her previous opinion. A man who could play the noble game from such ignoble motives was beyond the pale.

"Rollo is exceedingly good at golf," proceeded Mrs. Podmarsh. "He scores more than a hundred and twenty every time, while Mr. Burns, who is supposed to be one of the best players in the club, seldom manages to reach eighty. But Rollo is very modest — modesty is one of his best qualities — and you would never guess he was so skilful unless you were told."

"Well, Rollo darling, did you have a nice game? You didn't get your feet wet, I hope? This is Mary Kent, dear."

Rollo Podmarsh shook hands with Mary. And at her touch the strange dizzy feeling which had come over him at the sight of her suddenly became increased a thousand-fold. As I see that you are consulting your watch once more, I will not describe his emotions as exhaustively as I might. I will merely say that he had never felt anything resembling this sensation of dozed ecstasy since the occasion when a twenty-foot putt of his, which had been going well off the line, as his putts generally did, had hit a worm-cast sou'-sou'-east of the hole and popped in, giving him a snappy six. Rollo Podmarsh, as you will have divined, was in love at first sight. Which makes it all the sadder to think Mary at the moment was regarding him as an outcast and a blister.

Mrs. Podmarsh, having enfolded her son in a vehement embrace, drew back with a startled exclamation, sniffing.

"Rollo!" she cried. "You smell of tobacco smoke."

Rollo looked embarrassed.

"Well, the fact is, mother — ".

A hard protuberance in his coat-pocket attracted Mrs. Podmarsh's notice. She swooped and drew out a big-bowled pipe.

"Rollo!" she exclaimed, aghast.

"Well, the fact is mother — "

"Don't you know," cried Mrs. Podmarsh, "that smoking is poisonous, and injurious to the health?"

"Yes. But the fact is, mother — "

"It causes nervous dyspepsia, sleeplessness, gnawing of the stomach, headache, weak eyes, red spots on the skin, throat irritation, asthma, bronchitis, heart failure, lung trouble, catarrh, melancholy, neurasthenia, loss of memory, impaired will-power, rheumatism, lumbago, sciatica, neuritis, heartburn, torpid liver, loss of appetite, enervation, lassitude, lack of ambition, and falling out of hair."

"Yes, I know, mother. But the fact is, Ted Ray smokes all the time he's playing, and I thought it might improve my game."

And it was at these splendid words that Mary Kent felt for the first time that something might be made of Rollo Podmarsh. That she experienced one-millionth of the fervour which was gnawing at his vitals I will not say. A woman does not fall in love in a flash like a man. But at least she no longer regarded him with loathing. On the contrary, she found herself liking him. There was, she considered, the right stuff in Rollo. And if, as seemed probable from his mother's conversation, it would take a bit of digging to bring it up, well — she liked rescue-work and had plenty of time.

Mr. Arnold Bennett, in a recent essay, advises young bachelors to proceed with a certain caution in matters of the heart. They should, he asserts, first decide whether or not they are ready for love; then, whether it is better to marry earlier or later; thirdly, whether their ambitions are such that a wife will prove a hindrance to their career. These romantic preliminaries concluded, they may grab a girl and go to it. Rollo Podmarsh would have made a tough audience for these precepts. Since the days of Antony and Cleopatra probably no one had ever got more swiftly off the mark. One may say that he was in love before he had come within two yards of the girl. And each day that passed found him more nearly up to his eyebrows in the tender emotion.

He thought of Mary when he was changing his wet shoes; he dreamed of her while putting flannel next his skin; he yearned for her over the evening arrowroot. Why, the man was such a slave to his devotion that he actually went to the length of purloining small articles belonging to her. Two days after Mary's arrival Rollo Podmarsh was driving off the first tee with one of her handkerchiefs, a powder-puff, and a dozen hairpins secreted in his left breast-pocket. When dressing for dinner he used to take them out and look at them, and at night he slept with them under his pillow. Heavens, how he loved that girl!

One evening when they had gone out into the garden together to look at the new moon — Rollo, by his mother's advice, wearing a woollen scarf to protect his throat — he endeavoured to bring the conversation round to the important subject. Mary's last remark had been about earwigs.

Considered as a cue, it lacked a subtle something; but Rollo was not the man to be discouraged by that.

"Talking of earwigs, Miss Kent," he said, in a low musical voice, "have you ever been in love?"

Mary was silent for a moment before replying.

"Yes, once. When I was eleven. With a conjurer who came to perform at my birthday-party. He took a rabbit and two eggs out of my hair, and life seemed one grand sweet song."

"Never since then?"

"Never."

"Suppose — just for the sake of argument — suppose you ever did love any one — er — what sort of a man would it be?"

"A hero," said Mary, promptly.

"A hero?" said Rollo, somewhat taken aback. "What sort of hero?"

"Any sort. I could only love a really brave man — a man who had done some wonderful heroic action."

"Shall we go in?" said Rollo, hoarsely. "The air is a little chilly."

We have now, therefore, arrived at a period in Rollo Podmarsh's career which might have inspired those lines of Henley's about "the night that covers me, black as the pit from pole to pole." What with one thing and another, he was in an almost Job-like condition of despondency. I say "one thing and another," for it was not only hopeless love that weighed him down. In addition to being hopelessly in love, he was greatly depressed about his golf.

On Rollo in his capacity of golfer I have so far not dwelt. You have probably allowed yourself, in spite of the significant episode of the pipe, to dismiss him as one of those placid, contented — shall I say dilettante? — golfers who are so frequent in these degenerate days. Such was not the case. Outwardly placid, Rollo was consumed inwardly by an ever-burning fever of ambition. His aims were not extravagant.

He did not want to become amateur champion, nor even to win a monthly medal; but he did, with his whole soul, desire one of these days to go round the course in under a hundred. This feat accomplished, it was his intention to set the seal on his golfing career by playing a real money-match; and already he had selected his opponent, a certain Colonel Bodger, a tottery performer of advanced years who for the last decade had been a martyr to lumbago.

But it began to look as if even the modest goal he had marked out for himself were beyond his powers. Day after day he would step on to the first tee, glowing with zeal and hope, only to crawl home in the quiet evenfall with another hundred and twenty on his card. Little wonder, then, that he began to lose his appetite and would moan feebly at the sight of a poached egg.

With Mrs. Podmarsh sedulously watching over her son's health, you might have supposed that this inability on his part to teach the foodstuffs to take a joke would have caused consternation in the home. But it so happened that Rollo's mother had recently been reading a medical treatise in which an eminent physician stated that we all eat too much nowadays, and that the secret of a happy life is to lay off the carbohydrates to some extent. She was, therefore, delighted to observe the young man's moderation in the matter of food, and frequently held him up as an example to be noted and followed by little Lettice Willoughby, her grand-daughter, who was a good and consistent trencherwoman, particularly rough on the puddings. Little Lettice, I should mention, was the daughter of Rollo's sister Enid, who lived in the neighbourhood. Mrs. Willoughby had been compelled to go away on a visit a few days before and had left her child with Mrs. Podmarsh during her absence.

You can fool some of the people all the time, but Lettice Willoughby was not of the type that is easily deceived. A nice, old-fashioned child would no doubt have accepted without questioning her grandmother's dictum that roly-poly pudding could not fail to hand a devastating wallop to the blood-pressure, and that to take two helpings of it was practically equivalent to walking right into the family vault. A child with less decided opinions of her own would have been impressed by the spectacle of her uncle refusing sustenance, and would have received without demur the statement that he did it because he felt that abstinence was good for his health. Lettice was a modern child and knew better. She had had experience of this loss of appetite and its significance. The first symptom which had preceded the demise of poor old Ponto, who had recently handed in his portfolio after holding office for ten years as the Willoughby family dog, had been this same disinclination to absorb nourishment. Besides, she was an observant child, and had not failed to note the haggard misery in her uncle's eyes. She tackled him squarely on the subject one morning after breakfast. Rollo had retired into the more distant parts of the garden, and was leaning forward, when she found him, with his head buried in his hands.

"Hallo, uncle," said Lettice.

Rollo looked up wanly.

"Ah, child!" he said. He was fond of his niece.

"Aren't you feeling well, uncle?"

"Far, far from well."

"It's old age, I expect," said Lettice.

"I feel old," admitted Rollo. "Old and battered. Ah, Lettice, laugh and be gay while you can."

"All right, uncle."

"Make the most of your happy, careless, smiling, halcyon childhood."

"Right-o, uncle."

"When you get to my age, dear, you will realise that it is a sad, hopeless world. A world where, if you keep your head down, you forget to let the club-head lead: where even if you do happen by a miracle to keep 'em straight with your brassie, you blow up on the green and foozle a six-inch putt."

Lettice could not quite understand what Uncle Rollo was talking about, but she gathered broadly that she had been correct in supposing him to be in a bad state, and her warm, childish heart was filled with pity for him. She walked thoughtfully away, and Rollo resumed his reverie.

Into each life, as the poet says, some rain must fall. So much had recently been falling into Rollo's that, when Fortune at last sent along a belated sunbeam, it exercised a cheering effect out of all proportion to its size. By this I mean that when, some four days after his conversation with Lettice, Mary Kent asked him to play golf with her, he read into the invitation a significance which only a lover could have seen in it. I will not go so far as to say that Rollo Podmarsh looked on Mary Kent's suggestion that they should have a round together as actually tantamount to a revelation of undying love; but he certainly regarded it as a most encouraging sign. It seemed to him that things were beginning to move, that Rollo Preferred were on a rising market. Gone was the gloom of the past days. He forgot those sad, solitary wanderings of his in the bushes at the bottom of the garden; he forgot that his mother had bought him a new set of winter woollies which felt like horsehair; he forgot that for the last few evenings his arrowroot had tasted rummy. His whole mind was occupied with the astounding fact that she had voluntarily offered to play golf with him, and he walked out on to the first tee filled with a yeasty exhilaration which nearly caused him to burst into song.

"How shall we play?" asked Mary. "I am a twelve. What is your handicap?"

Rollo was under the disadvantage of not actually possessing a handicap. He had a sort of private system of bookkeeping of his own by which he took strokes over if they did not seem to him to be up to sample, and allowed himself five-foot putts at discretion. So he had never actually

handed in the three cards necessary for handicapping purposes.

"I don't exactly know," he said. "It's my ambition to get
round in under a hundred, but I've never managed it yet."

"Never?"

"Never! It's strange, but something always seems to go
wrong."

"Perhaps you'll manage it to-day," said Mary, encouragingly, so encouragingly that it was all that Rollo could do to
refrain from flinging himself at her feet and barking like a
dog. "Well, I'll start you two holes up, and we'll see how we
get on. Shall I take the honour?"

She drove off one of those fair-to-medium balls which go
with a twelve handicap. Not a great length, but nice and
straight.

"Splendid!" cried Rollo, devoutly.

"Oh, I don't know," said Mary. "I wouldn't call it anything
special."

Titanic emotions were surging in Rollo's bosom as he addressed his ball. He had never felt like this before, especially
on the first tee — where as a rule he found himself overcome
with a nervous humility.

"Oh, Mary! Mary!" he breathed to himself as he swung.

You who squander your golden youth fooling about on a
bowling-green will not understand the magic of those three
words. But if you were a golfer, you would realise that in
selecting just that invocation to breathe to himself Rollo Podmarsh had hit, by sheer accident, on the ideal method of
achieving a fine drive. Let me explain. The first two words,
tensely breathed, are just sufficient to take a man with the
proper slowness to the top of his swing; the first syllable of
the second "Mary" exactly coincides with the striking of the
ball; and that final "ry!" takes care of the follow-through. The
consequence was that Rollo's ball, instead of hopping down
the hill like an embarrassed duck, as was its usual practice,

sang off the tee with a scream like a shell, nodded in passing Mary's ball, where it lay some hundred and fifty yards down the course, and, carrying on from there, came to rest within easy distance of the green. For the first time in his golfing life Rollo Podmarsh had hit a nifty.

Mary followed the ball's flight with astonished eyes.

"But this will never do!" she exclaimed. "I can't possibly start you two up if you're going to do this sort of thing."

Rollo blushed.

"I shouldn't think it would happen again," he said. "I've never done a drive like that before."

"But it must happen again," said Mary, firmly. "This is evidently your day. If you don't get round in under a hundred to-day, I shall never forgive you."

Rollo shut his eyes, and his lips moved feverishly. He was registering a vow that, come what might, he would not fail her. A minute later he was holing out in three, one under bogey.

The second hole is the short lake-hole. Bogey is three, and Rollo generally did it in four; for it was his custom not to count any balls he might sink in the water, but to start afresh with one which happened to get over, and then take three putts. But to-day something seemed to tell him that he would not require the aid of this ingenious system. As he took his mashie from the bag, he *knew* that his first shot would soar successfully on to the green.

"Ah, Mary!" he breathed as he swung.

These subtleties are wasted on a worm, if you will pardon the expression, like yourself, who, possibly owing to a defective education, is content to spend life's springtime rolling wooden balls across a lawn; but I will explain that in altering and shortening his soliloquy at this juncture Rollo had done the very thing any good pro. would have recommended. If he had murmured, "Oh, Mary! Mary!" as before he would have over-swung. "Ah, Mary!" was exactly right for a half-swing with the mashie. His ball shot up in a beautiful arc, and trickled to within six inches of the hole.

Mary was delighted. There was something about this big, diffident man which had appealed from the first to everything in her that was motherly.

"Marvellous!" she said. "You'll get a two. Five for the first two holes! Why, you simply must get round under a hundred now." She swung, but too lightly; and her ball fell in the water. "I'll give you this," she said, without the slightest chagrin, for this girl had a beautiful nature. "Let's get on to the third. Four up! Why, you're wonderful!"

And not to weary you with too much detail, I will simply remark that, stimulated by her gentle encouragement, Rollo Podmarsh actually came off the ninth green with a medal score of forty-six for the half-round. A ten on the seventh had spoiled his card to some extent, and a nine on the eighth had not helped, but nevertheless here he was in forty-six, with the easier half of the course before him. He tingled all over — partly because he was wearing the new winter woollies to which I have alluded previously, but principally owing to triumph, elation, and love. He gazed at Mary as Dante might have gazed at Beatrice on one of his particularly sentimental mornings.

Mary uttered an exclamation.

"Oh, I've just remembered," she exclaimed. "I promised to write last night to Jane Simpson and give her that new formula for knitting jumpers. I think I'll 'phone her now from the club-house and then it'll be off my mind. You go on to the tenth, and I'll join you there."

Rollo proceeded over the brow of the hill to the tenth tee, and was filling in the time with practice-swings when he heard his name spoken.

"Good gracious, Rollo! I couldn't believe it was you at first."

He turned to see his sister, Mrs. Willoughby, the mother of the child Lettice.

"Hallo!" he said. "When did you get back?"

"Late last night. Why, it's extraordinary!"

"Hope you had a good time. What's extraordinary? Listen, Enid. Do you know what I've done? Forty-six for the first nine! Forty-six! And holing out every putt."

"Oh, then that accounts for it."

"Accounts for what?"

"Why, your looking so pleased with life. I got an idea from Letty, when she wrote to me, that you were at death's door. Your gloom seems to have made a deep impression on the child. Her letter was full of it."

Rollo was moved.

"Dear little Letty! She is wonderfully sympathetic."

"Well, I must be off now," said Enid Willoughby. "I'm late. Oh, talking of Letty. Don't children say the funniest things! She wrote in her letter that you were very old and wretched and that she was going to put you out of your misery."

"Ha ha ha!" laughed Rollo.

"We had to poison poor old Ponto the other day, you know, and poor little Letty was inconsolable till we explained to her that it was really the kindest thing to do, because he was so old and ill. But just imagine her thinking of wanting to end *your* sufferings!"

"Ha ha!" laughed Rollo. "Ha ha h —"

His voice trailed off into a broken gurgle. Quite suddenly a sinister thought had come to him.

The arrowroot had tasted rummy!

"Why, what on earth is the matter?" asked Mrs. Willoughby, regarding his ashen face.

Rollo could find no words. He yammered speechlessly. Yes, for several nights the arrowroot had tasted very rummy. Rummy! There was no other adjective. Even as he plied the spoon he had said to himself: "This arrowroot tastes rummy!" And — he uttered a sharp yelp as he remembered — it had been little Lettice who had brought it to him. He recollected being touched at the time by the kindly act.

"What *is* the matter, Rollo?" demanded Mrs. Willoughby, sharply. "Don't stand there looking like a dying duck."

"I am a dying duck," responded Rollo, hoarsely. "A dying man, I mean. Enid, that infernal child has poisoned me!"

"Don't be ridiculous! And kindly don't speak of her like that!"

"I'm sorry. I shouldn't blame her, I suppose. No doubt her motives were good. But the fact remains."

"Rollo, you're too absurd."

"But the arrowroot tasted rummy."

"I never knew you could be such an idiot," said his exasperated sister with sisterly outspokenness. "I thought you would think it quaint. I thought you would roar with laughter."

"I did — till I remembered about the rumminess of the arrowroot."

Mrs. Willoughby uttered an impatient exclamation and walked away.

Rollo Podmarsh stood on the tenth tee, a volcano of mixed emotions. Mechanically he pulled out his pipe and lit it. But he found that he could not smoke. In this supreme crisis of his life tobacco seemed to have lost its magic. He put the pipe back in his pocket and gave himself up to his thoughts. Now terror gripped him; anon a sort of gentle melancholy. It was so hard that he should be compelled to leave the world just as he had begun to hit 'em right.

And then in the welter of his thoughts there came one of practical value. To wit, that by hurrying to the doctor's without delay he might yet be saved. There might be antidotes.

He turned to go and there was Mary Kent standing beside him with her bright, encouraging smile.

"I'm sorry I kept you so long," she said. "It's your honour. Fire away, and remember that you've got to do this nine in fifty-three at the outside."

Rollo's thoughts flitted wistfully to the snug surgery where Dr. Brown was probably sitting at this moment surrounded by the finest antidotes.

"Do you know, I think I ought to — "

"Of course you ought to," said Mary. "If you did the first nine in forty-six, you can't possibly take fifty-three coming in."

For one long moment Rollo continued to hesitate — a moment during which the instinct of self-preservation seemed as if it must win the day. All his life he had been brought up to be nervous about his health, and panic gripped him. But there is a deeper, nobler instinct than that of self-preservation — the instictive desire of a golfer who is at the top of his form to go on and beat his medal-score record. And little by little this grand impulse began to dominate Rollo. If, he felt, he went off now to take antidotes, the doctor might possibly save his life; but reason told him that never again would he be likely to do the first nine in forty-six. He would have to start all over afresh.

Rollo Podmarsh hesitated no longer. With a pale, set face he teed up his ball and drove.

If I were telling this story to a golfer instead of to an excrescence — I use the word in the kindliest spirit — who spends his time messing about on a bowling-green, nothing would please me better than to describe shot by shot Rollo's progress over the remaining nine holes. Epics have been written with less material. But these details would, I am aware, be wasted on you. Let it suffice that by the time his last approach trickled on to the eighteenth green he had taken exactly fifty shots.

"Three for it!" said Mary Kent. "Steady now! Take it quite easy and be sure to lay your second dead."

It was prudent counsel, but Rollo was now thoroughly

above himself. He had got his feet wet in a puddle on the sixteenth, but he did not care. His winter woollies seemed to be lined with ants, but he ignored them. All he knew was that he was on the last green in ninety-six, and he meant to finish in style. No tame three putts for him! His ball was five yards away, but he aimed for the back of the hole and brought his putter down with a whack. Straight and true the ball sped, hit the tin, jumped high in the air, and fell into the hole with a rattle.

"Oo!" cried Mary.

Rollo Podmarsh wiped his forehead and leaned dizzily on his putter. For a moment, so intense is the fervour induced by the game of games, all he could think of was that he had gone round in ninety-seven. Then, as one waking from a trance, he began to appreciate his position. The fever passed, and a clammy dismay took possession of him. He had achieved his life's ambition; but what now? Already he was conscious of a curious discomfort within him. He felt as he supposed Italians of the Middle Ages must have felt after dropping in to take pot-luck with the Borgias. It was hard. He had gone round in ninety-seven, but he could never take the next step in the career which he had mapped out in his dreams — the money-match with the lumbago-stricken Colonel Bodger.

Mary Kent was fluttering round him, bubbling congratulations, but Rollo sighed.

"Thanks," he said. "Thanks very much. But the trouble is, I'm afraid I'm going to die almost immediately. I've been poisoned!"

"Poisoned!"

"Yes. Nobody is to blame. Everything was done with the best intentions. But there it is."

"But I don't understand."

Rollo explained. Mary listened pallidly.

"Are you sure?" she gasped.

"Quite sure," said Rollo, gravely. "The arrowroot tasted rummy."

"But arrowroot always does."

Rollo shook his head.

"No," he said. "It tastes like warm blotting-paper, but not rummy."

Mary was sniffing.

"Don't cry," urged Rollo, tenderly. "Don't cry."

"But I must. And I've come out without a handkerchief."

"Permit me," said Rollo, producing one of her best from his left breast-pocket.

"I wish I had a powder-puff," said Mary.

"Allow me," said Rollo. "And your hair has become a little disordered. If I may — " And from the same reservoir he drew a handful of hairpins.

Mary gazed at these exhibits with astonishment.

"But these are mine," she said.

"Yes. I sneaked them from time to time."

"But why?"

"Because I loved you," said Rollo. And in a few moving sentences which I will not trouble you with he went on to elaborate this theme.

Mary listened with her heart full of surging emotions, which I cannot possibly go into if you persist in looking at that damned watch of yours. The scales had fallen from her eyes. She had thought slightingly of this man because he had been a little over-careful of his health, and all the time he had had within him the potentiality of heroism. Something seemed to snap inside her.

"Rollo!" she cried, and flung herself into his arms.

"Mary!" muttered Rollo, gathering her up.

"I told you it was all nonsense," said Mrs. Willoughby, coming up at this tense moment and going on with the conversation where she had left off. "I've just seen Letty, and she said she meant to put you out of your misery but the chemist wouldn't sell her any poison, so she let it go."

Rollo disentangled himself from Mary.

"What?" he cried.

Mrs. Willoughby repeated her remarks.

"You're sure?" he said.

"Of course I'm sure."

"Then why did the arrowroot taste rummy?"

"I made inquiries about that. It seems that mother was worried about your taking to smoking, and she found an advertisement in one of the magazines about the Tobacco Habit Cured in Three Days by a secret method without the victim's knowledge. It was a gentle, safe, agreeable method of eliminating the nicotine poison from the system, strengthening the weakened membranes, and overcoming the craving; so she put some in your arrowroot every night."

There was a long silence. To Rollo Podmarsh it seemed as though the sun had suddenly begun to shine, the birds to sing, and the grasshoppers to toot. All Nature was one vast substantial smile. Down in the valley by the second hole he caught sight of Wallace Chesney's plus-fours gleaming as their owner stooped to play his shot, and it seemed to him that he had never in his life seen anything so lovely.

"Mary," he said, in a low, vibrant voice, "will you wait here for me? I want to go into the club-house for a moment."

"To change your wet shoes?"

"No!" thundered Rollo. "I'm never going to change my wet shoes again in my life." He felt in his pocket, and hurled a box of patent pills far into the undergrowth. "But I *am* going to change my winter woollies. And when I've put those dashed barbed-wire entanglements into the club-house furnace, I'm going to 'phone to old Colonel Bodger. I hear his lumbago's worse than ever. I'm going to fix up a match with him for a shilling a hole. And if I don't lick the boots off him you can break the engagement!"

"My hero!" murmured Mary.

Rollo kissed her, and with long, resolute steps strode to the club-house.

The Heel of Achilles

O

On the young man's face, as he sat sipping his ginger-ale in the club-house smoking-room, there was a look of disillusionment.

"Never again!" he said.

The Oldest Member glanced up from his paper.

"You are proposing to give up golf once more?" he queried.

"Not golf. Betting on golf." The Young Man frowned. "I've just been let down badly. Wouldn't you have thought I had a good thing, laying seven to one on McTavish against Robinson?"

"Undoubtedly," said the Sage. "The odds, indeed, generous as they are, scarcely indicate the former's superiority. Do you mean to tell me that the thing came unstitched?"

"Robinson won in a walk, after being three down at the turn."

"Strange! What happened?"

"Why, they looked in at the bar to have a refresher before starting for the tenth," said the young man, his voice quivering, "and McTavish suddenly discovered that there was a hole in his trouser-pocket and a dime had dropped out. He worried so frightfully about it that on the second nine he couldn't do a thing right. Went completely off his game and didn't win a hole."

The Sage shook his head gravely.

"If this is really going to be a lesson to you, my boy, never to bet on the result of a golf-match, it will be a blessing in disguise. There is no such thing as a certainty in golf. I wonder if I ever told you a rather curious episode in the career of Vincent Jopp?"

"*The* Vincent Jopp? The Chicago multi-millionaire?"

"The same. You never knew he once came within an ace of winning the American Amateur Championship, did you?"

"I never heard of his playing golf."

"He played for one season. After that he gave it up and has not touched a club since. Ring the bell and get me a small lime-juice, and I will tell you all."

It was long before your time (said the Oldest Member) that the events which I am about to relate took place. I had just come down from Harvard, and was feeling particularly pleased with myself because I had secured the job of private and confidential secretary to Vincent Jopp, then a man in the early thirties, busy in laying the foundations of his present remarkable fortune. He engaged me, and took me with him to Chicago.

Jopp was, I think, the most extraordinary personality I have encountered in a long and many-sided life. He was admirably equipped for success in finance, having the steely eye and square jaw without which it is hopeless for a man to enter that line of business. He possessed also an overwhelming confidence in himself, and the ability to switch a cigar from one corner of his mouth to the other without wiggling his ears, which, as you know, is the stamp of the true Monarch of the Money Market. He was the nearest approach to the financier on the films, the fellow who makes his jaw-muscles jump when he is telephoning, that I have ever seen.

Like all successful men, he was a man of method. He kept a pad on his desk on which he would scribble down his appointments, and it was my duty on entering the office each morning to take this pad and type its contents neatly in a loose-leaved ledger. Usually, of course, these entries referred to business appointments and deals which he was contemplating, but one day I was interested to note, against the date May 3rd, the entry:

Propose to Amelia.

I was interested, as I say, but not surprised. Though a man of steel and iron, there was nothing of the celibate about Vincent Jopp. He was one of those men who marry early and often. On three separate occasions before I joined his service he had jumped off the dock, to scramble back to shore again later by means of the Divorce Court lifebelt. Scattered here and there about the country there were three ex-Mrs. Jopps, drawing their monthly envelope, and now, it seemed, he contemplated the addition of a fourth to the platoon.

I was not surprised, I say, at this resolve of his. What did seem a little remarkable to me was the thorough way in which he had thought the thing out. This iron-willed man recked nothing of possible obstacles. Under the date of June 1st was the entry:

Marry Amelia;

while in March of the following year he had arranged to have his first-born christened Thomas Reginald. Later on, the short-coating of Thomas Reginald was arranged for, and there was a note about sending him to school. Many hard things have been said of Vincent Jopp, but nobody has ever accused him of not being a man who looked ahead.

On the morning of May 4th Jopp came into the office, looking, I fancied, a little thoughtful. He sat for some moments staring before him with his brow a trifle furrowed; then he seemed to come to himself. He rapped his desk.

"Hi! You!" he said. It was thus that he habitually addressed me.

"Mr. Jopp?" I replied.

"What's golf?"

I had at that time just succeeded in getting my handicap down into single figures, and I welcomed the opportunity of dilating on the noblest of pastimes. But I had barely begun my eulogy when he stopped me.

"It's a game, is it?"

"I suppose you could call it that," I said, "but it is an off-hand way of describing the holiest — "

"How do you play it?"

"Pretty well," I said. "At the beginning of the season I didn't seem able to keep 'em straight at all, but lately I've been doing fine. Getting better every day. Whether it was that I was moving my head or gripping too tightly with the right hand — "

"Keep the reminiscences for your grandchildren during the long winter evenings," he interrupted, abruptly, as was his habit. "What I want to know is what a fellow does when he plays golf. Tell me in as few words as you can just what it's all about."

"You hit a ball with a stick till it falls into a hole."

"Easy!" he snapped. "Take dictation."

I produced my pad.

"May the fifth, take up golf. What's an Amateur Championship?"

"It is the annual competition to decide which is the best player among the amateurs. There is also a Professional Championship, and an Open event."

"Oh, there are golf professionals, are there? What do they do?"

"They teach golf."

"Which is the best of them?"

"Sandy McHoots won both British and American Open events last year."

"Wire him to come here at once."

"But McHoots is in Inverlochty, in Scotland."

"Never mind. Get him; tell him to name his own terms. When is the Amateur Championship?"

"I think it is on September the twelfth this year."

"All right, take dictation. September twelfth, win Amateur Championship."

I stared at him in amazement, but he was not looking at me.

"Got that?" he said. "September thir — Oh, I was forgetting! Add September twelfth, corner wheat. September thirteenth, marry Amelia."

"Marry Amelia," I echoed, moistening my pencil.

"Where do you play this — what's-its-name — golf?"

"There are clubs all over the country. I belong to the Wissahicky Glen."

"That a good place?"

"Very good."

"Arrange to-day for my becoming a member."

Sandy McHoots arrived in due course, and was shown into the private office.

"Mr. McHoots?" said Vincent Jopp.

"Mphm!" said the Open Champion.

"I have sent for you, Mr. McHoots, because I hear that you are the greatest living exponent of this game of golf."

"Aye," said the champion, cordially. "I am that."

"I wish you to teach me the game. I am already somewhat behind schedule owing to the delay incident upon your long journey, so let us start at once. Name a few of the most important points in connection with the game. My secretary will make notes of them, and I will memorise them. In this way we shall save time. Now, what is the most important thing to remember when playing golf?"

"Keep your heid still."

"A simple task."

"Na sae simple as it soonds."

"Nonsense!" said Vincent Jopp, curtly. "If I decide to keep my head still, I shall keep it still. What next?"

"Keep your e'e on the ba'."

"It shall be attended to. And the next?"

"Dinna press."

"I won't. And to resume."

Mr. McHoots ran through a dozen of the basic rules, and I took them down in shorthand. Vincent Jopp studied the list. "Very good. Easier than I had supposed. On the first tee at Wissahicky Glen at eleven sharp to-morrow, Mr. McHoots. Hi! You!"

"Sir?" I said.

"Go out and buy me a set of clubs, a red jacket, a cloth cap, a pair of spiked shoes, and a ball."

"One ball?"

"Certainly. What need is there of more?"

"It sometimes happens," I explained, "that a player who is learning the game fails to hit his ball straight, and then he often loses it in the rough at the side of the fairway."

"Absurd!" said Vincent Jopp. "If I set out to drive my ball straight, I shall drive it straight. Good morning, Mr. McHoots. You will excuse me now. I am busy cornering Woven Textiles."

Golf is in its essence a simple game. You laugh in a sharp, bitter, barking manner when I say this, but nevertheless it is true. Where the average man goes wrong is in making the game difficult for himself. Observe the non-player, the man who walks round with you for the sake of the fresh air. He will hole out with a single care-free flick of his umbrella the twenty-foot putt over which you would ponder and hesitate for a full minute before sending it right off the line. Put a driver in his hands, and he pastes the ball into the next county without a thought. It is only when he takes to the game in earnest that he becomes self-conscious and anxious, and tops his shots even as you and I. A man who could retain through his golfing career the almost scornful confidence of the non-player would be unbeatable. Fortunately such an attitude of mind is beyond the scope of human nature.

It was not, however, beyond the scope of Vincent Jopp, the superman. Vincent Jopp was, I am inclined to think, the only golfer who ever approached the game in a spirit of Pure Reason. I have read of men who, never having swum in their lives, studied a text-book on their way down to the swimming bath, mastered its contents, and dived in and won the big race. In just such a spirit did Vincent Jopp start to play golf. He committed McHoots's hints to memory, and then went out on the links and put them into practice. He came to the tee with a clear picture in his mind of what he had to do, and he did it. He was not intimidated, like the average novice, by the thought that if he pulled in his hands he would slice, or if he gripped too tightly with the right he would pull. Pulling in the hands was an error, so he did not pull in his hands. Gripping too tightly was a defect, so he did not grip too tightly. With that weird concentration which had served him so well in business he did precisely what he had set out to do — no less and no more. Golf with Vincent Jopp was an exact science.

The annals of the game are studded with the names of those who have made rapid progress in their first season. Colonel Quill, we read in our Vardon, took up golf at the age of fifty-six, and by devising an ingenious machine consisting of a fishing-line and a sawn-down bedpost was enabled to keep his head so still that he became a scratch player before the end of the year. But no one, I imagine, except Vincent Jopp, has ever achieved scratch on his first morning on the links.

The main difference, we are told, between the amateur and the professional golfer is the fact that the latter is always aiming at the pin, while the former has in his mind a vague

picture of getting somewhere reasonably near it. Vincent
Jopp invariably went for the pin. He tried to hole out from
anywhere inside two hundred and twenty yards. The only
occasion on which I ever heard him express any chagrin or
disappointment was during the afternoon round on his first
day out, when from the tee on the two hundred and eighty
yard seventh he laid his ball within six inches of the hole.

"A marvellous shot!" I cried, genuinely stirred.

"Too much to the right," said Vincent Jopp, frowning.

He went on from triumph to triumph. He won the
monthly medal in May, June, July, August, and September.
Towards the end of May he was heard to complain that Wissahicky Glen was not a sporting course. The Greens Committee sat up night after night trying to adjust his handicap so
as to give other members an outside chance against him. The
golf experts of the daily papers wrote columns about his play.
And it was pretty generally considered throughout the country that it would be a pure formality for anyone else to enter
against him in the Amateur Championship — an opinion
which was borne out when he got through into the final
without losing a hole. A safe man to have betted on, you
would have said. But mark the sequel.

The Amateur Championship was held that year in Detroit.
I had accompanied my employer there; for, though engaged
on this nerve-wearing contest, he refused to allow his business to be interfered with. As he had indicated in his schedule, he was busy at the time cornering wheat; and it was my
task to combine the duties of caddy and secretary. Each day
I accompanied him round the links with my note-book and
his bag of clubs, and the progress of his various matches
was somewhat complicated by the arrival of a stream of
telegraph-boys bearing important messages. He would read
these between the strokes and dictate replies to me, never,
however, taking more than the five minutes allowed by the

rules for an interval between strokes. I am inclined to think that it was this that put the finishing touch on his opponents' discomfiture. It is not soothing for a nervous man to have the game hung up on the green while his adversary dictates to his caddy a letter beginning "Yours of the 11th inst. received and contents noted. In reply would state — " This sort of thing puts a man off his game.

I was resting in the lobby of our hotel after a strenuous day's work, when I found that I was being paged. I answered the summons, and was informed that a lady wished to see me. Her card bore the name "Miss Amelia Merridew." Amelia! The name seemed familiar. Then I remembered. Amelia was the name of the girl Vincent Jopp intended to marry, the fourth of the long line of Mrs. Jopps. I hurried to present myself, and found a tall, slim girl, who was plainly labouring under a considerable agitation.

"Miss Merridew?" I said.

"Yes," she murmured. "My name will be strange to you."

"Am I right," I queried, "in supposing that you are the lady to whom Mr. Jopp — "

"I am! I am!" she replied. "And, oh, what shall I do?"

"Kindly give me particulars," I said, taking out my pad from force of habit.

She hesitated a moment, as if afraid to speak.

"You are caddying for Mr. Jopp in the Final to-morrow?" she said at last.

"I am."

"Then could you — would you mind — would it be giving you too much trouble if I asked you to shout 'Boo!' at him when he is making his stroke, if he looks like winning?"

I was perplexed.

"I don't understand."

"I see that I must tell you all. I am sure you will treat what I say as absolutely confidential."

"Certainly."

"I am provisionally engaged to Mr. Jopp."

"Provisionally?"

She gulped.

"Let me tell you my story. Mr. Jopp asked me to marry him, and I would rather do anything on earth than marry him. But how could I say 'No!' with those awful eyes of his boring me through? I knew that if I said 'No,' he would argue me out of it in two minutes. I had an idea. I gathered that he had never played golf, so I told him that I would marry him if he won the Amateur Championship this year. And now I find that he has been a golfer all along, and, what is more, a plus man! It isn't fair!"

"He was not a golfer when you made that condition," I said. "He took up the game on the following day."

"Impossible! How could he have become as good as he is in this short time?"

"Because he is Vincent Jopp! In his lexicon there is no such word as impossible."

She shuddered.

"What a man! But I can't marry him," she cried. "I want to marry somebody else. Oh, won't you help me? Do shout 'Boo!' at him when he is starting his down-swing!"

I shook my head.

"It would take more than a single 'Boo!' to put Vincent Jopp off his stroke."

"But won't you try it?"

"I cannot. My duty is to my employer."

"Oh, do!"

"No, no. Duty is duty, and paramount with me. Besides, I have a hundred dollars down on him to win."

The stricken girl uttered a faint moan, and tottered away.

I was in our suite shortly after dinner that night, going over some of the notes I had made that day, when the telephone rang. Jopp was out at the time, taking a short stroll with his after-dinner cigar. I unhooked the receiver, and a female voice spoke.

"Is that Mr. Jopp?"

"Mr. Jopp's secretary speaking. Mr. Jopp is out."

"Oh, it's nothing important. Will you say that Mrs. Luella Mainprice Jopp called up to wish him luck? I shall be on the course to-morrow to see him win the final."

I returned to my notes. Soon afterwards the telephone rang again.

"Vincent, dear?"

"Mr. Jopp's secretary speaking."

"Oh, will you say that Mrs. Jane Jukes Jopp called up to wish him luck? I shall be there to-morrow to see him play."

I resumed my work. I had hardly started when the telephone rang for the third time.

"Mr. Jopp?"

"Mr. Jopp's secretary speaking."

"This is Mrs. Agnes Parsons Jopp. I just called up to wish him luck. I shall be looking on to-morrow."

I shifted my work nearer to the telephone-table so as to be ready for the next call. I had heard that Vincent Jopp had only been married three times, but you never knew.

Presently Jopp came in.

"Anybody called up?" he asked.

"Nobody on business. An assortment of your wives were on the wire wishing you luck. They asked me to say that they will be on the course to-morrow."

For a moment it seemed to me that the man's iron repose was shaken.

"Luella?" he asked.

"She was the first."

"Jane?"

"And Jane."

"And Agnes?"

"Agnes," I said, "is right."

"H'm!" said Vincent Jopp. And for the first time since I had known him I thought that he was ill at ease.

The day of the final dawned bright and clear. At least, I was not awake at the time to see, but I suppose it did; for at nine o'clock, when I came down to breakfast, the sun was shining brightly. The first eighteen holes were to be played before lunch, starting at eleven. Until twenty minutes before the hour Vincent Jopp kept me busy taking dictation, partly on matters connected with his wheat deal and partly on a signed article dealing with the Final, entitled "How I Won." At eleven sharp we were out on the first tee.

Jopp's opponent was a nice-looking young man, but obviously nervous. He giggled in a distraught sort of way as he shook hands with my employer.

"Well, may the best man win," he said.

"I have arranged to do so," replied Jopp, curtly, and started to address his ball.

There was a large crowd at the tee, and, as Jopp started his down-swing, from somewhere on the outskirts of this crowd there came suddenly a musical "Boo!" It rang out in the clear morning air like a bugle.

I had been right in my estimate of Vincent Jopp. His forceful stroke never wavered. The head of his club struck the ball, despatching it a good two hundred yards down the middle of the fairway. As we left the tee I saw Amelia Merridew being led away with bowed head by two members of the Greens Committee. Poor girl! My heart bled for her. And yet, after all, Fate had been kind in removing her from the scene, even in custody, for she could hardly have borne to watch the proceedings. Vincent Jopp made rings around his antagonist. Hole after hole he won in his remorseless, machine-like way, until when lunch-time came at the end of the eighteenth he was ten up. All the other holes had been halved.

It was after lunch, as we made our way to the first tee, that the advance-guard of the Mrs. Jopps appeared in the person of Luella Mainprice Jopp, a kittenish little woman with blonde hair and a Pekinese dog. I remembered reading in the papers that she had divorced my employer for persistent and aggravated mental cruelty, calling witnesses to bear out her statement that he had said he did not like her in pink, and that on two separate occasions had insisted on her dog eating the leg of a chicken instead of the breast; but Time, the great healer, seemed to have removed all bitterness, and she greeted him affectionately.

"Wassums going to win great big championship against nasty rough strong man?" she said.

"Such," said Vincent Jopp, "is my intention. It was kind of you, Luella, to trouble to come and watch me. I wonder if you know Mrs. Agnes Parsons Jopp?" he said, courteously, indicating a kind-looking, motherly woman who had just come up. "How are you, Agnes?"

"If you had asked me that question this morning, Vincent," replied Mrs. Agnes Parsons Jopp, "I should have been obliged to say that I felt far from well. I had an odd throbbing feeling in the left elbow, and I am sure my temperature was above the normal. But this afternoon I am a little better. How are you, Vincent?"

Although she had, as I recalled from the reports of the case, been compelled some years earlier to request the Court to sever her marital relations with Vincent Jopp on the ground of calculated and inhuman brutality, in that he had callously refused, in spite of her pleadings, to take old Dr. Bennett's Tonic Swamp-Juice three times a day, her voice, as she spoke, was kind and even anxious. Badly as this man had treated her — and I remember hearing that several of the jury had been unable to restrain their tears when she was in the witness-box giving her evidence — there still seemed to linger some remnants of the old affection.

"I am quite well, thank you, Agnes," said Vincent Jopp.

"Are you wearing your liver-pad?"

A frown flitted across my employer's strong face.

"I am not wearing my liver-pad," he replied, brusquely.

"Oh, Vincent, how rash of you!"

He was about to speak, when a sudden exclamation from his rear checked him. A genial-looking woman in a sports coat was standing there, eyeing him with a sort of humorous horror.

"Well, Jane," he said.

I gathered that this was Mrs. Jane Jukes Jopp, the wife who had divorced him for systematic and ingrowing fiendishness on the ground that he had repeatedly outraged her feelings by wearing a white waistcoat with a dinner-jacket. She continued to look at him dumbly, and then uttered a sort of strangled, hysterical laugh.

"Those legs!" she cried. "Those legs!"

Vincent Jopp flushed darkly. Even the strongest and most silent of us have our weaknesses, and my employer's was the rooted idea that he looked well in knickerbockers. It was not my place to try to dissuade him, but there was no doubt that they did not suit him. Nature, in bestowing upon him a massive head and a jutting chin, had forgotten to finish him off at the other end. Vincent Jopp's legs were skinny.

"You poor dear man!" went on Mrs. Jane Jukes Jopp. "What practical joker ever lured you into appearing in public in knickerbockers?"

"I don't object to the knickerbockers," said Mrs. Agnes Parsons Jopp, "but when he foolishly comes out in quite a strong east wind without his liver-pad — "

"Little Tinky-Ting don't need no liver-pad, he don't," said Mrs. Luella Mainprice Jopp, addressing the animal in her arms, "because he was his muzzer's pet, he was."

I was standing quite near to Vincent Jopp, and at this moment I saw a bead of perspiration spring out on his forehead, and into his steely eyes there came a positively hunted look. I could understand and sympathise. Napoleon himself would have wilted if he had found himself in the midst of a trio of females, one talking baby-talk, another fussing about his health, and the third making derogatory observations of his lower limbs. Vincent Jopp was becoming unstrung.

"May as well be starting, shall we?"

It was Jopp's opponent who spoke. There was a strange, set look on his face — the look of a man whose back is against the wall. Ten down on the morning's round, he had drawn on his reserves of courage and was determined to meet the inevitable bravely.

Vincent Jopp nodded absently, then turned to me.

"Keep those women away from me," he whispered tensely. "They'll put me off my stroke!"

"Put *you* off your stroke!" I exclaimed, incredulously.

"Yes, me! How the deuce can I concentrate, with people babbling about liver-pads, and — and knickerbockers all round me? Keep them away!"

He started to address his ball, and there was a weak uncertainty in the way he did it that prepared me for what was to come. His club rose, wavered, fell; and the ball, badly topped, trickled two feet and sank into a cuppy lie.

"Is that good or bad?" inquired Mrs. Luella Mainprice Jopp.

A sort of desperate hope gleamed in the eye of the other competitor in the final. He swung with renewed vigour. His ball sang through the air, and lay within chip-shot distance of the green.

"At the very least," said Mrs. Agnes Parsons Jopp, "I hope, Vincent, that you are wearing flannel next your skin."

I heard Jopp give a stifled groan as he took his spoon from the bag. He made a gallant effort to retrieve the lost ground, but the ball struck a stone and bounded away into the long grass to the side of the green. His opponent won the hole.

We moved to the second tee.

"Now, *that* young man," said Mrs. Jane Jukes Jopp, indicating her late husband's blushing antagonist, "is quite right to wear knickerbockers. He can carry them off. But a glance in the mirror must have shown you that you — "

"I'm sure you're feverish, Vincent," said Mrs. Agnes Parsons Jopp, solicitously. "You are quite flushed. There is a wild gleam in your eyes."

"Muzzer's pet's got little buttons of eyes, that don't never have no wild gleam in zem because he's muzzer's own darling, he was!" said Mrs. Luella Mainprice Jopp.

A hollow groan escaped Vincent Jopp's ashen lips.

I need not recount the play hole by hole, I think. There are some subjects that are too painful. It was pitiful to watch Vincent Jopp in his downfall. By the end of the first nine his lead had been reduced to one, and his antagonist, rendered a new man by success, was playing magnificent golf. On the next hole he drew level. Then with a superhuman effort Jopp contrived to halve the eleventh, twelfth, and thirteenth. It seemed as though his iron will might still assert itself, but on the fourteenth the end came.

He had driven a superb ball, outdistancing his opponent by a full fifty yards. The latter played a good second to within a few feet of the green. And then, as Vincent Jopp was shaping for his stroke, Luella Mainprice gave tongue.

"Vincent!"

"Well?"

"Vincent, that other man — bad man — not playing fair. When your back was turned just now, he gave his ball a great bang. *I* was watching him."

"At any rate," said Mrs. Agnes Parsons Jopp, "I do hope, when the game is over, Vincent, that you will remember to cool slowly."

"Flesho!" cried Mrs. Jane Jukes Jopp triumphantly. "I've been trying to remember the name all the afternoon. I saw about it in one of the papers. The advertisements speak most highly of it. You take it before breakfast and again before retiring, and they guarantee it to produce firm, healthy flesh on the most sparsely-covered limbs in next to no time. Now, *will* you remember to get a bottle to-night? It comes in two sizes, the dollar (or large) size and the smaller at fifty cents. Irvin Cobb writes that he used it regularly for years."

Vincent Jopp uttered a quavering moan, and his hand, as he took the mashie from his bag, was trembling like an aspen.

Ten minutes later, he was on his way back to the club-house, a beaten man.

And so (concluded the Oldest Member) you see that in golf there is no such thing as a soft snap. You can never be certain of the finest player. Anything may happen to the greatest expert at any stage of the game. In a recent competition George Duncan took eleven shots over a hole which eighteen-handicap men generally do in five. No! Back horses or go down to Throgmorton Street and try to take it away from the Rothschilds, and I will applaud you as a shrewd and cautious financier. But to bet at golf is pure gambling.

Rodney Fails to Qualify

O

There was a sound of revelry by night, for the first Saturday
in June had arrived and the Golf Club was holding its
monthly dance. Fairy lanterns festooned the branches of the
chestnut trees on the terrace above the ninth green, and
from the big dining-room, cleared now of its tables and
chairs, came a muffled slithering of feet and the plaintive
sound of saxophones moaning softly like a man who has just
missed a short putt. In a basket-chair in the shadows, the
Oldest Member puffed a cigar and listened, well content. His
was the peace of the man who has reached the age when he
is no longer expected to dance.

A door opened, and a young man came out of the club-
house. He stood on the steps with folded arms, gazing to left
and right. The Oldest Member, watching him from the darkness, noted that he wore an air of gloom. His brow was furrowed and he had the indefinable look of one who has been
smitten in the spiritual solar plexus.

Yes, where all around him was joy, jollity, and song, this
young man brooded.

The sound of a high tenor voice, talking rapidly and enter-
tainingly on the subject of modern Russian thought, now
intruded itself on the peace of the night. From the farther
end of the terrace a girl came into the light of the lantern,
her arm in that of a second young man. She was small and
pretty, he tall and intellectual. The light shone on his forehead and glittered on his tortoiseshell-rimmed spectacles.

FORE!

The girl was gazing up at him with reverence and adoration, and at the sight of these twain the youth on the steps appeared to undergo some sort of spasm. His face became contorted and he wobbled. Then, with a gesture of sublime despair, he tripped over the mat and stumbled back into the club-house. The couple passed on and disappeared, and the Oldest Member had the night to himself, until the door opened once more and the club's courteous and efficient secretary trotted down the steps. The scent of the cigar drew him to where the Oldest Member sat, and he dropped into the chair beside him.

"Seen young Ramage to-night?" asked the secretary.

"He was standing on those steps only a moment ago," replied the Oldest Member. "Why do you ask?"

"I thought perhaps you might have had a talk with him and found out what's the matter. Can't think what's come to him to-night. Nice, civil boy as a rule, but just now, when I was trying to tell him about my short approach on the fifth this afternoon, he was positively abrupt. Gave a sort of hollow gasp and dashed away in the middle of a sentence."

The Oldest Member sighed.

"You must overlook his brusqueness," he said. "The poor lad is passing through a trying time. A short while back I was the spectator of a little drama that explains everything. Mabel Patmore is flirting disgracefully with that young fellow Purvis."

"Purvis? Oh, you mean the man who won the club Bowls Championship last week?"

"I can quite believe that he may have disgraced himself in the manner you describe," said the Sage, coldly. "I know he plays that noxious game. And it is for that reason that I hate to see a nice girl like Mabel Patmore, who only needs a little more steadiness off the tee to become a very fair golfer, wasting her time on him. I suppose his attraction lies in the fact that he has a great flow of conversation, while poor

Ramage is, one must admit, more or less of a dumb Isaac.
Girls are too often snared by a glib tongue. Still, it is a pity,
a great pity. The whole affair recalls irresistibly to my mind
the story — "

The secretary rose with a whirr like a rocketing pheasant.

" — the story," continued the Sage, "of Jane Packard, William Bates, and Rodney Spelvin — which, as you have never
heard it, I will now proceed to relate."

"Can't stop now, much as I should like — "

"It is a theory of mine," proceeded the Oldest Member,
attaching himself to the other's coat-tails, and pulling him
gently back into his seat, "that nothing but misery can come
of the union between a golfer and an outcast whose soul has
not been purified by the noblest of games. This is well exemplified by the story of Jane Packard, William Bates, and Rodney Spelvin."

"All sorts of things to look after — "

"That is why I am hoping so sincerely that there is nothing
more serious than a temporary flirtation in this business of
Mabel Patmore and bowls-playing Purvis. A girl in whose life
golf has become a factor, would be mad to trust her happiness
to a blister whose idea of enjoyment is trundling wooden
balls across a lawn. Sooner or later he is certain to fail her in
some crisis. Lucky for her if this failure occurs before the
marriage knot has been inextricably tied and so opens her
eyes to his inadequacy — as was the case in the matter of Jane
Packard, William Bates, and Rodney Spelvin. I will now,"
said the Oldest Member, "tell you all about Jane Packard,
William Bates, and Rodney Spelvin."

The secretary uttered a choking groan.

"I shall miss the next dance," he pleaded.

"A bit of luck for some nice girl," said the Sage, equably.

He tightened his grip on the other's arm.

*

FORE!

Jane Packard and William Bates (said the Oldest Member) were not, you must understand, officially engaged. They had grown up together from childhood, and there existed between them a sort of understanding — the understanding being that, if ever William could speed himself up enough to propose, Jane would accept him, and they would settle down and live stodgily and happily ever after. For William was not one of your rapid wooers. In his affairs of the heart he moved somewhat slowly and ponderously, like a motor-lorry, an object which both in physique and temperament he greatly resembled. He was an extraordinarily large, powerful, ox-like young man, who required plenty of time to make up his mind about any given problem. I have seen him in the club dining-room musing with a thoughtful frown for fifteen minutes on end while endeavouring to weigh the rival merits of a chump chop and a sirloin steak as a luncheon dish. A placid, leisurely man, I might almost call him lymphatic. I *will* call him lymphatic. He was lymphatic.

The first glimmering of an idea that Jane might possibly be a suitable wife for him had come to William some three years before this story opens. Having brooded on the matter tensely for six months, he then sent her a bunch of roses. In the October of the following year, nothing having occurred to alter his growing conviction that she was an attractive girl, he presented her with a two-pound box of assorted chocolates. And from then on his progress, though not rapid, was continuous, and there seemed little reason to doubt that, should nothing come about to weaken Jane's regard for him, another five years or so would see the matter settled.

And it did not appear likely that anything would weaken Jane's regard. They had much in common, for she was a calm, slow-moving person, too. They had a mutual devotion to golf, and played together every day; and the fact that their handicaps were practically level formed a strong bond. Most divorces, as you know, spring from the fact that the husband is too markedly superior to his wife at golf; this leading him, when she starts criticising his relations, to say bitter and unforgivable things about her mashie-shots. Nothing of this kind could happen with William and Jane. They would build their life on a solid foundation of sympathy and understanding. The years would find them consoling and encouraging each other, happy married lovers. If, that is to say, William ever got round to proposing.

It was not until the fourth year of this romance that I detected the first sign of any alteration in the schedule. I had happened to call on the Packards one afternoon and found them all out except Jane. She gave me tea and conversed for a while, but she seemed distrait. I had known her since she wore rompers, so felt entitled to ask if there was anything wrong.

"Not exactly wrong," said Jane, and she heaved a sigh.

"Tell me," I said.

She heaved another sigh.

"Have you ever read *The Love that Scorches*, by Luella Periton Phipps?" she asked.

I said I had not.

"I got it out of the library yesterday," said Jane, dreamily, "and finished it at three this morning in bed. It is a very, very beautiful book. It is all about the desert and people riding on camels and a wonderful Arab chief with stern, yet tender, eyes, and a girl called Angela, and oases and dates and mirages, and all like that. There is a chapter where the Arab chief seizes the girl and clasps her in his arms and she feels his hot breath searing her face and he flings her on his horse and they ride off and all around was sand and night, and the mysterious stars. And somehow — oh, I don't know — "

She gazed yearningly at the chandelier.

"I wish mother would take me to Algiers next winter," she murmured, absently. "It would do her rheumatism so much good."

I went away frankly uneasy. These novelists, I felt, ought to be more careful. They put ideas into girls' heads and made them dissatisfied. I determined to look William up and give him a kindly word of advice. It was no business of mine, you may say, but they were so ideally suited to one another that it seemed a tragedy that anything should come between them. And Jane was in a strange mood. At any moment, I felt, she might take a good, square look at William and wonder what she could ever have seen in him. I hurried to the boy's cottage.

"William," I said, "as one who dandled you on his knee when you were a baby, I wish to ask you a personal question. Answer me this, and make it snappy. Do you love Jane Packard?"

A look of surprise came into his face, followed by one of intense thought. He was silent for a space.

"Who, me?" he said at length.

"Yes, you."

"Jane Packard?"

"Yes, Jane Packard."

"Do I love Jane Packard?" said William, assembling the material and arranging it neatly in his mind.

He pondered for perhaps five minutes.

"Why, of course I do," he said.

"Splendid!"

"Devotedly, dash it!"

"Capital."

"You might say madly."

I tapped him on his barrel-like chest.

"Then my advice to you, William Bates, is to tell her so."

"Now that's rather a brainy scheme," said William, looking at me admiringly. "I see exactly what you're driving at. You mean it would kind of settle things, and all that?"

"Precisely."

"Well, I've got to go away for a couple of days to-morrow

— it's the Invitation Tournament at Squashy Hollow — but I'll be back on Wednesday. Suppose I take her out on the links on Wednesday and propose?"

"A very good idea."

"At the sixth hole, say?"

"At the sixth hole would do excellently."

"Or the seventh?"

"The sixth would be better. The ground slopes from the tee, and you would be hidden from view by the dog-leg turn."

"Something in that."

"My own suggestion would be that you somehow contrive to lead her into that large bunker to the left of the sixth fairway."

"Why?"

"I have reason to believe that Jane would respond more readily to your wooing were it conducted in some vast sandy waste. And there is another thing," I proceeded, earnestly, "which I must impress upon you. See that there is nothing tame or tepid about your behaviour when you propose. You must show zip and romance. In fact, I strongly recommend you, before you even say a word to her, to seize her and clasp her in your arms and let your hot breath sear her face."

"Who, me?" said William.

"Believe me, it is what will appeal to her most."

"But, I say! Hot breath, I mean! Dash it all, you know, what?"

"I assure you it is indispensable."

"Seize her?" said William blankly.

"Precisely."

"Clasp her in my arms?"

"Just so."

William plunged into silent thought once more.

"Well, you *know*, I suppose," he said at length. "You've

had experience, I take it. Still — Oh, all right, I'll have a stab at it."

"There spoke the true William Bates!" I said. "Go to it, lad, and Heaven speed your wooing!"

In all human schemes — and it is this that so often brings failure to the subtlest strategists — there is always the chance of the Unknown Factor popping up, that unforeseen X for which we have made no allowance and which throws our whole plan of campaign out of gear. I had not anticipated anything of the kind coming along to mar the arrangements on the present occasion; but when I reached the first tee on the Wednesday afternoon to give William Bates that last word of encouragement, which means so much, I saw that I had been too sanguine. William had not yet arrived, but Jane was there, and with her a tall, slim, dark-haired, sickeningly romantic-looking youth in faultlessly fitting serge. A stranger to me. He was talking to her in a musical undertone, and she seemed to be hanging on his words. Her beautiful eyes were fixed on his face, and her lips slightly parted. So absorbed was she that it was not until I spoke that she became aware of my presence.

"William not arrived yet?"

She turned with a start.

"William? Hasn't he? Oh! No, not yet. I don't suppose he will be long. I want to introduce you to Mr. Spelvin. He has come to stay with the Wyndhams for a few weeks. He is going to walk round with us."

Naturally this information came as a shock to me, but I masked my feelings and greeted the young man with a well-assumed cordiality.

"Mr. George Spelvin, the actor?" I asked, shaking hands.

"My cousin," he said. "My name is Rodney Spelvin. I do not share George's histrionic ambitions. If I have any claim to — may I say renown? — it is as a maker of harmonies."

"A composer, eh?"

"Verbal harmonies," explained Mr. Spelvin. "I am, in my humble fashion, a poet."

"He writes the most beautiful poetry," said Jane, warmly. "He has just been reciting some of it to me."

"Oh, that little thing?" said Mr. Spelvin, deprecatingly. "A mere *morceau*. One of my juvenilia."

"It was too beautiful for words," persisted Jane.

"Ah, you," said Mr. Spelvin, "have the soul to appreciate it. I could wish that there were more like you, Miss Packard. We singers have much to put up with in a crass and materialistic world. Only last week a man, a coarse editor, asked me what my sonnet, 'Wine of Desire,' *meant.*" He laughed indulgently. "I gave him answer, 'twas a sonnet, not a mining prospectus."

"It would have served him right," said Jane, heatedly, "if you had pasted him one on the nose!"

At this point a low whistle behind me attracted my attention, and I turned to perceive William Bates towering against the sky-line.

"Hoy!" said William.

I walked to where he stood, leaving Jane and Mr. Spelvin in earnest conversation with their heads close together.

"I say," said William, in a rumbling undertone, "who's the bird with Jane?"

"A man named Spelvin. He is visiting the Wyndhams. I suppose Mrs. Wyndham made them acquainted."

"Looks a bit of a Gawd-help-us," said William critically.

"He is going to walk round with you."

It was impossible for a man of William Bates's temperament to start, but his face took on a look of faint concern.

"Walk round with us?"

"So Jane said."

"But look here," said William. "I can't possibly seize her and clasp her in my arms and do all that hot-breath stuff with this pie-faced exhibit hanging round on the outskirts."

"No, I fear not."

"Postpone it, then, what?" said William, with unmistakable relief. "Well, as a matter of fact, it's probably a good thing. There was a most extraordinary fine steak-and-kidney pudding at lunch, and, between ourselves, I'm not feeling what you might call keyed up to anything in the nature of a romantic scene. Some other time, eh?"

I looked at Jane and the Spelvin youth, and a nameless apprehension swept over me. There was something in their attitude which I found alarming. I was just about to whisper a warning to William not to treat this new arrival too lightly, when Jane caught sight of him and called him over and a moment later they set out on their round.

I walked away pensively. This Spelvin's advent, coming immediately on top of that book of desert love, was undeniably sinister. My heart sank for William, and I waited at the club-house to have a word with him, after his match. He came in two hours later, flushed and jubilant.

"Played the game of my life!" he said. "We didn't hole out all the putts, but, making allowance for everything, you can chalk me up an eighty-three. Not so bad, eh? You know the eighth hole? Well, I was a bit short with my drive, and found my ball lying badly for the brassie, so I took my driving-iron and with a nice easy swing let the pill have it so squarely on the seat of the pants that it flew — "

"Where is Jane?" I interrupted.

"Jane? Oh, the bloke Spelvin has taken her home."

"Beware of him, William!" I whispered tensely. "Have a care, young Bates! If you don't look out, you'll have him stealing Jane from you. Don't laugh. Remember that I saw them together before you arrived. She was gazing into his eyes as a desert maiden might gaze into the eyes of a sheik. You don't seem to realise, wretched William Bates, that Jane is an extremely romantic girl. A fascinating stranger like this, coming suddenly into her life, may well snatch her away from you before you know where you are."

"That's all right," said William, lightly. "I don't mind admitting that the same idea occurred to me. But I made judicious inquiries on the way round, and found out that the fellow's a poet. You don't seriously expect me to believe that there's any chance of Jane falling in love with a poet?"

He spoke incredulously, for there were three things in the world that he held in the smallest esteem — slugs, poets, and caddies with hiccups.

"I think it extremely possible, if not probable," I replied.

"Nonsense!" said William. "And, besides, the man doesn't play golf. Never had a club in his hand, and says he never wants to. That's the sort of fellow he is."

At this, I confess, I did experience a distinct feeling of relief. I could imagine Jane Packard, stimulated by exotic literature, committing many follies, but I was compelled to own that I could not conceive of her giving her heart to one who not only did not play golf but had no desire to play it. Such a man, to a girl of her fine nature and correct upbringing, would be beyond the pale. I walked home with William in a calm and happy frame of mind.

I was to learn but one short week later that Woman is the unfathomable, incalculable mystery, the problem we men can never hope to solve.

The week that followed was one of much festivity in our village. There were dances, picnics, bathing-parties, and all the other adjuncts of high summer. In these William Bates played but a minor part. Dancing was not one of his gifts. He swung, if called upon, an amiable shoe, but the disposition in the neighbourhood was to refrain from calling upon him; for he had an incurable habit of coming down with his full weight upon his partner's toes, and many a fair girl had had to lie up for a couple of days after collaborating with him in a fox-trot.

Picnics, again, bored him, and he always preferred a round on the links to the merriest bathing-party. The consequence was that he kept practically aloof from the revels, and all through the week Jane Packard was squired by Rodney Spelvin. With Spelvin she swayed over the waxed floor; with Spelvin she dived and swam; and it was Spelvin who, with zealous hand, brushed ants off her mayonnaise and squashed wasps with a chivalrous teaspoon. The end was inevitable. Apart from anything else, the moon was at its full and many of these picnics were held at night. And you know what that means. It was about ten days later that William Bates came to me in my little garden with an expression on his face like a man who didn't know it was loaded.

"I say," said William, "you busy?"

I emptied the remainder of the water-can on the lobelias, and was at his disposal.

"I say," said William, "rather a rotten thing has happened. You know Jane?"

I said I knew Jane.

"You know Spelvin?"

I said I knew Spelvin.

"Well, Jane's gone and got engaged to him," said William, aggrieved.

"What?"

"It's a fact."

"Already?"

"Absolutely. She told me this morning. And what I want to know," said the stricken boy, sitting down thoroughly unnerved on a basket of strawberries, "is, where do I get off?"

My heart bled for him, but I could not help reminding him that I had anticipated this.

"You should not have left them so much alone together," I said. "You must have known that there is nothing more conducive to love than the moon in June. Why, songs have been written about it. In fact, I cannot at the moment recall a song that has not been written about it."

"Yes, but how was I to guess that anything like this would happen?" cried William, rising and scraping strawberries off his person. "Who would ever have supposed Jane Packard would leap off the dock with a fellow who doesn't play golf?"

"Certainly, as you say, it seems almost incredible. You are sure you heard her correctly? When she told you about the engagement, I mean. There was no chance that you could have misunderstood?"

"Not a bit of it. As a matter of fact, what led up to the thing, if you know what I mean, was me proposing to her myself. I'd been thinking a lot during the last ten days over what you said to me about that, and the more I thought of it the more of a sound egg the notion seemed. So I got her alone up at the club-house and said, 'I say, old girl, what about it?' and she said, 'What about what?' and I said, 'What about marrying me? Don't if you don't want to, of course,' I said, 'but I'm bound to say it looks pretty good to me.' And then she said she loved another — this bloke Spelvin, to wit. A nasty jar, I can tell you, it was. I was just starting off on a round, and it made me hook my putts on every green."

"But did she say specifically that she was engaged to Spelvin?"

"She said she loved him."

"There may be hope. If she is not irrevocably engaged the fancy may pass. I think I will go and see Jane and make tactful inquiries."

"I wish you would," said William. "And, I say, you haven't any stuff that'll take strawberry-juice off a fellow's trousers, have you?"

My interview with Jane that evening served only to confirm the bad news. Yes, she was definitely engaged to the man Spelvin. In a burst of girlish confidence she told me some of the details of the affair.

"The moon was shining and a soft breeze played in the trees," she said. "And suddenly he took me in his arms, gazed deep into my eyes, and cried, 'I love you! I worship you! I adore you! You are the tree on which the fruit of my life hangs; my mate; my woman; predestined to me since the first star shone up in yonder sky!' "

"Nothing," I agreed, "could be fairer than that. And then?" I said, thinking how different it all must have been from William Bates's miserable, limping proposal.

"Then we fixed it up that we would get married in September."

"You are sure you are doing wisely?" I ventured.

Her eyes opened.

"Why do you say that?"

"Well, you know, whatever his other merits — and no doubt they are numerous — Rodney Spelvin does *not* play golf."

"No, but he's very broad-minded about it."

I shuddered. Women say these things so lightly.

"Broad-minded?"

"Yes. He has no objection to my going on playing. He says he likes my pretty enthusiasms."

There seemed nothing more to say on that subject.

"Well," I said, "I am sure I wish you every happiness. I had hoped, of course — but never mind that."

"What?"

"I had hoped, as you insist on my saying it, that you and William Bates — "

A shadow passed over her face. Her eyes grew sad.

"Poor William! I'm awfully sorry about that. He's a dear."

"A splendid fellow," I agreed.

"He has been so wonderful about the whole thing. So many men would have gone off and shot grizzly bears or something. But William just said 'Right-o!' in a quiet voice, and he's going to caddy for me at Mossy Heath next week."

"There is good stuff in the boy."

"Yes." She sighed. "If it wasn't for Rodney — Oh, well!"

I thought it would be tactful to change the subject.

"So you have decided to go to Mossy Heath again?"

"Yes. And I'm really going to qualify this year."

The annual Invitation Tournament at Mossy Heath was one of the most important fixtures of our local female golfing year. As is usual with these affairs, it began with a medal-play qualifying round, the thirty-two players with the lowest net scores then proceeding to fight it out during the remainder of the week by match-play. It gratified me to hear Jane speak so confidently of her chances, for this was the fourth year she had entered, and each time, though she had started out with the brightest prospects, she had failed to survive the qualifying round. Like so many golfers, she was fifty per cent better at match-play than at medal-play. Mossy Heath, being a championship course, is full of nasty pitfalls, and on each of the three occasions on which she had tackled it one very bad hole had undone all her steady work on the other seventeen and ruined her card. I was delighted to find her so undismayed by failure.

"I am sure you will," I said. "Just play your usual careful game."

"It doesn't matter what sort of a game I play this time," said Jane, jubilantly. "I've just heard that there are only thirty-two entries this year, so that everybody who finishes is bound to qualify. I have simply got to get round somehow, and there I am."

"It would seem somewhat superfluous in these circumstances to play a qualifying round at all."

"Oh, but they must. You see, there are prizes for the best three scores, so they have to play it. But isn't it a relief to know that, even if I come to grief on that beastly seventh, as I did last year, I shall still be all right?"

"It is, indeed. I have a feeling that once it becomes a matter of match-play you will be irresistible."

"I do hope so. It would be lovely to win with Rodney looking on."

"Will he be looking on?"

"Yes. He's going to walk round with me. Isn't it sweet of him?"

Her *fiancé*'s name having slid into the conversation again, she seemed inclined to become eloquent about him. I left her, however, before she could begin. To one so strongly pro-William as myself, eulogistic prattle about Rodney Spelvin was repugnant. I disapproved entirely of this infatuation of hers. I am not a narrow-minded man; I quite appreciate the fact that non-golfers are entitled to marry; but I could not countenance their marrying potential winners of the Ladies' Invitation Tournament at Mossy Heath.

The Greens Committee, as greens committees are so apt to do in order to justify their existence, have altered the Mossy Heath course considerably since the time of which I am speaking, but they have left the three most poisonous holes untouched. I refer to the fourth, the seventh, and the fifteenth. Even a soulless Greens Committee seems to have realised that golfers, long-suffering though they are, can be pushed too far, and that the addition of even a single extra bunker to any of these dreadful places would probably lead to armed riots in the club-house.

Jane Packard had done well on the first three holes, but as she stood on the fourth tee she was conscious, despite the fact that this seemed to be one of her good days, of a certain nervousness; and oddly enough, great as was her love for Rodney Spelvin, it was not his presence that gave her courage, but the sight of William Bates's large, friendly face and the sound of his pleasant voice urging her to keep her bean down and refrain from pressing.

As a matter of fact, to be perfectly truthful, there was

beginning already to germinate within her by this time a faint but definite regret that Rodney Spelvin had decided to accompany her on this qualifying round. It was sweet of him to bother to come, no doubt, but still there was something about Rodney that did not seem to blend with the holy atmosphere of a championship course. He was the one romance of her life and their souls were bound together for all eternity, but the fact remained that he did not appear to be able to keep still while she was making her shots, and his light humming, musical though it was, militated against accuracy on the green. He was humming now as she addressed her ball, and for an instant a spasm of irritation shot through her. She fought it down bravely and concentrated on her drive, and when the ball soared over the cross-bunker she forgot her annoyance. There is nothing so mellowing, so conducive to sweet and genial thoughts, as a real juicy one straight down the middle, and this was a pipterino.

"Nice work," said William Bates, approvingly.

Jane gave him a grateful smile and turned to Rodney. It was his appreciation that she wanted. He was not a golfer, but even he must be able to see that her drive had been something out of the common.

Rodney Spelvin was standing with his back turned, gazing out over the rolling prospect, one hand shading his eyes.

"That vista there," said Rodney. "That calm, wooded hollow, bathed in the golden sunshine. It reminds me of the island valley of Avilion — "

"Did you see my drive, Rodney?"

" — where falls not rain nor hail nor any snow, nor ever wind blows loudly. Eh? Your drive? No, I didn't."

Again Jane Packard was aware of that faint, wistful regret. But this was swept away a few moments later in the ecstasy of a perfect iron-shot which plunked her ball nicely on to the green. The last time she had played this hole she had taken seven, for all round the plateau green are sinister sand-bunkers, each beckoning the ball into its hideous depths; and now she was on in two and life was very sweet. Putting was her strong point, so that there was no reason why she should not get a snappy four on one of the nastiest holes on the course. She glowed with a strange emotion as she took her putter, and as she bent over her ball the air seemed filled with soft music.

It was only when she started to concentrate on the line of her putt that this soft music began to bother her. Then, listening, she became aware that it proceeded from Rodney Spelvin. He was standing immediately behind her, humming an old French love-song. It was the sort of old French love-song to which she could have listened for hours in some scented garden under the young May moon, but on the green of the fourth at Mossy Heath it got right in amongst her nerve-centres.

"Rodney, *please!*"

"Eh?"

Jane found herself wishing that Rodney Spelvin would not say "Eh?" whenever she spoke to him.

"Do you mind not humming?" said Jane. "I want to putt."

"Putt on, child, putt on," said Rodney Spelvin, indulgently. "I don't know what you mean, but, if it makes you happy to putt, putt to your heart's content."

Jane bent over her ball again. She had got the line now. She brought back her putter with infinite care.

"My God!" exclaimed Rodney Spelvin, going off like a bomb.

Jane's ball, sharply jabbed, shot past the hole and rolled on about three yards. She spun round in anguish. Rodney Spelvin was pointing at the horizon.

"*What* a bit of colour!" he cried. "Did you ever see such a bit of colour?"

"Oh, Rodney!" moaned Jane.

"Eh?"

Jane gulped and walked to her ball. Her fourth putt trickled into the hole.

"Did you win?" said Rodney Spelvin, amiably.

Jane walked to the fifth tee in silence.

The fifth and sixth holes at Mossy Heath are long, but they offer little trouble to those who are able to keep straight. It is as if the architect of the course had relaxed over these two in order to ensure that his malignant mind should be at its freshest and keenest when he came to design the pestilential seventh. This seventh, as you may remember, is the hole at which Sandy McHoots, then Open Champion, took an eleven on an important occasion. It is a short hole, and a full mashie will take you nicely on to the green, provided you can carry the river that frolics just beyond the tee and seems to plead with you to throw it a ball to play with. Once on the green, however, the problem is to stay there. The green itself is about the size of a drawing-room carpet, and in the summer, when the ground is hard, a ball that has not the maximum of back-spin is apt to touch lightly and bound off into the river beyond; for this is an island green, where the stream bends like a serpent. I refresh your memory with these facts in order that you may appreciate to the full what Jane Packard was up against.

The woman with whom Jane was partnered had the honour, and drove a nice high ball which fell into one of the bunkers to the left. She was a silent, patient-looking woman, and she seemed to regard this as perfectly satisfactory. She withdrew from the tee and made way for Jane.

"Nice work!" said William Bates, a moment later. For Jane's ball, soaring in a perfect arc, was dropping, it seemed on the very pin.

"Oh, Rodney, look!" cried Jane.

"Eh?" said Rodney Spelvin.

His remark was drowned in a passionate squeal of agony

from his betrothed. The most poignant of all tragedies had occurred. The ball, touching the green, leaped like a young lamb, scuttled past the pin, and took a running dive over the cliff.

There was a silence. Jane's partner, who was seated on the bench by the sand-box reading a pocket edition in limp leather of Vardon's *What Every Young Golfer Should Know*, with which she had been refreshing herself at odd moments all through the round, had not observed the incident. William Bates, with the tact of a true golfer, refrained from comment. Jane was herself swallowing painfully. It was left to Rodney Spelvin to break the silence.

"Good!" he said.

Jane Packard turned like a stepped-on worm.

"What do you mean, good?"

"You hit your ball farther than she did."

"I sent it into the river," said Jane, in a low, toneless voice.

"Capital!" said Rodney Spelvin, delicately masking a yawn with two fingers of his shapely right hand. "Capital! Capital!"

Her face contorted with pain, Jane put down another ball.

"Playing three," she said.

The student of Vardon marked the place in her book with her thumb, looked up, nodded, and resumed her reading.

"Nice w — " began William Bates, as the ball soared off the tee, and checked himself abruptly. Already he could see that the unfortunate girl had put too little beef into it. The ball was falling, falling. It fell. A crystal fountain flashed up towards the sun. The ball lay floating on the bosom of the stream, only some few feet short of the island. But, as has been well pointed out, that little less and how far away!

"Playing five!" said Jane, between her teeth.

"What," inquired Rodney Spelvin, chattily, lighting a cigarette, "is the record break?"

"Playing *five*," said Jane, with a dreadful calm, and gripped her mashie.

"Half a second," said William Bates, suddenly. "I say, I believe you could play that last one from where it floats. A good crisp slosh with a niblick would put you on, and you'd be there in four, with a chance for a five. Worth trying, what? I mean, no sense in dropping strokes unless you have to."

Jane's eyes were gleaming. She threw William a look of infinite gratitude.

"Why, I believe I could!"

"Worth having a dash."

"There's a boat down there!"

"I could row," said William.

"I could stand in the middle and slosh," cried Jane.

"And what's-his-name — *that*," said William, jerking his head in the direction of Rodney Spelvin, who was strolling up and down behind the tee, humming a gay Venetian barcarolle, "could steer."

"William," said Jane, fervently, "you're a darling."

"Oh, I don't know," said William, modestly.

"There's no one like you in the world. Rodney!"

"Eh?" said Rodney Spelvin.

"We're going out in that boat. I want you to steer."

Rodney Spelvin's face showed appreciation of the change of programme. Golf bored him, but what could be nicer than a gentle row in a boat.

"Capital!" he said. "Capital! Capital!"

There was a dreamy look in Rodney Spelvin's eyes as he leaned back with the tiller-ropes in his hands. This was just his idea of the proper way of passing a summer afternoon. Drifting lazily over the silver surface of the stream. His eyes closed. He began to murmur softly:

"All to-day the slow sleek ripples hardly bear up shoreward, Charged with sighs more light than laughter, faint and fair, Like a woodland lake's weak wavelets lightly lingering forward, Soft and listless as the — Here! Hi!"

FORE!

For at this moment the silver surface of the stream was violently split by a vigorously-wielded niblick, the boat lurched drunkenly, and over his Panama-hatted head and down his grey-flannelled torso there descended a cascade of water.

"Here! Hi!" cried Rodney Spelvin.

He cleared his eyes and gazed reproachfully. Jane and William Bates were peering into the depths.

"I missed it," said Jane.

"There she spouts!" said William, pointing. "Ready?"

Jane raised her niblick.

"Here! Hi!" bleated Rodney Spelvin, as a second cascade poured damply over him.

He shook the drops off his face, and perceived that Jane was regarding him with hostility.

"I do wish you wouldn't talk just as I am swinging," she said, pettishly. "Now you've made me miss it again! If you can't keep quiet, I wish you wouldn't insist on coming round with one. Can you see it, William?"

"There she blows," said William Bates.

"Here! You aren't going to do it *again*, are you?" cried Rodney Spelvin.

Jane bared her teeth.

"I'm going to get that ball on to the green if I have to stay here all night," she said.

Rodney Spelvin looked at her and shuddered. Was this the quiet, dreamy girl he had loved? This Mænad? Her hair was lying in damp wisps about her face, her eyes were shining with an unearthly light.

"No, but really — " he faltered.

Jane stamped her foot.

"What *are* you making all this fuss about, Rodney?" she snapped. "Where is it, William?"

"There she dips," said William. "Playing six."

"Playing six."

"Let her go," said William.

"Let her go it is!" said Jane.

A perfect understanding seemed to prevail between these two.

Splash!

The woman on the bank looked up from her Vardon as Rodney Spelvin's agonised scream rent the air. She saw a boat upon the water, a man rowing the boat, another man, hatless, gesticulating in the stern, a girl beating the water with a niblick. She nodded placidly and understandingly. A niblick was the club she would have used herself in such circumstances. Everything appeared to her entirely regular and orthodox. She resumed her book.

Splash!

"Playing fifteen," said Jane.

"Fifteen is right," said William Bates.

Splash! Splash! Splash!

"Playing forty-four."

"Forty-four is correct."

Splash! Splash! Splash! Splash!

"Eighty-three?" said Jane, brushing the hair out of her eyes.

"No. Only eighty-two," said William Bates.

"Where is it?"

"There she drifts."

A dripping figure rose violently in the stern of the boat, spouting water like a public fountain. For what seemed to him like an eternity Rodney Spelvin had ducked and spluttered and writhed, and now it came to him abruptly that he was through. He bounded from his seat, and at the same time Jane swung with all the force of her supple body. There was a splash beside which all the other splashes had been as nothing. The boat overturned and went drifting away. Three bodies plunged into the stream. Three heads emerged from the water.

The woman on the bank looked absently in their direction. Then she resumed her book.

"It's all right," said William Bates, contentedly. "We're in our depth."

"My bag!" cried Jane. "My bag of clubs!"

"Must have sunk," said William.

"Rodney," said Jane, "my bag of clubs is at the bottom somewhere. Dive under and swim about and try to find it."

"It's bound to be around somewhere," said William Bates encouragingly.

Rodney Spelvin drew himself up to his full height. It was not an easy thing to do, for it was muddy where he stood, but he did it.

"Damn your bag of clubs!" he bellowed, lost to all shame. "I'm going home!"

With painful steps, tripping from time to time and vanishing beneath the surface, he sloshed to the shore. For a moment he paused on the bank, silhouetted against the summer sky, then he was gone.

Jane Packard and William Bates watched him go with amazed eyes.

"I never would have dreamed," said Jane, dazedly, "that he was that sort of man."

"A bad lot," said William Bates.

"The sort of man to be upset by the merest trifle!"

"Must have a naturally bad disposition," said William Bates.

"Why, if a little thing like this could make him so rude and brutal and horrid, it wouldn't be *safe* to marry him!"

"Taking a big chance," agreed William Bates. "Sort of fellow who would water the cat's milk and kick the baby in the face." He took a deep breath and disappeared. "Here are your clubs, old girl," he said, coming to the surface again. "Only wanted a bit of looking for."

"Oh, William," said Jane, "you are the most wonderful man on earth!"

"Would you go as far as that?" said William.

"I was mad, mad, ever to get engaged to that brute!"

"Now there," said William Bates, removing an eel from his left breast-pocket, "I'm absolutely with you. Thought so all along, but didn't like to say so. What I mean is, a girl like you — keen on golf and all that sort of thing — ought to marry a chap like me — keen on golf and everything of that description."

"William," cried Jane, passionately, detaching a newt from her right ear, "I will!"

"Silly nonsense, when you come right down to it, your marrying a fellow who doesn't play golf. Nothing in it."

"I'll break off the engagement the moment I get home."

"You couldn't make a sounder move, old girl."

"William!"

"Jane!"

The woman on the bank, glancing up as she turned a page, saw a man and a girl embracing, up to their waists in water. It seemed to have nothing to do with her. She resumed her book.

Jane looked lovingly into William's eyes.

"William," she said, "I think I have loved you all my life."

"Jane," said William, "I'm dashed sure I've loved *you* all *my* life. Meant to tell you so a dozen times, but something always seemed to come up."

"William," said Jane, "you're an angel and a darling. Where's the ball?"

"There she pops."

"Playing eighty-four?"

"Eighty-four it is," said William. "Slow back, keep your eye on the ball, and don't press."

The woman on the bank began Chapter Twenty-five.

The Heart of a Goof

O

It was a morning when all nature shouted "Fore!" The breeze, as it blew gently up from the valley, seemed to bring a message of hope and cheer, whispering of chip-shots holed and brassies landing squarely on the meat. The fairway, as yet unscarred by the irons of a hundred dubs, smiled greenly up at the azure sky; and the sun, peeping above the trees, looked like a giant golf-ball perfectly lofted by the mashie of some unseen god and about to drop dead by the pin of the eighteenth. It was the day of the opening of the course after the long winter, and a crowd of considerable dimensions had collected at the first tee. Plus fours gleamed in the sunshine, and the air was charged with happy anticipation.

In all that gay throng there was but one sad face. It belonged to the man who was waggling his driver over the new ball perched on its little hill of sand. This man seemed careworn, hopeless. He gazed down the fairway, shifted his feet, waggled, gazed down the fairway again, shifted the dogs once more, and waggled afresh. He waggled as Hamlet might have waggled, moodily, irresolutely. Then, at last, he swung, and, taking from his caddie the niblick which the intelligent lad had been holding in readiness from the moment when he had walked on to the tee, trudged wearily off to play his second.

The Oldest Member, who had been observing the scene with a benevolent eye from his favourite chair on the terrace, sighed.

"Poor Jenkinson," he said, "does not improve."

"No," agreed his companion, a young man with open features and a handicap of six. "And yet I happen to know that
he has been taking lessons all the winter at one of those
indoor places."

"Futile, quite futile," said the Sage with a shake of his
snowy head. "There is no wizard living who could make that
man go round in an average of sevens. I keep advising him
to give up the game."

"You!" cried the young man, raising a shocked and startled
face from the driver with which he was toying. "*You* told him
to give up golf! Why I thought — "

"I understand and approve of your horror," said the Oldest
Member, gently. "But you must bear in mind that Jenkinson's is not an ordinary case. You know and I know scores of
men who have never broken a hundred and twenty in their
lives, and yet contrive to be happy, useful members of society. However badly they may play, they are able to forget.
But with Jenkinson it is different. He is not one of those who
can take it or leave it alone. His only chance of happiness lies
in complete abstinence. Jenkinson is a goof."

"A what?"

"A goof," repeated the Sage. "One of those unfortunate
beings who have allowed this noblest of sports to get too
great a grip upon them, who have permitted it to eat into
their souls, like some malignant growth. The goof, you must
understand, is not like you and me. He broods. He becomes
morbid. His goofery unfits him for the battles of life. Jenkinson, for example, was once a man with a glowing future in
the hay, corn and feed business, but a constant stream of
hooks, tops and slices gradually made him so diffident and
mistrustful of himself, that he let opportunity after opportunity slip, with the result that other, sterner, hay, corn and
feed merchants passed him in the race. Every time he had
the chance to carry through some big deal in hay, or to

execute some flashing *coup* in corn and feed, the fatal diffidence generated by a hundred rotten rounds would undo
him. I understand his bankruptcy may be expected at any
moment."

"My golly!" said the young man, deeply impressed. "I hope
I never become a goof. Do you mean to say there is really no
cure except giving up the game?"

The Oldest Member was silent for a while.

"It is curious that you should have asked that question," he
said at last, "for only this morning I was thinking of the one
case in my experience where a goof was enabled to overcome his deplorable malady. It was owing to a girl, of course.
The longer I live, the more I come to see that most things are.
But you will, no doubt, wish to hear the story from the beginning."

The young man rose with the startled haste of some wild
creature, which, wandering through the undergrowth, per-
ceives the trap in his path.

"I should love to," he mumbled, "only I shall be losing my
place at the tee."

"The goof in question," said the Sage, attaching himself
with quiet firmness to the youth's coat-button, "was a man of
about your age, by name Ferdinand Dibble. I knew him well.
In fact, it was to me — "

"Some other time, eh?"

"It was to me," proceeded the Sage, placidly, "that he
came for sympathy in the great crisis of his life, and I am not
ashamed to say that when he had finished laying bare his soul
to me there were tears in my eyes. My heart bled for the
boy."

"I bet it did. But — "

The Oldest Member pushed him gently back into his seat.

"Golf," he said, "is the Great Mystery. Like some capricious goddess — "

The young man, who had been exhibiting symptoms of

feverishness, appeared to become resigned. He sighed softly.

"Did you ever read 'The Ancient Mariner'?" he said.

"Many years ago," said the Oldest Member. "Why do you ask?"

"Oh, I don't know," said the young man. "It just occurred to me."

Golf (resumed the Oldest Member) is the Great Mystery. Like some capricious goddess, it bestows its favours with what would appear an almost fat-headed lack of method and discrimination. On every side we see big two-fisted he-men floundering round in three figures, stopping every few minutes to let through little shrimps with knock knees and hollow cheeks, who are tearing off snappy seventy-fours. Giants of finance have to accept a stroke per from their junior clerks. Men capable of governing empires fail to control a small, white ball, which presents no difficulties whatever to others with one ounce more brain than a cuckoo-clock. Mysterious, but there it is. There was no apparent reason why Ferdinand Dibble should not have been a competent golfer. He had strong wrists and a good eye. Nevertheless, the fact remains that he was a dub. And on a certain evening in June I realised that he was also a goof. I found it out quite suddenly as the result of a conversation which we had on this very terrace.

I was sitting here that evening thinking of this and that, when by the corner of the club-house I observed young Dibble in conversation with a girl in white. I could not see who she was, for her back was turned. Presently they parted and Ferdinand came slowly across to where I sat. His air was dejected. He had had the boots licked off him earlier in the afternoon by Jimmy Fothergill, and it was to this that I attributed his gloom. I was to find out in a few moments that I was partly but not entirely correct in this surmise. He took the next chair to mine, and for several minutes sat staring moodily down into the valley.

"I've just been talking to Barbara Medway," he said, suddenly breaking the silence.

"Indeed?" I said. "A delightful girl."

"She's going away for the summer to Marvis Bay."

"She will take the sunshine with her."

"You bet she will!" said Ferdinand Dibble, with extraordinary warmth, and there was another long silence.

Presently Ferdinand uttered a hollow groan.

"I love her, dammit!" he muttered brokenly. "Oh, golly, how I love her!"

I was not surprised at his making me the recipient of his confidences like this. Most of the young folk in the place brought their troubles to me sooner or later.

"And does she return your love?"

"I don't know. I haven't asked her."

"Why not? I should have thought the point not without its interest for you."

Ferdinand gnawed the handle of his putter distractedly.

"I haven't the nerve," he burst out at length. "I simply can't summon up the cold gall to ask a girl, least of all an angel like her, to marry me. You see, it's like this. Every time I work myself up to the point of having a dash at it, I go out and get trimmed by some one giving me a stroke a hole. Every time I feel I've mustered up enough pep to propose, I take ten on a bogey three. Every time I think I'm in good mid-season form for putting my fate to the test, to win or lose it all, something goes all blooey with my swing, and I slice into the rough at every tee. And then my self-confidence leaves me. I become nervous, tongue-tied, diffident. I wish to goodness I knew the man who invented this infernal game. I'd strangle him. But I suppose he's been dead for ages. Still, I could go and jump on his grave."

It was at this point that I understood all, and the heart within me sank like lead. The truth was out. Ferdinand Dibble was a goof.

"Come, come, my boy," I said, though feeling the uselessness of any words. "Master this weakness."

"I can't."

"Try!"

"I have tried."

He gnawed his putter again.

"She was asking me just now if I couldn't manage to come to Marvis Bay, too," he said.

"That surely is encouraging? It suggests that she is not entirely indifferent to your society."

"Yes, but what's the use? Do you know," a gleam coming into his eyes for a moment, "I have a feeling that if I could ever beat some really fairly good player — just once — I could bring the thing off." The gleam faded. "But what chance is there of that?"

It was a question which I did not care to answer. I merely patted his shoulder sympathetically, and after a little while he left me and walked away. I was still sitting there, thinking over his hard case, when Barbara Medway came out of the club-house.

She, too, seemed grave and preoccupied, as if there was something on her mind. She took the chair which Ferdinand had vacated, and sighed wearily.

"Have you ever felt," she asked, "that you would like to bang a man on the head with something hard and heavy? With knobs on?"

I said I had sometimes experienced such a desire, and asked if she had any particular man in mind. She seemed to hesitate for a moment before replying, then, apparently, made up her mind to confide in me. My advanced years carry with them certain pleasant compensations, one of which is that nice girls often confide in me. I frequently find myself enrolled as a father-confessor on the most intimate matters by beautiful creatures from whom many a younger man would give his eyeteeth to get a friendly word. Besides, I had known Barbara since she was a child. Frequently — though not recently — I had given her her evening bath. These things form a bond.

"Why are men such chumps?" she exclaimed.

"You still have not told me who it is that has caused these harsh words. Do I know him?"

"Of course you do. You've just been talking to him."

"Ferdinand Dibble? But why should you wish to bang Ferdinand Dibble on the head with something hard and heavy with knobs on?"

"Because he's such a goop."

"You mean a goof?" I queried, wondering how she could have penetrated the unhappy man's secret.

"No, a goop. A goop is a man who's in love with a girl and won't tell her so. I am as certain as I am of anything that Ferdinand is fond of me."

"Your instinct is unerring. He has just been confiding in me on that very point."

"Well, why doesn't he confide in *me*, the poor fish?" cried the high-spirited girl, petulantly flicking a pebble at a passing grasshopper. "I can't be expected to fling myself into his arms unless he gives some sort of a hint that he's ready to catch me."

"Would it help if I were to repeat to him the substance of this conversation of ours?"

"If you breathe a word of it, I'll never speak to you again," she cried. "I'd rather die an awful death than have any man think I wanted him so badly that I had to send relays of messengers begging him to marry me."

I saw her point.

"Then I fear," I said, gravely, "that there is nothing to be done. One can only wait and hope. It may be that in the years to come Ferdinand Dibble will acquire a nice lissom, wristy swing, with the head kept rigid and the right leg firmly braced and — "

"What are you talking about?"

"I was toying with the hope that some sunny day Ferdi-nand Dibble would cease to be a goof."

"You mean a goop?"

"No, a goof. A goof is a man who — " And I went on to explain the peculiar psychological difficulties which lay in the way of any declaration of affection on Ferdinand's part.

"But I never heard of anything so ridiculous in my life," she ejaculated. "Do you mean to say that he is waiting till he is good at golf before he asks me to marry him?"

"It is not quite so simple as that," I said sadly. "Many bad golfers marry, feeling that a wife's loving solicitude may im-prove their game. But they are rugged, thick-skinned men, not sensitive and introspective, like Ferdinand. Ferdinand has allowed himself to become morbid. It is one of the chief merits of golf that non-success at the game induces a certain amount of decent humility, which keeps a man from pluming himself too much on any petty triumphs he may achieve in other walks of life; but in all things there is a happy mean, and with Ferdinand this humility has gone too far. It has taken all the spirit out of him. He feels crushed and worth-less. He is grateful to caddies when they accept a tip instead of drawing themselves up to their full height and flinging the money in his face."

"Then do you mean that things have got to go on like this for ever?"

I thought for a moment.

"It is a pity," I said, "that you could not have induced Ferdinand to go to Marvis Bay for a month or two."

"Why?"

"Because it seems to me, thinking the thing over, that it is just possible that Marvis Bay might cure him. At the hotel there he would find collected a mob of golfers — I used the term in its broadest sense, to embrace the paralytics and the men who play left-handed — whom even he would be able to beat. When I was last at Marvis Bay, the hotel links were a sort of Sargasso Sea into which had drifted all the pitiful flotsam and jetsam of golf. I have seen things done on that course at which I shuddered and averted my eyes — and I am not a weak man. If Ferdinand can polish up his game so as to go round in a fairly steady hundred and five, I fancy there is hope. But I understand he is not going to Marvis Bay."

"Oh yes, he is," said the girl.

"Indeed! He did not tell me that when we were talking just now."

"He didn't know it then. He will when I have had a few words with him."

And she walked with firm steps back into the club-house.

It has been well said that there are many kinds of golf, beginning at the top with the golf of professionals and the best amateurs and working down through the golf of ossified men to that of Scotch University professors. Until recently this last was looked upon as the lowest possible depth; but nowadays, with the growing popularity of summer hotels, we are able to add a brand still lower, the golf you find at places like Marvis Bay.

To Ferdinand Dibble, coming from a club where the standard of play was rather unusually high, Marvis Bay was a revelation, and for some days after his arrival there he went about dazed, like a man who cannot believe it is really true. To go out on the links at this summer resort was like entering a new world. The hotel was full of stout, middle-aged men, who, after a misspent youth devoted to making money, had taken to a game at which real proficiency can only be acquired by those who start playing in their cradles and keep their weight down. Out on the course each morning you could see representatives of every nightmare style that was ever invented. There was the man who seemed to be attempting to deceive his ball and lull it into a false security by looking away from it and then making a lightning slash in the apparent hope of catching it off its guard. There was the man who wielded his mid-iron like one killing snakes. There was the man who addressed his ball as if he were stroking a cat, the man who drove as if he were cracking a whip, the man who brooded over each shot like one whose heart is bowed down by bad news from home, and the man who scooped with his mashie as if he were ladling soup. By the end of the first week Ferdinand Dibble was the acknowledged champion of the place. He had gone through the entire menagerie like a bullet through a cream puff.

First, scarcely daring to consider the possibility of success, he had taken on the man who tried to catch his ball off its guard and had beaten him five up and four to play. Then, with gradually growing confidence, he tackled in turn the Cat-Stroker, the Whip-Cracker, the Heart Bowed Down, and the Soup-Scooper, and walked all over their faces with spiked shoes. And as these were the leading local amateurs, whose prowess the octogenarians and the men who went round in bath-chairs vainly strove to emulate, Ferdinand Dibble was faced on the eighth morning of his visit by the startling fact that he had no more worlds to conquer. He was monarch of all he surveyed, and, what is more, had won his first trophy, the prize in the great medal-play handicap tournament, in which he had nosed in ahead of the field by two strokes, edging out his nearest rival, a venerable old gentleman, by means of a brilliant and unexpected four on the last hole. The prize was a handsome pewter mug, about the size of the old oaken bucket, and Ferdinand used to go to his room immediately after dinner to croon over it like a mother over her child.

You are wondering, no doubt, why, in these circumstances, he did not take advantage of the new spirit of exhilarated pride which had replaced his old humility and instantly pro-

pose to Barbara Medway. I will tell you. He did not propose
to Barbara because Barbara was not there. At the last moment she had been detained at home to nurse a sick parent
and had been compelled to postpone her visit for a couple of
weeks. He could, no doubt, have proposed in one of the daily
letters which he wrote to her, but somehow, once he started
writing, he found that he used up so much space describing
his best shots on the links that day that it was difficult to
squeeze in a declaration of undying passion. After all, you can
hardly cram that sort of thing into a postscript.

He decided, therefore, to wait till she arrived, and meanwhile pursued his conquering course. The longer he waited
the better, in one way, for every morning and afternoon that
passed was adding new layers to his self-esteem. Day by day
in every way he grew chestier and chestier.

Meanwhile, however, dark clouds were gathering. Sullen
mutterings were to be heard in corners of the hotel lounge,
and the spirit of revolt was abroad. For Ferdinand's chestiness had not escaped the notice of his defeated rivals. There
is nobody so chesty as a normally unchesty man who suddenly becomes chesty, and I am sorry to say that the chestiness which had come to Ferdinand was the aggressive type
of chestiness which breeds enemies. He had developed a
habit of holding the game up in order to give his opponent
advice. The Whip-Cracker had not forgiven, and never
would forgive, his well-meant but galling criticism of his
back-swing. The Scooper, who had always scooped since the
day when, at the age of sixty-four, he subscribed to the Correspondence Course which was to teach him golf in twelve
lessons by mail, resented being told by a snip of a boy that
the mashie-stroke should be a smooth, unhurried swing. The
Snake-Killer — But I need not weary you with a detailed
recital of these men's grievances; it is enough to say that they

all had it in for Ferdinand, and one night, after dinner, they met in the lounge to decide what was to be done about it.

A nasty spirit was displayed by all.

"A mere lad telling me how to use my mashie!" growled the Scooper. "Smooth and unhurried my left eyeball! I get it up, don't I? Well, what more do you want?"

"I keep telling him that mine is the old, full St. Andrew swing," muttered the Whip-Cracker, between set teeth, "but he won't listen to me."

"He ought to be taken down a peg or two," hissed the Snake-Killer. It is not easy to hiss a sentence without a single "s" in it, and the fact that he succeeded in doing so shows to what a pitch of emotion the man had been goaded by Ferdinand's maddening air of superiority.

"Yes, but what can we do?" queried an octogenarian, when this last remark had been passed on to him down his ear-trumpet.

"That's the trouble," sighed the Scooper. "What can we do?" And there was a sorrowful shaking of heads.

"I know!" exclaimed the Cat-Stroker, who had not hitherto spoken. He was a lawyer, and a man of subtle and sinister mind. "I have it! There's a boy in my office — young Parsloe — who could beat this man Dibble hollow. I'll wire him to come down here and we'll spring him on this fellow and knock some of the conceit out of him."

There was a chorus of approval.

"But are you sure he can beat him?" asked the Snake-Killer, anxiously. "It would never do to make a mistake."

"Of course I'm sure," said the Cat-Stroker. "George Parsloe once went round in ninety-four."

"Many changes there have been since 'ninety-four," said the octogenarian, nodding sagely. "Ah, many, many changes. None of these motor-cars then, tearing about and killing — "

Kindly hands led him off to have an egg-and-milk, and the

remaining conspirators returned to the point at issue with bent brows.

"Ninety-four?" said the Scooper, incredulously. "Do you mean counting every stroke?"

"Counting every stroke."

"Not conceding himself any putts?"

"Not one."

"Wire him to come at once," said the meeting with one voice.

That night the Cat-Stroker approached Ferdinand, smooth, subtle, lawyer-like.

"Oh, Dibble," he said, "just the man I wanted to see. Dibble, there's a young friend of mine coming down here who goes in for golf a little. George Parsloe is his name. I was wondering if you could spare time to give him a game. He is just a novice, you know."

"I shall be delighted to play a round with him," said Ferdinand, kindly.

"He might pick up a pointer or two from watching you," said the Cat-Stroker.

"True, true," said Ferdinand.

"Then I'll introduce you when he shows up."

"Delighted," said Ferdinand.

He was in excellent humour that night, for he had had a letter from Barbara saying that she was arriving on the next day but one.

It was Ferdinand's healthy custom of a morning to get up in good time and take a dip in the sea before breakfast. On the morning of the day of Barbara's arrival, he arose, as usual, donned his flannels, took a good look at the cup, and started out. It was a fine, fresh morning, and he glowed both externally and internally. As he crossed the links, for the nearest route to the water was through the fairway of the seventh, he was whistling happily and rehearsing in his mind the opening sentences of his proposal. For it was his firm resolve that night after dinner to ask Barbara to marry him. He was proceeding over the smooth turf without a care in the world, when there was a sudden cry of "Fore!" and the next moment a golf ball, missing him by inches, sailed up the fairway and came to a rest fifty yards from where he stood. He looked round and observed a figure coming towards him from the tee.

The distance from the tee was fully a hundred and thirty yards. Add fifty to that, and you have a hundred and eighty yards. No such drive had been made on the Marvis Bay links since their foundation, and such is the generous spirit of the true golfer that Ferdinand's first emotion, after the not inexcusable spasm of panic caused by the hum of the ball past his ear, was one of cordial admiration. By some kindly miracle, he supposed, one of his hotel acquaintances had been permitted for once in his life to time a drive right. It was only when the other man came up that there began to steal over him a sickening apprehension. The faces of all those who hewed divots on the hotel course were familiar to him, and the fact that this fellow was a stranger seemed to point with dreadful certainty to his being the man he had agreed to play.

"Sorry," said the man. He was a tall, strikingly handsome youth, with brown eyes and a dark moustache.

"Oh, that's all right," said Ferdinand. "Er — do you always drive like that?"

"Well, I generally get a bit longer ball, but I'm off my drive this morning. It's lucky I came out and got this practice. I'm playing a match to-morrow with a fellow named Dibble, who's a local champion, or something."

"Me," said Ferdinand, humbly.

"Eh? Oh, you?" Mr. Parsloe eyed him appraisingly. "Well, may the best man win."

As this was precisely what Ferdinand was afraid was going to happen, he nodded in a sickly manner and tottered off to his bathe. The magic had gone out of the morning. The sun

still shone, but in a silly, feeble way; and a cold and depressing wind had sprung up. For Ferdinand's inferiority complex, which had seemed cured for ever, was back again,
doing business at the old stand.

How sad it is in this life that the moment to which we have
looked forward with the most glowing anticipation so often
turns out on arrival, flat, cold, and disappointing. For ten days
Barbara Medway had been living for that meeting with Ferdinand, when, getting out of the train, she would see him
popping about on the horizon with the lovelight sparkling in
his eyes and words of devotion trembling on his lips. The
poor girl never doubted for an instant that he would unleash
his pent-up emotions inside the first five minutes, and her
only worry was lest he should give an embarrassing publicity
to the sacred scene by falling on his knees on the station
platform.

"Well, here I am at last," she cried gaily.

"Hullo!" said Ferdinand, with a twisted smile.

The girl looked at him, chilled. How could she know that
his peculiar manner was due entirely to the severe attack of
cold feet resultant upon his meeting with George Parsloe
that morning? The interpretation which she placed upon it
was that he was not glad to see her. If he had behaved like
this before, she would, of course, have put it down to ingrowing goofery, but now she had his written statements to prove
that for the last ten days his golf had been one long series of
triumphs.

"I got your letters," she said, persevering bravely.

"I thought you would," said Ferdinand, absently.

"You seem to have been doing wonders."

"Yes."

There was a silence.

"Have a nice journey?" said Ferdinand.

"Very," said Barbara.

She spoke coldly, for she was madder than a wet hen. She saw it all now. In the ten days since they had parted, his love, she realised, had waned. Some other girl, met in the romantic surroundings of this picturesque resort, had supplanted her in his affections. She knew how quickly Cupid gets off the mark at a summer hotel, and for an instant she blamed herself for ever having been so ivory-skulled as to let him come to this place alone. Then regret was swallowed up in wrath, and she became so glacial that Ferdinand, who had been on the point of telling her the secret of his gloom, retired into his shell and conversation during the drive to the hotel never soared above a certain level. Ferdinand said the sunshine was nice and Barbara said yes, it was nice, and Ferdinand said it looked pretty on the water, and Barbara said yes, it did look pretty on the water, and Ferdinand said he hoped it was not going to rain, and Barbara said yes, it would be a pity if it rained. And then there was another lengthy silence.

"How is my uncle?" asked Barbara at last.

I omitted to mention that the individual to whom I have referred as the Cat-Stroker was Barbara's mother's brother, and her host at Marvis Bay.

"Your uncle?"

"His name is Tuttle. Have you met him?"

"Oh yes. I've seen a good deal of him. He has got a friend staying with him," said Ferdinand, his mind returning to the matter nearest his heart. "A fellow named Parsloe."

"Oh, is George Parsloe here? How jolly!"

"Do you know him?" barked Ferdinand, hollowly. He would not have supposed that anything could have added to his existing depression, but he was conscious now of having slipped a few rungs farther down the ladder of gloom. There had been a horribly joyful ring in her voice. Ah, well, he reflected morosely, how like life it all was! We never know what the morrow may bring forth. We strike a good patch and are beginning to think pretty well of ourselves, and along comes a George Parsloe.

"Of course I do," said Barbara. "Why, there he is."

The cab had drawn up at the door of the hotel, and on the porch George Parsloe was airing his graceful person. To Ferdinand's fevered eye he looked like a Greek god, and his inferiority complex began to exhibit symptoms of elephantiasis. How could he compete at love or golf with a fellow who looked as if he had stepped out of the movies and considered himself off his drive when he did a hundred and eighty yards?

"Geor-gee!" cried Barbara, blithely. "Hullo, George!"

"Why, hullo, Barbara!"

They fell into pleasant conversation, while Ferdinand hung miserably about in the offing. And presently, feeling that his society was not essential to their happiness, he slunk away.

George Parsloe dined at the Cat-Stroker's table that night, and it was with George Parsloe that Barbara roamed in the moonlight after dinner. Ferdinand, after a profitless hour at the billiard-table, went early to his room. But not even the rays of the moon, glinting on his cup, could soothe the fever in his soul. He practised putting sombrely into his tooth-glass for a while; then, going to bed, fell at last into a troubled sleep.

Barbara slept late the next morning and breakfasted in her room. Coming down towards noon, she found a strange emptiness in the hotel. It was her experience of summer hotels that a really fine day like this one was the cue for half the inhabitants to collect in the lounge, shut all the windows, and talk about conditions in the jute industry. To her surprise, though the sun was streaming down from a cloudless sky, the only occupant of the lounge was the octogenarian with the ear-trumpet. She observed that he was chuckling to himself in a senile manner.

"Good morning," she said, politely, for she had made his acquaintance on the previous evening.

"Hey?" said the octogenarian, suspending his chuckling and getting his trumpet into position.

"I said 'Good morning!' " roared Barbara into the receiver.

"Hey?"

"Good morning!"

"Ah! Yes, it's a very fine morning, a very fine morning. If it wasn't for missing my bun and glass of milk at twelve sharp," said the octogenarian, "I'd be down on the links. That's where I'd be, down on the links. If it wasn't for missing my bun and glass of milk."

This refreshment arriving at this moment he dismantled the radio outfit and began to restore his tissues.

"Watching the match," he explained, pausing for a moment in his bun-mangling.

"What match?"

The octogenarian sipped his milk.

"What match?" repeated Barbara.

"Hey?"

"What match?"

The octogenarian began to chuckle again and nearly swallowed a crumb the wrong way.

"Take some of the conceit out of him," he gurgled.

"Out of who?" asked Barbara, knowing perfectly well that she should have said "whom."

"Yes," said the octogenarian.

"Who is conceited?"

"Ah! This young fellow, Dibble. Very conceited. I saw it in his eye from the first, but nobody would listen to me. Mark my words, I said, that boy needs taking down a peg or two. Well, he's going to be this morning. Your uncle wired to young Parsloe to come down, and he's arranged a match between them. Dibble — " Here the octogenarian choked again and had to rinse himself out with milk, "Dibble doesn't know that Parsloe once went round in ninety-four!"

"What?"

Everything seemed to go black to Barbara. Through a murky mist she appeared to be looking at a Negro octogenarian sipping ink. Then her eyes cleared, and she found herself clutching for support at the back of the chair. She understood now. She realised why Ferdinand had been so distrait, and her whole heart went out to him in a spasm of maternal pity. How she had wronged him!

"Take some of the conceit out of him," the octogenarian was mumbling, and Barbara felt a sudden sharp loathing for the old man. For two pins she could have dropped a beetle in his milk. Then the need for action roused her. What action? She did not know. All she knew was that she must act.

"Oh!" she cried.

"Hey?" said the octogenarian, bringing his trumpet to the ready.

But Barbara had gone.

It was not far to the links, and Barbara covered the distance on flying feet. She reached the club-house, but the course was empty except for the Scooper, who was preparing to drive off the first tee. In spite of the fact that something seemed to tell her subconsciously that this was one of the sights she ought not to miss, the girl did not wait to watch. Assuming that the match had started soon after breakfast, it must by now have reached one of the holes on the second nine. She ran down the hill, looking to left and right, and was presently aware of a group of spectators clustered about a green in the distance. As she hurried towards them they moved away, and now she could see Ferdinand advancing to the next tee. With a thrill that shook her whole body she realised that he had the honour. So he must have won one hole, at any rate. Then she saw her uncle.

"How are they?" she gasped.

Mr. Tuttle seemed moody. It was apparent that things were not going altogether to his liking.

"All square at the fifteenth," he replied, gloomily.

"All square!"

"Yes. Young Parsloe," said Mr. Tuttle with a sour look in the direction of that lissom athlete, "doesn't seem to be able to do a thing right on the greens. He has been putting like a sheep with the botts."

From the foregoing remark of Mr. Tuttle you will, no doubt, have gleaned at least a clue to the mystery of how Ferdinand Dibble had managed to hold his long-driving adversary up to the fifteenth green, but for all that you will probably consider that some further explanation of this amazing state of affairs is required. Mere bad putting on the part of George Parsloe is not, you feel, sufficient to cover the matter entirely. You are right. There was another very important factor in the situation — to wit, that by some extraordinary chance Ferdinand Dibble had started right off from the first tee, playing the game of a lifetime. Never had he made such drives, never chipped his chip so shrewdly.

About Ferdinand's driving there was as a general thing a fatal stiffness and over-caution which prevented success. And with his chip-shots he rarely achieved accuracy owing to his habit of rearing his head like the lion of the jungle just before the club struck the ball. But to-day he had been swinging with a careless freedom, and his chips had been true and clean. The thing had puzzled him all the way round. It had not elated him, for, owing to Barbara's aloofness and the way in which she had gambolled about George Parsloe like a young lamb in the springtime, he was in too deep a state of dejection to be elated by anything. And now, suddenly, in a flash of clear vision, he perceived the reason why he had been playing so well to-day. It was just because he was not elated. It was simply because he was so profoundly miserable.

That was what Ferdinand told himself as he stepped off the sixteenth, after hitting a screamer down the centre of the fairway, and I am convinced that he was right. Like so many indifferent golfers, Ferdinand Dibble had always made the game hard for himself by thinking too much. He was a deep student of the works of the masters, and whenever he prepared to play a stroke he had a complete mental list of all the mistakes which it was possible to make. He would remember how Taylor had warned against dipping the right shoulder, how Vardon had inveighed against any movement of the head; he would recall how Ray had mentioned the tendency to snatch back the club, how Braid had spoken sadly of those who sin against their better selves by stiffening the muscles and heaving.

The consequence was that when, after waggling in a frozen manner till mere shame urged him to take some definite course of action, he eventually swung, he invariably proceeded to dip his right shoulder, stiffen his muscles, heave, and snatch back the club, at the same time raising his head sharply as in the illustrated plate ("Some Frequent Faults of Beginners — No. 3 — Lifting the Bean") facing page thirty-four of James Braid's *Golf Without Tears*. Today he had been so preoccupied with his broken heart that he had made his shots absently, almost carelessly, with the result that at least one in every three had been a lallapaloosa.

Meanwhile, George Parsloe had driven off and the match was progressing. George was feeling a little flustered by now. He had been given to understand that this bird Dibble was a hundred-at-his-best man, and all the way round the fellow had been reeling off fives in great profusion, and had once actually got a four. True, there had been an occasional six, and even a seven, but that did not alter the main fact that the man was making the dickens of a game of it. With the haughty spirit of one who had once done a ninety-four,

George Parsloe had anticipated being at least three up at the turn. Instead of which he had been two down, and had to fight strenuously to draw level.

Nevertheless, he drove steadily and well, and would certainly have won the hole had it not been for his weak and sinful putting. The same defect caused him to halve the seventeenth, after being on in two, with Ferdinand wandering in the desert and only reaching the green with his fourth. Then, however, Ferdinand holed out from a distance of seven yards, getting a five; which George's three putts just enabled him to equal.

Barbara had watched the proceedings with a beating heart. At first she had looked on from afar; but now, drawn as by a magnet, she approached the tee. Ferdinand was driving off. She held her breath. Ferdinand held his breath. And all around one could see their respective breaths being held by George Parsloe, Mr. Tuttle, and the enthralled crowd of spectators. It was a moment of the acutest tension, and it was broken by the crack of Ferdinand's driver as it met the ball and sent it hopping along the ground for a mere thirty yards. At this supreme crisis in the match Ferdinand Dibble had topped.

George Parsloe teed up his ball. There was a smile of quiet satisfaction on his face. He snuggled the driver in his hands, and gave it a preliminary swish. This, felt George Parsloe, was where the happy ending came. He could drive as he had never driven before. He would so drive that it would take his opponent at least three shots to catch up with him. He drew back his club with infinite caution, poised it at the top of the swing —

"I always wonder — " said a clear, girlish voice, ripping the silence like the explosion of a bomb.

George Parsloe started. His club wobbled. It descended. The ball trickled into the long grass in front of the tee. There was a grim pause.

"You were saying, Miss Medway — " said George Parsloe, in a small, flat voice.

"Oh, I'm so sorry," said Barbara. "I'm afraid I put you off."

"A little, perhaps. Possibly the merest trifle. But you were saying you wondered about something. Can I be of any assistance?"

"I was only saying," said Barbara, "that I always wonder why tees are called tees."

George Parsloe swallowed once or twice. He also blinked a little feverishly. His eyes had a dazed, staring expression.

"I'm afraid I cannot tell you offhand," he said, "but I will make a point of consulting some good encyclopædia at the earliest opportunity."

"Thank you so much."

"Not at all. It will be a pleasure. In case you were thinking of inquiring at the moment when I am putting why greens are called greens, may I venture the suggestion now that it is because they are green?"

And, so saying, George Parsloe stalked to his ball and found it nestling in the heart of some shrub of which, not being a botanist, I cannot give you the name. It was a close-knit, adhesive shrub, and it twined its tentacles so lovingly around George Parsloe's niblick that he missed his first shot altogether. His second made the ball rock, and his third dislodged it. Playing a full swing with his brassie and being by now a mere cauldron of seething emotions he missed his fourth. His fifth came to within a few inches of Ferdinand's drive, and he picked it up and hurled it from him into the rough as if it had been something venomous.

"Your hole and match," said George Parsloe, thinly.

Ferdinand Dibble sat beside the glittering ocean. He had hurried off the course with swift strides the moment George Parsloe had spoken those bitter words. He wanted to be alone with his thoughts.

They were mixed thoughts. For a moment joy at the reflection that he had won a tough match came irresistibly to the surface, only to sink again as he remembered that life, whatever its triumphs, could hold nothing for him now that Barbara Medway loved another.

"Mr. Dibble!"

He looked up. She was standing at his side. He gulped and rose to his feet.

"Yes?"

There was a silence.

"Doesn't the sun look pretty on the water?" said Barbara.

Ferdinand groaned. This was too much.

"Leave me," he said, hollowly. "Go back to your Parsloe, the man with whom you walked in the moonlight beside this same water."

"Well, why shouldn't I walk with Mr. Parsloe in the moonlight beside this same water?" demanded Barbara, with spirit.

"I never said," replied Ferdinand, for he was a fair man at heart, "that you shouldn't walk with Mr. Parsloe beside this same water. I simply said you did walk with Mr. Parsloe beside this same water."

"I've a perfect right to walk with Mr. Parsloe beside this same water," persisted Barbara. "He and I are old friends."

Ferdinand groaned again.

"Exactly! There you are! As I suspected. Old friends. Played together as children, and what not, I shouldn't wonder."

"No, we didn't. I've only known him five years. But he is engaged to be married to my greatest chum, so that draws us together."

Ferdinand uttered a strangled cry.

"Parsloe engaged to be married!"

"Yes. The wedding takes place next month."

"But look here." Ferdinand's forehead was wrinkled. He

was thinking tensely. "Look here," said Ferdinand, a close reasoner. "If Parsloe's engaged to your greatest chum, he can't be in love with *you.*"

"No."

"And you aren't in love with him?"

"No."

"Then, by gad," said Ferdinand, "how about it?"

"What do you mean?"

"Will you marry me?" bellowed Ferdinand.

"Yes."

"You will?"

"Of course I will."

"Darling!" cried Ferdinand.

"There is only one thing that bothers me a bit," said Ferdinand, thoughtfully, as they strolled together over the scented meadows, while in the trees above them a thousand birds trilled Mendelssohn's Wedding March.

"What is that?"

"Well, I'll tell you," said Ferdinand. "The fact is, I've just discovered the great secret of golf. You can't play a really hot game unless you're so miserable that you don't worry over your shots. Take the case of a chip-shot, for instance. If you're really wretched, you don't care where the ball is going and so you don't raise your head to see. Grief automatically prevents pressing and over-swinging. Look at the top-notchers. Have you ever seen a happy pro?"

"No. I don't think I have."

"Well, then!"

"But pros are all Scotchmen," argued Barbara.

"It doesn't matter. I'm sure I'm right. And the darned thing is that I'm going to be so infernally happy all the rest of my life that I suppose my handicap will go up to thirty or something."

Barbara squeezed his hand lovingly.

"Don't worry, precious," she said, soothingly. "It will be all right. I am a woman, and, once we are married, I shall be able to think of at least a hundred ways of snootering you to such an extent that you'll be fit to win the Amateur Championship."

"You will?" said Ferdinand, anxiously. "You're sure?"

"Quite, quite sure, dearest," said Barbara.

"My angel!" said Ferdinand.

He folded her in his arms, using the interlocking grip.

A Mixed Threesome

O

It was the holiday season, and during the holidays the Greens Committees have decided that the payment of one hundred dollars shall entitle fathers of families not only to infest the course themselves, but also to decant their nearest and dearest upon it in whatever quantity they please. All over the links, in consequence, happy, laughing groups of children had broken out like a rash. A wan-faced adult, who had been held up for ten minutes while a drove of issue quarrelled over whether little Claude had taken two hundred or two hundred and twenty approach shots to reach the ninth green sank into a seat beside the Oldest Member.

"What luck?" inquired the Sage.

"None to speak of," returned the other, moodily. "I thought I had bagged a small boy in a Lord Fauntleroy suit on the sixth, but he ducked. These children make me tired. They should be bowling their hoops in the road. Golf is a game for grown-ups. How can a fellow play, with a platoon of progeny blocking him at every hole?"

The Oldest Member shook his head. He could not subscribe to these sentiments.

No doubt (said the Oldest Member) the summer golf-child is, from the point of view of the player who likes to get round the course in a single afternoon, something of a trial; but, personally, I confess, it pleases me to see my fellow human beings — and into this category golf-children, though at the moment you may not be broad-minded enough to admit it, undoubtedly fall — taking to the noblest of games at an early age. Golf, like measles, should be caught young, for, if postponed to riper years, the results may be serious. Let me tell you the story of Mortimer Sturgis, which illustrates what I mean rather aptly.

Mortimer Sturgis, when I first knew him, was a carefree man of thirty-eight, of amiable character and independent means, which he increased from time to time by judicious ventures on the Stock Exchange. Although he had never played golf, his had not been altogether an ill-spent life. He swung a creditable racket at tennis, was always ready to contribute a baritone solo to charity concerts, and gave freely to the poor. He was what you might call a golden-mean man, good-hearted rather than magnetic, with no serious vices and no heroic virtues. For a hobby, he had taken up the collecting of porcelain vases, and he was engaged to Betty Weston, a charming girl of twenty-five, a lifelong friend of mine.

I liked Mortimer. Everybody liked him. But, at the same time, I was a little surprised that a girl like Betty should have become engaged to him. As I said before, he was not magnetic; and magnetism, I thought, was the chief quality she would have demanded in a man. Betty was one of those ardent, vivid girls, with an intense capacity for hero-worship, and I would have supposed that something more in the nature of a plumed knight or a corsair of the deep would have been her ideal. But, of course, if there is a branch of modern industry where the demand is greater than the supply, it is the manufacture of knights and corsairs; and nowadays a girl, however flaming her aspirations, has to take the best she can get. I must admit that Betty seemed perfectly content with Mortimer.

Such, then, was the state of affairs when Eddie Denton arrived, and the trouble began.

I was escorting Betty home one evening after a tea-party

at which we had been fellow-guests, when, walking down the road, we happened to espy Mortimer. He broke into a run when he saw us, and galloped up, waving a piece of paper in his hand. He was plainly excited, a thing which was unusual in this well-balanced man. His broad, good-humoured face was working violently.

"Good news!" he cried. "Good news! Dear old Eddie's back!"

"Oh, how nice for you, dear!" said Betty. "Eddie Denton is Mortimer's best friend," she explained to me. "He has told me so much about him. I have been looking forward to his coming home. Mortie thinks the world of him."

"So will you, when you know him," cried Mortimer. "Dear old Eddie! He's a wonder! The best fellow on earth! There's nobody like Eddie! He landed yesterday. Just home from Central Africa. He's an explorer, you know," he said to me. "Spends all his time in places where it's death for a white man to go."

"An explorer!" I heard Betty breathe, as if to herself. I was not so impressed, I fear, as she was. Explorers, as a matter of fact, leave me a trifle cold. It has always seemed to me that the difficulties of their life are greatly exaggerated — generally by themselves. In a large country like Africa, for instance, I should imagine that it was almost impossible for a man not to get somewhere if he goes on long enough. Give *me* the fellow who can plunge into the bowels of the earth at Times Square and find the right subway train with nothing but a lot of misleading signs to guide him. However, we are not all constituted alike in this world, and it was apparent from the flush on her cheek and the light in her eyes that Betty admired explorers.

"I wired to him at once," went on Mortimer, "and insisted on his coming down here. It's two years since I saw him. You don't know how I have looked forward, dear, to you and Eddie meeting. He is just your sort. I know how romantic you are and keen on adventure and all that. Well, you should hear Eddie tell the story of how he brought down the bull *bongo* with his last cartridge after all the *pongos,* or native bearers, had fled into the *dongo,* or undergrowth."

"I should love to!" whispered Betty, her eyes glowing. I suppose to an impressionable girl these things really are of absorbing interest. For myself, *bongos* intrigue me even less than *pongos,* while *dongos* frankly bore me. "When do you expect him?"

"He will get my wire to-night. I'm hoping we shall see the dear old fellow to-morrow afternoon some time. How surprised old Eddie will be to hear that I'm engaged. He's such a confirmed bachelor himself. He told me once that he considered the wisest thing ever said by human tongue was the Swahili proverb — 'Whoso taketh a woman into his kraal depositeth himself straightway in the *wongo.*' *Wongo,* he tells me, is a sort of broth composed of herbs and meat-bones, corresponding to our soup. You must get Eddie to give it you in the original Swahili. It sounds even better."

I saw the girl's eyes flash, and there came into her face that peculiar set expression which married men know. It passed in an instant, but not before it had given me material for thought which lasted me all the way to my house and into the silent watches of the night. I was fond of Mortimer Sturgis, and I could see trouble ahead for him as plainly as though I had been a palmist reading his hand at two guineas a visit. There are other proverbs fully as wise as the one which Mortimer had translated from the Swahili, and one of the wisest is that quaint old East London saying, handed down from one generation of costermongers to another, and whispered at midnight in the wigwams of the whelk-sellers: "Never introduce your donah to a pal." In those seven words is contained the wisdom of the ages.

I could read the future so plainly. What but one thing could happen after Mortimer had influenced Betty's imagination with his stories of his friend's romantic career, and added the finishing touch by advertising him as a woman-hater? He might just as well have asked for his ring back at once. My heart bled for Mortimer.

I happened to call at his house on the second evening of the explorer's visit, and already the mischief had been done.

Denton was one of those lean, hard-bitten men with smouldering eyes and a brick-red complexion. He looked what he was, the man of action and enterprise. He had the wiry frame and strong jaw without which no explorer is complete, and Mortimer, beside him, seemed but a poor, soft product of our hot-house civilisation. Mortimer, I forgot to say, wore glasses; and, if there is one time more than another when a man should not wear glasses, it is while a strong-faced, keen-eyed wanderer in the wilds is telling a beautiful girl the story of his adventures.

For this was what Denton was doing. My arrival seemed to have interrupted him in the middle of a narrative. He shook my hand in a strong, silent sort of way, and resumed:

"Well, the natives seemed fairly friendly, so I decided to stay the night."

I made a mental note never to seem fairly friendly to an explorer. If you do, he always decides to stay the night.

"In the morning they took me down to the river. At this point it widens into a *kongo*, or pool, and it was here, they told me, that the crocodile mostly lived, subsisting on the native oxen — the short-horned *jongos* — which, swept away by the current while crossing the ford above, were carried down on the *longos*, or rapids. It was not, however, till the second evening that I managed to catch sight of his ugly snout above the surface. I waited around, and on the third day I saw him suddenly come out of the water and heave his whole length on to a sandbank in mid-stream and go to sleep in the sun. He was certainly a monster — fully thirty — you have never been in Central Africa, have you, Miss Weston? No? You ought to go there! — fully fifty feet from tip to tail. There he lay, glistening. I shall never forget the sight."

He broke off to light a cigarette. I heard Betty draw in her breath sharply. Mortimer was beaming through his glasses with the air of the owner of a dog which is astonishing a drawing-room with its clever tricks.

"And what did you do then, Mr. Denton?" asked Betty, breathlessly.

"Yes, what did you do then, old chap?" said Mortimer.

Denton blew out the match and dropped it on the ash-tray.

"Eh? Oh," he said, carelessly, "I swam across and shot him."

"Swam across and shot him!"

"Yes. It seemed to me that the chance was too good to be missed. Of course, I might have had a pot at him from the bank, but the chances were I wouldn't have hit him in a vital place. So I swam across to the sandbank, put the muzzle of my gun in his mouth, and pulled the trigger. I have rarely seen a crocodile so taken aback."

"But how dreadfully dangerous!"

"Oh, danger!" Eddie Denton laughed lightly. "One drops into the habit of taking a few risks out there, you know. Talking of danger, the time when things really did look a little nasty was when the wounded *gongo* cornered me in a narrow *tongo* and I only had a pocket-knife with everything in it broken except the corkscrew and the thing for taking stones out of horses' hoofs. It was like this — "

I could bear no more. I am a tender-hearted man, and I made some excuse and got away. From the expression on the girl's face I could see that it was only a question of days before she gave her heart to this romantic newcomer.

As a matter of fact, it was on the following afternoon that she called on me and told me that the worst had happened. I had known her from a child, you understand, and she always confided her troubles to me.

"I want your advice," she began. "I'm so wretched!"

She burst into tears. I could see the poor girl was in a highly nervous condition, so I did my best to calm her by describing how I had once done the long hole in four. My friends tell me that there is no finer soporific, and it seemed as though they may be right, for presently, just as I had reached the point where I laid my approach-putt dead from a distance of thirty feet, she became quieter. She dried her eyes, yawned once or twice, and looked at me bravely.

"I love Eddie Denton!" she said.

"I feared as much. When did you feel this coming on?"

"It crashed on me like a thunderbolt last night after dinner. We were walking in the garden, and he was just telling me how he had been bitten by a poisonous *zongo,* when I seemed to go all giddy. When I came to myself I was in Eddie's arms. His face was pressed against mine, and he was gargling."

"Gargling?"

"I thought so at first. But he reassured me. He was merely speaking in one of the lesser-known dialects of the Walla-Walla natives of eastern Uganda, into which he always drops in moments of great emotion. He soon recovered sufficiently to give me a rough translation, and then I knew that he loved me. He kissed me. I kissed him. We kissed each other."

"And where was Mortimer all this while?"

"Indoors, cataloguing his collection of vases."

For a moment, I confess, I was inclined to abandon Mortimer's cause. A man, I felt, who could stay indoors cataloguing vases while his *fiancée* wandered in the moonlight with explorers deserved all that was coming to him. I overcame the feeling.

"Have you told him?"

"Of course not."

"You don't think it might be of interest to him?"

"How can I tell him? It would break his heart. I am awfully fond of Mortimer. So is Eddie. We would both die rather than do anything to hurt him. Eddie is the soul of honour. He agrees with me that Mortimer must never know."

"Then you aren't going to break off your engagement?"

"I couldn't. Eddie feels the same. He says that, unless something can be done, he will say good-bye to me and creep far, far away to some distant desert, and there, in the great stillness, broken only by the cry of the prowling *yongo,* try to forget."

"When you say 'unless something can be done,' what do you mean? What can be done?"

"I thought you might have something to suggest. Don't you think it possible that somehow Mortimer might take it into his head to break the engagement himself?"

"Absurd! He loves you devotedly."

"I'm afraid so. Only the other day I dropped one of his best vases, and he just smiled and said it didn't matter."

"I can give you even better proof than that. This morning Mortimer came to me and asked me to give him secret lessons in golf."

"Golf! But he despises golf."

"Exactly. But he is going to learn it for your sake."

"But why secret lessons?"

"Because he wants to keep it a surprise for your birthday. Now can you doubt his love?"

"I am not worthy of him!" she whispered.

The words gave me an idea.

"Suppose," I said, "we could convince Mortimer of that!"

"I don't understand."

"Suppose, for instance, he could be made to believe that you were, let us say, a dipsomaniac."

She shook her head. "He knows that already."

"What!"

"Yes; I told him I sometimes walked in my sleep."

"I mean a secret drinker."

"Nothing will induce me to pretend to be a secret drinker."

"Then a drug-fiend?" I suggested, hopefully.

"I hate medicine."

"I have it!" I said. "A kleptomaniac."

"What is that?"

"A person who steals things."

"Oh, that's horrid."

"Not at all. It's a perfectly ladylike thing to do. You don't know you do it."

"But, if I don't know I do it, how do I know I do it?"

"I beg your pardon?"

"I mean, how can I tell Mortimer I do it if I don't know?"

"You don't tell him. I will tell him. I will inform him to-morrow that you called on me this afternoon and stole my watch and" — I glanced about the room — "my silver match-box."

"I'd rather have that little vinaigrette."

"You don't get either. I merely say you stole it. What will happen?"

"Mortimer will hit you with a cleek."

"Not at all. I am an old man. My white hairs protect me. What he will do is to insist on confronting me with you and asking you to deny the foul charge."

"And then?"

"Then you admit it and release him from his engagement."

She sat for a while in silence. I could see that my words had made an impression.

"I think it's a splendid idea. Thank you very much." She rose and moved to the door. "I knew you would suggest something wonderful." She hesitated. "You don't think it would make it sound more plausible if I really took the vinaigrette?" she added, a little wistfully.

"It would spoil everything," I replied, firmly, as I reached for the vinaigrette and locked it carefully in my desk.

She was silent for a moment, and her glance fell on the carpet. That, however, did not worry me. It was nailed down.

"Well, good-bye," she said.

"*Au revoir*," I replied. "I am meeting Mortimer at six-thirty to-morrow. You may expect us round at your house at about eight."

Mortimer was punctual at the tryst next morning. When I reached the tenth tee he was already there. We exchanged a brief greeting and I handed him a driver, outlined the essentials of grip and swing, and bade him go to it.

"It seems a simple game," he said, as he took his stance. "You're sure it's fair to have the ball sitting up on top of a young sand-hill like this?"

"Perfectly fair."

"I mean, I don't want to be coddled because I'm a beginner."

"The ball is always teed up for the drive," I assured him.

"Oh, well, if you say so. But it seems to me to take all the element of sport out of the game. Where do I hit it?"

"Oh, straight ahead."

"But isn't it dangerous? I mean, suppose I smash a window in that house over there?"

He indicated a charming bijou residence some five hundred yards down the fairway.

"In that case," I replied, "the owner comes out in his pajamas and offers you the choice between some nuts and a cigar."

He seemed reassured, and began to address the ball.

I watched him curiously. I never put a club into the hand of a beginner without something of the feeling of the sculptor who surveys a mass of shapeless clay. I experience the emotions of a creator. Here, I say to myself, is a semi-sentient being into whose soulless carcass I am breathing life. A moment before, he was, though technically living, a mere clod. A moment hence he will be a golfer.

While I was still occupied with these meditations Mortimer swung at the ball. The club, whizzing down, brushed the surface of the rubber sphere, toppling it off the tee and propelling it six inches with a slight slice on it.

"Damnation!" said Mortimer, unravelling himself.

I nodded approvingly. His drive had not been anything to write to the golfing journals about, but he was picking up the technique of the game.

"What happened then?"

I told him in a word.

"Your stance was wrong, and your grip was wrong, and you moved your head, and swayed your body, and took your eye off the ball, and pressed, and forgot to use your wrists, and swung back too fast, and let the hands get ahead of the club, and lost your balance, and omitted to pivot on the ball of the left foot, and bent your right knee."

He was silent for a moment.

"There is more in this pastime," he said, "than the casual observer would suspect."

I have noticed, and I suppose other people have noticed, that in the golf education of every man there is a definite point at which he may be said to have crossed the dividing line — the Rubicon, as it were — that separates the golfer from the non-golfer. This moment comes immediately after his first good drive. In the ninety minutes in which I instructed Mortimer Sturgis that morning in the rudiments of the game, he made every variety of drive known to science; but it was not till we were about to leave that he made a good one.

A monument before he had surveyed his blistered hands with sombre disgust.

"It's no good," he said. "I shall never learn this beast of a game. And I don't want to either. It's only fit for lunatics. Where's the sense in it? Hitting a rotten little ball with a stick! If I want exercise, I'll take a stick and go and rattle it along the railings. There's something *in* that! Well, let's be getting along. No good wasting the whole morning out here."

"Try one more drive, and then we'll go."

"All right. If you like. No sense in it, though."

He teed up the ball, took a careless stance, and flicked moodily. There was a sharp crack, the ball shot off the tee, flew a hundred yards in a dead straight line never ten feet above the ground, soared another seventy yards in a graceful arc, struck the turf, rolled, and came to rest within easy mashie distance of the green.

"Splendid!" I cried.

The man seemed stunned.

"How did that happen?"

I told him very simply.

"Your stance was right, and your grip was right, and you kept your head still, and didn't sway your body, and never took your eye off the ball, and slowed back, and let the arms come well through, and rolled the wrists, and let the club-head lead, and kept your balance, and pivoted on the ball of the left foot, and didn't duck the right knee."

"I see," he said. "Yes, I thought that must be it."

"Now let's go home."

"Wait a minute. I just want to remember what I did while it's fresh in my mind. Let me see, this was the way I stood. Or was it more like this? No, like this." He turned to me, beaming. "What a great idea it was, my taking up golf! It's all nonsense what you read in the comic papers about people foozling all over the place and breaking clubs and all that. You've only to exercise a little reasonable care. And what a corking game it is! Nothing like it in the world! I wonder if Betty is up yet. I must go round and show her how I did that drive. A perfect swing, with every ounce of weight, wrist, and muscle behind it. I meant to keep it a secret from the dear girl till I had really learned, but of course I *have* learned now. Let's go round and rout her out."

He had given me my cue. I put my hand on his shoulder and spoke sorrowfully.

"Mortimer, my boy, I fear I have bad news for you."

"Slow back — keep the head — What's that? Bad news?"

"About Betty."

"About Betty? What about her? Don't sway the body — keep the eye on the — "

"Prepare yourself for a shock, my boy. Yesterday afternoon Betty called to see me. When she had gone I found that she had stolen my silver matchbox."

"Stolen your matchbox?"

"Stolen my matchbox."

"Oh, well, I dare say there were faults on both sides," said Mortimer. "Tell me if I sway my body this time."

"You don't grasp what I have said! Do you realise that Betty, the girl you are going to marry, is a kleptomaniac?"

"A kleptomaniac!"

"That is the only possible explanation. Think what this means, my boy. Think how you will feel every time your wife says she is going out to do a little shopping! Think of yourself, left alone at home, watching the clock, saying to yourself, 'Now she is lifting a pair of silk stockings!' 'Now she is hiding gloves in her umbrella!' 'Just about this moment she is getting away with a pearl necklace!' "

"Would she do that?"

"She would! She could not help herself. Or, rather, she could not refrain from helping herself. How about it, my boy?"

"It only draws us closer together," he said.

I was touched, I own. My scheme had failed, but it had proved Mortimer Sturgis to be of pure gold. He stood gazing down the fairway, wrapped in thought.

"By the way," he said, meditatively, "I wonder if the dear girl ever goes to any of those sales — those auction-sales, you know, where you're allowed to inspect the things the day before? They often have some pretty decent vases."

He broke off and fell into a reverie.

From this point onward Mortimer Sturgis proved the truth of what I said to you about the perils of taking up golf at an advanced age. A lifetime of observing my fellow-creatures has convinced me that Nature intended us all to be golfers. In every human being the germ of golf is implanted at birth, and suppression causes it to grow and grow till — it may be at forty, fifty, sixty — it suddenly bursts its bonds and sweeps over the victim like a tidal wave. The wise man, who begins to play in childhood, is enabled to let the poison exude gradually from his system, with no harmful results. But a man like Mortimer Sturgis, with thirty-eight golfless years behind him, is swept off his feet. He is carried away. He loses all sense of proportion. He is like the fly that happens to be sitting on the wall of the dam just when the crack comes.

Mortimer Sturgis gave himself up without a struggle to an orgy of golf such as I have never witnessed in any man. Within two days of that first lesson he had accumulated a collection of clubs large enough to have enabled him to open a shop; and he went on buying them at the rate of two and three a day. On Sundays, when religious scruples would not permit him to buy clubs, he was like a lost spirit. True, he would do his regular four rounds on the day of rest, but he never felt happy. The thought, as he sliced into the rough, that the patent wooden-faced cleek which he intended to purchase next morning might have made all the difference, completely spoiled his enjoyment.

I remember him calling me up on the telephone at three o'clock one morning to tell me that he had solved the problem of putting. He intended in future, he said, to use a croquet mallet, and he wondered that no one had ever thought of it before. The sound of his broken groan when I informed him that croquet mallets were against the rules haunted me for days.

His golf library kept pace with his collection of clubs. He bought all the standard works, subscribed to all the golfing papers, and, when he came across a paragraph in a magazine to the effect that Mr. Hutchings, a British ex-amateur champion, did not begin to play till he was past forty, and that his opponent in the final, Mr. S. H. Fry, had never held a club till his thirty-fifth year, he had it engraved on vellum and framed and hung up beside his shaving-mirror.

And Betty, meanwhile? She, poor child, stared down the years into a bleak future, in which she saw herself parted for ever from the man she loved, and the golf-widow of another for whom — even when he won a medal for lowest net at a weekly handicap with a score of a hundred and three minus twenty-four — she could feel nothing warmer than respect. Those were dreary days for Betty. We three — she and I and Eddie Denton — often talked over Mortimer's strange obsession. Denton said that, except that Mortimer had not come out in pink spots, his symptoms were almost identical with those of the dreaded *mongo-mongo,* the scourge of the West African hinterland. Poor Denton! He had already booked his passage for Africa, and spent hours looking in the atlas for good deserts.

In every fever of human affairs there comes at last the crisis. We may emerge from it healed or we may plunge into still deeper depths of soul-sickness; but always the crisis comes. I was privileged to be present when it came in the affairs of Mortimer Sturgis and Betty Weston.

I had gone into the club-house one afternoon at an hour when it is usually empty, and the first thing I saw, as I entered the main room, which looks out on the ninth green, was

Mortimer. He was grovelling on the floor, and I confess that, when I caught sight of him, my heart stood still. I feared that his reason, sapped by dissipation, had given way. I knew that for weeks, day in and day out, the niblick had hardly ever been out of his hand, and no constitution can stand that.

He looked up as he heard my footstep.

"Hallo," he said. "Can you see a ball anywhere?"

"A ball?" I backed away, reaching for the door-handle. "My dear boy," I said, soothingly, "you have made a mistake. Quite a natural mistake. One anybody would have made. But, as a matter of fact, this is the club-house. The links are outside there. Why not come away with me very quietly and let us see if we can't find some balls on the links? If you will wait here a moment, I will call up Doctor Smithson. He was telling me only this morning that he wanted a good spell of ball-hunting to put him in shape. You don't mind if he joins us?"

"It was a Silver King with my initials on it," Mortimer went on, not heeding me. "I got on the ninth green in eleven with a nice mashie-niblick, but my approach-putt was a little too strong. It came in through that window."

I perceived for the first time that one of the windows facing the course was broken, and my relief was great. I went down on my knees and helped him in his search. We ran the ball to earth finally inside the piano.

"What's the local rule?" inquired Mortimer. "Must I play it where it lies, or may I tee up and lose a stroke? If I have to play it where it lies, I suppose a niblick would be the club?"

It was at this moment that Betty came in. One glance at her pale, set face told me that there was to be a scene, and I would have retired, but that she was between me and the door.

"Hallo, dear," said Mortimer, greeting her with a friendly waggle of his niblick. "I'm bunkered in the piano. My approach-putt was a little strong, and I over-ran the green."

"Mortimer," said the girl, tensely, "I want to ask you one question."

"Yes, dear? I wish, darling, you could have seen my drive at the eighth just now. It was a pip!"

Betty looked at him steadily.

"Are we engaged," she said, "or are we not?"

"Engaged? Oh, to be married? Why, of course. I tried the open stance for a change, and — "

"This morning you promised to take me for a ride. You never appeared. Where were you?"

"Just playing golf."

"Golf! I'm sick of the very name!"

A spasm shook Mortimer.

"You mustn't let people hear you saying things like that!" he said. "I somehow felt, the moment I began my up-swing, that everything was going to be all right. I — "

"I'll give you one more chance. Will you take me for a drive in your car this evening?"

"I can't."

"Why not? What are you doing?"

"Just playing golf!"

"I'm tired of being neglected like this!" cried Betty, stamping her foot. Poor girl, I saw her point of view. It was bad enough for her being engaged to the wrong man, without having him treat her as a mere acquaintance. Her conscience fighting with her love for Eddie Denton had kept her true to Mortimer, and Mortimer accepted the sacrifice with an absent-minded carelessness which would have been galling to any girl. "We might just as well not be engaged at all. You never take me anywhere."

"I asked you to come with me to watch the Open Championship."

"Why don't you ever take me to dances?"

"I can't dance."

"You could learn."

"But I'm not sure if dancing is a good thing for a fellow's game. You never hear of any first-class pro. dancing. James Barnes doesn't dance."

"Well, my mind's made up. Mortimer, you must choose between golf and me."

"But, darling, I went round in a hundred and one yesterday. You can't expect a fellow to give up golf when he's at the top of his game."

"Very well. I have nothing more to say. Our engagement is at an end."

"Don't throw me over, Betty," pleaded Mortimer, and there was that in his voice which cut me to the heart. "You'll make me so miserable. And, when I'm miserable, I always slice my approach shots."

Betty Weston drew herself up. Her face was hard.

"Here is your ring!" she said, and swept from the room.

For a moment after she had gone Mortimer remained very still, looking at the glistening circle in his hand. I stole across the room and patted his shoulder.

"Bear up, my boy, bear up!" I said.

He looked at me piteously.

"Stymied!" he muttered.

"Be brave!"

He went on, speaking as if to himself.

"I had pictured — ah, how often I had pictured! — our little home! Hers and mine. She sewing in her arm-chair, I practising putts on the hearth-rug — " He choked. "While in the corner, little Harry Vardon Sturgis played with little J. H. Taylor Sturgis. And round the room — reading, busy with their childish tasks — little George Duncan Sturgis, Abe Mitchell Sturgis, Harold Hilton Sturgis, Edward Ray Sturgis, Horace Hutchinson Sturgis, and little James Braid Sturgis."

"My boy! My boy!" I cried.

"What's the matter?"

"Weren't you giving yourself rather a large family?"
He shook his head moodily.

"Was I?" he said, dully. "I don't know. What's par?"
There was a silence.

"And yet — " he said, at last, in a low voice. He paused. An odd, bright look had come into his eyes. He seemed suddenly to be himself again, the old, happy, Mortimer Sturgis I had known so well. "And yet," he said, "who knows? Perhaps it is all for the best. They might all have turned out tennis-players!" He raised his niblick again, his face aglow. "Playing thirteen!" he said. "I think the game here would be to chip out through the door and work round the club-house to the green, don't you?"

Little remains to be told. Betty and Eddie have been happily married for years. Mortimer's handicap is now down to eighteen, and he is improving all the time. He was not present at the wedding, being unavoidably detained by a medal tournament; but, if you turn up the files and look at the list of presents, which were both numerous and costly, you will see — somewhere in the middle of the column, the words:

STURGIS, J. MORTIMER.
Two dozen Silver King Golf-balls and one patent
Sturgis Aluminum Self-Adjusting, Self-Compensat-
ing Putting-Cleek.

Excelsior

O

Alfred Jukes and Wilberforce Bream had just holed out at the end of their match for the club championship, the latter sinking a long putt to win, and the young man sitting with the Oldest Member on the terrace overlooking the eighteenth green said that though this meant a loss to his privy purse of ten dollars, his confidence in Jukes remained unimpaired. He still considered him a better golfer than Bream.

The Sage nodded without much enthusiasm.

"You may be right," he agreed. "But I would not call either of them a good golfer."

"They're both scratch."

"True. But it is not mere technical skill that makes a man a good golfer, it is the golfing soul. These two have not the proper attitude of seriousness towards the game. Jukes once returned to the club-house in the middle of a round because there was a thunderstorm and his caddy got struck by lightning, and I have known Bream to concede a hole for the almost frivolous reason that he had sliced his ball into a hornet's nest and was reluctant to play it where it lay. This was not the Bewstridge spirit."

"The what spirit?"

"The spirit that animated Horace Bewstridge, the finest golfer I have ever known."

"Was he scratch?"

"Far from it. His handicap was twenty-four. But though his ball was seldom in the right place, his heart was. When I think what Horace Bewstridge went through that day he battled for the President's Cup, I am reminded of the poem 'Excelsior,' by the late Henry Wadsworth Longfellow, with which you are doubtless familiar."

"I used to recite it as a child."

"I am sorry I missed the treat," said the Oldest Member courteously. "Then you will recall how its hero, in his struggle to reach the heights, was laid stymie after stymie, and how in order to achieve his aim, he had to give up all idea of resting his head upon the maiden's breast, though cordially invited to do so. A tear, if you remember, stood in his bright blue eye, but with a brief 'Excelsior!' he intimated that no business could result. Virtually the same thing that happened to Horace Bewstridge."

"You know," said the young man, "I've always thought that Excelsior bird a bit of a fathead. I mean to say, what was there in it for him? As far I can make out, just the walk."

"Suppose he had been trying to win his first cup?"

"I don't recollect anything being said about any cup. Do they give cups for climbing mountains 'mid snow and ice?"

"We are getting a little muddled," said the Oldest Member. "You appear to be discussing the youth with the banner and the clarion voice, while I am talking about Horace Bewstridge. It may serve to clear the air and disperse the fog of misunderstanding if I tell you the latter's story. And in order that you shall miss none of the finer shades, I must begin by dwelling upon his great love for Vera Witherby."

It was only after the thing had been going on for some time (said the Oldest Member) that I learned of this secret romance in Horace's life. As a rule, the Romeos who live about here are not backward in confiding in me when they fall in love. Indeed, I sometimes feel that I shall have to begin keeping them off with a stick. But Bewstridge was reticent. It was purely by chance that I became aware of his passion.

Excelsior

One rather breezy morning, I was sitting almost exactly where we are sitting now, thinking of this and that, when I observed fluttering towards me across the terrace a sheet of paper. It stopped against my foot, and I picked it up and read its contents. They ran as follows:

MEM

OLD B. Ribs. But watch eyes.
MA B. Bone up on pixies. Flowers. Insects.
I. Symp. breeziness.
A. Concil. If poss. p., but w.o. for s.d.a.

That was all, and I studied it with close attention and, I must confess, a certain amount of alarm. There had been a number of atom-bomb spy scares in the papers recently, and it occurred to me that this might be a secret code, possibly containing information about some local atoms.

It was then that I saw Horace Bewstridge hurrying towards me. He appeared agitated.

"Have you seen a piece of paper?" he asked.

"Would this be it?"

He took it, and seemed to hesitate for a moment.

"I suppose you're wondering what it's all about?"

I admitted to a certain curiosity, and he hesitated again. Then there crept into his eyes the look which I have seen so often in the eyes of young men. I saw that he was about to confide in me. And presently out it all came, like beer from a bottle. He was in love with Vera Witherby, the niece of one Ponsford Botts, a resident in the neighbourhood.

In putting it like that, I am giving you the thing in condensed form, confining myself to the gist. Horace Bewstridge was a little long-winded about it all, going rather deeply into his emotions and speaking at some length about her eyes, which he compared to twin stars. It was several minutes before I was able to enquire how he was making out.

"Have you told your love?" I asked.

FORE!

"Not yet," said Horace Bewstridge. "I goggle a good deal, but for the present am content to leave it at that. You see, I'm working this thing on a system. All the nibs will tell you that everything is done by propaganda nowadays, and that your first move, if you want to get anywhere, must be to rope in a *bloc* of friendly neutrals. I start, accordingly, by making myself solid with the family. I give them the old salve, get them rooting for me, and thus ensure an impressive build-up. Only then do I take direct action and edge into what you might call the *blitzkrieg.* This paper contains notes for my guidance."

"With reference to administering the salve?"

"Exactly."

I took the document from him, and glanced at it again.

"What," I asked, "does 'Old B. Ribs. But watch eyes' signify?"

"Quite simple. Old Botts tells dialect stories about Irishmen named Pat and Mike, and you laugh when he prods you in the ribs. But sometimes he doesn't prod you in the ribs, merely stands there looking pop-eyed. One has to be careful about that."

"Under the heading 'Ma B.,' I see you say: 'Bone up on pixies.' You add the words 'flowers' and 'insects.' "

"Yes. All that is vitally important. Mrs. Botts, I am sorry to say, is a trifle on the whimsy side. Perhaps you have read her books? They are three in number — *My Chums the Pixies, How to Talk to the Flowers,* and *Many of My Best Friends Are Mosquitoes.* The programme calls for a good working knowledge of them all."

"Who is 'I,' against whose name you have written the phrase: 'Symp. breeziness'?"

"That is little Irwin Botts, the son of the house. He is in love with Dorothy Lamour, and not making much of a go of it. He talks to me about her, and I endeavour to be breezily sympathetic."

"And 'A'?"

"Their poodle, Alphonse. The note is to remind me to conciliate him. He is a dog of wide influence, and cannot be ignored."

" 'If poss. p., but w.o. for s.d.a.'?"

"If possible, pat, but watch out for sudden dash at ankles. He is extraordinarily quick on his feet."

I handed back the paper.

"Well," I said, "it all seems a little elaborate, and I should have thought better results would have been obtained by having a direct pop at the girl, but I wish you luck."

In the days which followed, I kept a watchful eye on Horace, for his story had interested me strangely. Now and then, I would see him pacing the terrace with Ponsford Botts at his side and catch references to Pat and Mike, together with an occasional "Begorrah," and I noted how ringing was his guffaw as the other suddenly congealed with bulging eyes.

Once, as I strolled along the road, I heard a noise like machine-gun fire and turned the corner to find him slapping little Irwin's shoulder in a breezy, elder-brotherly manner. His pockets were generally bulging with biscuits for Alphonse, and from time to time he would come and tell me how he was getting along with Mrs. Botts's books. These, he confessed, called for all that he had of resolution and fortitude, but he told me that he was slowly mastering their contents and already knew a lot more about pixies than most people.

It would all have been easier, he said, if he had been in a position to be able to concentrate his whole attention upon them. But of course he had his living to earn and could not afford to neglect his office work. He held a subordinate post in the well-known firm of R. P. Crumbles Inc., purveyors of Silver Sardines (The Sardine with A Soul), and R. P. Crumbles was a hard taskmaster. And, in addition to this, he had entered for the annual handicap competition known as the President's Cup.

It was upon this latter topic, as the date of the tourney drew near, that he spoke almost as frequently and eloquently as upon the theme of his love. He had been playing golf, it appeared, for some seven years, and up till now had never come within even measurable distance of winning a trophy. Generally, he said, it was his putting that dished him. But recently, as the result of reading golf books, he had adopted a super-scientific system, and was now hoping for the best.

It was a stimulating experience to listen to his fine, frank enthusiasm. He spoke of the President's Cup as some young knight of King Arthur's Round Table might have spoken of the Holy Grail. And it was consequently with peculiar satisfaction that I noted his success in the early rounds. Step by step, he won his way into the semi-finals in his bracket, and was enabled to get triumphantly through that critical test owing to the fortunate circumstance of his opponent tripping over a passing cat on the eve of the match and spraining his ankle.

Many members of the club would, of course, have been fully competent to defeat Horace Bewstridge if they had sprained both ankles or even broken both arms, but Mortimer Gooch, his antagonist, was not one of these. He scratched, and Horace walked over into the final.

His chances now, it seemed to me, were extremely good. According to how the semi-final in the other bracket went, he would be playing either Peter Willard, who would be as clay in his hands, or a certain Sir George Copstone, a visiting Englishman whom his employer, R. P. Crumbles, had put up for the club, and who by an odd coincidence was residing as a guest at the house of Ponsford Botts. I had watched this hand across the sea in action, and was convinced that Horace, provided he did not lose his nerve, could trim him nicely.

A meeting on the fifteenth green the afternoon before the

match enabled me to convey these views to the young fellow. We were there to watch the finish of the opposition semi-final, and when Sir George Copstone had won this, I linked my arm in Horace's and told him that in my opinion the thing was in the bag.

"If Peter Willard, our most outstanding golfing cripple, can take this man to the fifteenth, your victory should be a certainty."

"Peter was receiving thirty-eight."

"You could give him fifty. What is this Copstone? A twenty-four like yourself, is he not?"

"Yes."

"Then you need feel no anxiety, my boy," I said, for when I give a pep talk I like it to be a pep talk. "If you are not too busy to-night reading about pixies, you might be looking around your living-room for a spot to put that cup."

He snorted devoutly, and I think he was about to burst into one of those ecstatic monologues of his, but at this moment we reached the terrace. And, as we did so, a harsh, metallic voice called his name, and I perceived, standing at some little distance, a beetle-browed man of formidable aspect, who looked like a cartoon of Capital in a Labour paper. He was smoking a large cigar, with which he beckoned to Horace Bewstridge imperiously, and Horace, leaving my side, ambled up to him like a spaniel. From the fact that, as he ambled, he was bleating "Oh, good evening, Mr. Crumbles. Yes, Mr. Crumbles. I'm coming, Mr. Crumbles," I deduced that this was the eminent sardine fancier who provided him with his weekly envelope.

Their conversation was not an extended one. R. P. Crumbles spoke rapidly and authoritatively for some moments, emphasising his remarks with swift, captain-of-industry prods at Horace's breastbone, and then he turned on his heel and strode off in a strong, economic royalist sort of way, and Horace came back to where I stood.

Now, I had noticed once or twice during the interview that the young fellow had seemed to totter on his axis, and as he drew nearer, his pallid face, with its starting eyes and drooping jaw, told me that all was not well.

"That was my boss," he said, in a low, faint voice.

"So I had guessed. Why did he call the conference?"

Horace Bewstridge beat his breast.

"It's about Sir George Copstone."

"What about him?"

Horace Bewstridge clutched his hair.

"Apparently this Copstone runs a vast system of chain stores throughout the British Isles, and old Crumbles has been fawning on him ever since his arrival in the hope of getting him to take on the Silver Sardine and propagate it over there. He says that this is a big opportunity for the dear old firm and that it behoves all of us to do our bit and push it along. So — "

"So — ?"

Horace Bewstridge rent his pullover.

"So," he whispered hoarsely, "I've got to play Customer's Golf to-morrow and let the man win that cup."

"Horace!" I cried.

I would have seized his hand and pressed it, but it was not there. Horace Bewstridge had left me. All that my eye encountered was a swirl of dust and his flying form disappearing in the direction of the bar. I understood and sympathized. There are moments in the life of every man when human consolation cannot avail and only two or three quick will meet the case.

I did not see him again until we met next afternoon on the first tee for the start of the final.

You, being a newcomer here (said the Oldest Member) may possibly have formed an erroneous impression regarding this President's Cup of which I have been speaking. Its name, I admit, is misleading, suggesting as it does the guerdon of some terrific tourney battled for by the cream of the local golfing talent. One pictures perspiring scratch men straining every nerve and history being made by amateur champions.

As a matter of fact, it is open for competition only to those whose handicap is not lower than twenty-four, and excites little interest outside the ranks of the submerged tenth who play for it. As a sporting event on our fixture list, as I often have to explain, it may be classed somewhere between the Grandmothers' Umbrella and the All-Day Sucker competed for by children who have not passed their seventh year.

The final, accordingly, did not attract a large gate. In fact, I think I was the only spectator. I was thus enabled to obtain an excellent view of the contestants and to follow their play to the best advantage. And, as on the previous occasions when I had watched him perform, I found myself speculating with no little bewilderment as to how Horace's opponent had got that way.

Sir George Copstone was one of those tall, thin, bony Englishmen who seem to have been left over from the eighteen-sixties. He did not actually wear long sidewhiskers of the type known as Piccadilly Weepers, nor did he really flaunt a fore-and-aft deer-stalker cap of the type affected by Sherlock Holmes, but you got the illusion that this was so, and it was partly the unnerving effect of his appearance on his opponents that had facilitated his making his way into the final. But what had been the basic factor in his success was his method of play.

A deliberate man, this Copstone. Before making a shot, he would inspect his enormous bag of clubs and take out one after another, slowly, as if he were playing spillikens. Having at length made his selection, he would stand motionless beside his ball, staring at it for what seemed an eternity. Only after one had begun to give up hope that life would ever again animate the rigid limbs, would he start his stroke. He was affectionately known on our links as The Frozen Horror.

Even in normal circumstances, a sensitive, highly-strung young man like Horace Bewstridge might well have found himself hard put to it to cope with such an antagonist. And when you take into consideration the fact that he had received those special instructions from the front office, it is not surprising that he should have failed in the opening stages of the encounter to give of his best. The fourth hole found him four down, and one had the feeling that he was lucky not to be five.

At this point, however, there occurred one of those remarkable changes of fortune which are so common in golf and which make it the undisputed king of games. Teeing up at the fifth, Sir George Copstone appeared suddenly to have become afflicted with some form of shaking palsy. Where before he had stood addressing his ball like Lot's wife just after she had been turned into a pillar of salt, he now wriggled like an Ouled Naïl dancer in the throes of colic. Nor did his condition improve as the match progressed. His movements took on an even freer abandon. To cut a long story short, which I am told is a thing I seldom do, he lost four holes in a row, and they came to the ninth all square.

And it was here that I observed an almost equally surprising change in the demeanour of Horace Bewstridge.

Until this moment, Horace had been going through the motions with something of the weary moodiness of a Volga boatman, his face drawn, his manner listless. But now he had become a different man. As he advanced to the ninth tee, his eyes gleamed, his ears wiggled and his lips were set. He looked like a Volga boatman who has just learned that Stalin has purged his employer.

I could see what had happened. Intoxicated with this unexpected success, he was beginning to rebel against those instructions from up top. The almost religious fervour which comes upon a twenty-four-handicap man when he sees a chance of winning his first cup had him in its grip. Who, he was asking himself, was R. P. Crumbles? The man who paid him his salary and could fire him out on his ear, yes, but was money everything? Suppose he won this cup and starved in the gutter, I could almost hear him murmuring, would not that be better than losing the cup and getting his three square a day?

And when on the ninth green, by pure accident, he sank a thirty-foot putt, I saw his lips move and I knew what he was saying to himself. It was the word "Excelsior."

It was as he stood gaping at the hole into which his ball had disappeared that Sir George Copstone spoke for the first time.

"Jolly good shot, what?" said Sir George, a gallant sportsman. "Right in the old crevasse, what, what? I say, look here," he went on, jerking his shoulders in a convulsive gesture, "do you mind if I go and shake out the underlinen? Got a beetle or something down my back."

"Certainly," said Horace.

"Won't keep you long. I'll just strip off the next-the-skins and spring upon it unawares."

He performed another complicated writhing movement, and was about to leave us, when along came R. P. Crumbles.

"How's it going?" asked R. P. Crumbles.

"Eh? What? Going? Oh, one down at the turn."

"He is?"

"No, I am," said Sir George. "He, in sharp contradistinction, is one up. Sank a dashed fine putt on this green. Thirty feet, if an inch. Well, excuse me, I'll just buzz off and bash this beetle."

He hastened away, twitching in every limb, and R. P. Crumbles turned to Horace. His face was suffused.

"Do I get no co-operation, Bewstridge?" he demanded.

"What the devil do you mean by being one up? And what's all this nonsense about thirty-foot putts? How dare you sink thirty-foot putts?"

I could have told him that Horace was in no way responsible for what had occurred and that the thing must be looked on as an Act of God, but I hesitated to wound the young man's feelings, and R. P. Crumbles continued.

"Thirty-foot putts, indeed! Have you forgotten what I told you?"

Horace Bewstridge met his accusing glare without a tremor. His face was like granite. His eyes shone with a strange light.

"I have not forgotten the inter-office memo to which you refer," he said, in a firm, quiet voice. "But I am ignoring it. I intend to trim the pants off this stranger in our midst."

"You do, and see what happens."

"I don't care what happens."

"Bewstridge," said R. P. Crumbles, "nine more holes remain to be played. During these nine holes, think well. I shall be waiting on the eighteenth to see the finish. I shall hope to find," he added significantly, "that the match has ended before then."

He walked away, and I think I have never seen the back of any head look more sinister. Horace, however, merely waved his putter defiantly, as if it had been a banner with a strange device and the other an old man recommending him not to try a pass.

"Nuts to you, R. P. Crumbles!" he cried, with a strange dignity. "Fire me, if you will. This is the only chance I shall ever have of winning a cup, and I'm going to do it."

I stood for a moment motionless. This revelation of the nobility of this young man's soul had stunned me. Then I hurried to where he stood, and gripped his hand. I was still shaking it, when an arch contralto voice spoke behind us.

"Good afternoon, Mr. Bewstridge."

Mrs. Botts was in our midst. She was accompanied by her husband, Ponsford, her son Irwin, and her dog, Alphonse.

"How is the match going?" asked Mrs. Botts.

Horace explained the position of affairs.

"We shall all be on the eighteenth green, to see the finish," said Mrs. Botts. "But you really must not beat Sir George. That would be very naughty. Where is Sir George?"

As she spoke, Sir George Copstone appeared, looking quite his old self again.

"Bashed him!" he said. "Whopping big chap. Put up the dickens of a struggle. But I settled him in the end. He'll think twice before he tackles a Sussex Copstone again."

Mrs. Botts uttered a girlish scream.

"Somebody attacked you, Sir George?"

"I should say so. Whacking great brute of a beetle. But I fixed him."

"You killed a beetle?"

"Well, stunned him, at any rate. Technical knockout."

"But, Sir George, don't you remember what Coleridge said — He prayeth best who loveth best all things both great and small?"

"Not beetles?"

"Of course. Some of my closest chums are beetles."

The other seemed amazed.

"This friend of yours, this Coleridge, really says — he positively asserts that we ought to love beetles?"

"Of course."

"Even when they get under the vest and start doing buck and wing dances along the spine?"

"Of course."

"Sounds a bit of a silly ass to me. Not the sort of chap one would care to know. Well, come on, Bewstridge, let's be moving, what? I say," went on Sir George, as they passed out of earshot, "do you know that old geezer? Potty, what? Over in England, we'd have her in a padded cell before she could say 'Pip, pip.' Beetles, egad! Coleridge, forsooth! And do you know what she said to me this morning? Told me to be careful where I stepped on the front lawn, because it was full of pixies. Can't stand that husband of hers, either. Always talking rot about Irishmen. And what price the son and heir? There's a young blister for you. And as for that flea storage depot she calls a dog . . . Well, I'll tell you. If I'd known what I was letting myself in for, staying at her house, I'd have gone to a hotel. Carry on, Bewstridge. It's your honour."

It was perhaps the exhilaration due to hearing these frank criticisms of a quartette whom he had never liked, though he had striven to love them for Vera Witherby's sake, that lent zip to Horace's drive from the tenth tee. Normally, he was a man who alternated between a weak slice and a robust hook, but on this occasion his ball looked neither to right nor left. He pasted it straight down the middle, and with such vehemence that he had no difficulty in winning the hole and putting himself two up.

But now the tide of fortune began to change again. His recent victory over the beetle had put Sir George Copstone right back into the old mid-season form. Once more he had become the formidable Frozen Horror whose deliberate methods of play had caused three stout men to succumb before his onslaught in the preliminary rounds. With infinite caution, like one suspecting a trap of some kind, he selected clubs from his bulging bag; with unremitting concentration he addressed and struck his ball. And for a while there took place as stern a struggle as I have ever witnessed on the links.

But gradually Sir George secured the upper hand. Little by little he recovered the ground he had lost. He kept turning in steady sevens, and came a time when Horace began to take nines. The strain had uncovered his weak spot. His putting touch had left him.

I could see what was wrong, of course. He was being much too scientific. He was remembering the illustrated plates in the golf books and trying to make the club head move from Spot A through Line B to ball C and that is always a fatal thing for a high handicap man to do. I have talked to a great many of our most successful high handicap men, and they all assured me that the only way in which it was possible to obtain results was to shut the eyes, breathe a short prayer and loose off into the unknown.

Still, there it was, and there was nothing that could be done about it. Horace went on studying the line and taking the Bobby Jones stance and all the rest of it, and gradually, as I say, Sir George recovered the ground he had lost. One down on the thirteenth, he squared the match at the fifteenth, and it was only by holing out a fortunate brassie shot to win on the seventeenth that Horace was enabled to avoid defeat by two and one. As it was, they came to the eighteenth on level terms, and everything, therefore, depended on what Fate held in store for them there.

I had a melancholy feeling that the odds were all in favour of the older man. At the time of which I am speaking, the eighteenth was not the long hole which we are looking at as we sit here, but that short, tricky one which is now the ninth — the one where you stand at the foot of the hill and pop the ball up vertically with a mashie, trusting that you will not overdrive and run across the green into the deep chasm on the other side. At such a hole, a cautious, calculating player like Sir George Copstone inevitably has the advantage over a younger and more ardent antagonist, who is apt to put too much beef behind his tee shot.

My fear, however, that Horace would fall into this error was not fulfilled. His ball soared in a perfect arc, and one could see at a glance that it must have dropped very near the pin. Sir George's effort, though sound and scholarly, was not in the same class, and there could be no doubt that on reaching the summit we should find that he was away. And so it proved. The first thing I saw as I arrived, was a group consisting of Ponsford Botts, little Irwin Botts and the poodle, Alphonse; the second, Horace's ball lying some two feet from the flag; the third, that of his opponent at least six feet beyond it.

Sir George, a fighter to the last, putted to within a few inches of the hole, and I heard Horace draw a deep breath.

"This for it," he said. And, as he spoke, there was a rapid pattering of feet, and what looked like a bundle of black cotton-wool swooped past him, seized the ball in its slavering jaws and bore it away. At this crucial moment, with Horace Bewstridge's fortunes swaying in the balance, the poodle Alphonse had got the party spirit.

The shocked "Hoy!" that sprang from my lips must have sounded to the animal like the Voice of Conscience, for he started visibly and dropped the ball. I had at least prevented him from going to the last awful extreme of carrying it down into the abyss.

But the spot where he had dropped it, was on the very edge of the green, and Horace Bewstridge stood motionless, with ashen face. Once before, in the course of this match, he had sunk a putt of this length, but he was doubting if that sort of thing happened twice in a lifetime. He would have to concentrate, concentrate. With knitted brow, he knelt down to study the line. And, as he did so, Alphonse began to bark.

Horace rose. Almost as clearly as if he had given them verbal utterance, I could read the thoughts that were passing through his mind.

This dog, he was saying to himself, was the apple of Irwin Botts's eye. It was also the apple of Ponsford Botts's eye. To seek it out and kick it in the slats, therefore, would be to shoot that system of his to pieces beyond repair. Irwin Botts would look at him askance. Ponsford Botts would look at him askance. And if they looked at him askance, Vera Witherby would look at him askance, too, for they were presumably the apples of her eye, just as Alphonse was the apple of theirs.

On the other hand, he could not putt with a noise like that going on.

He made his decision. If he should lose Vera Witherby, it would be most unfortunate, but not so unfortunate as losing the President's Cup. Horace Bewstridge, as I have said, was a golfer.

The next moment, the barking had broken off in a sharp yelp, and Alphonse was descending into the chasm like a falling star. Horace returned to his ball, and resumed his study of the line.

The Bottses, Irwin and Ponsford, had been stunned witnesses of the assault. They now gave tongue simultaneously.

"Hey!" cried Irwin Botts.

"Hi!" cried Ponsford Botts.

Horace frowned meditatively at the hole. Even apart from the length of it, it was a difficult shot. He would have to allow for the undulations of the green. There was a nasty little slope there to the right. That must be taken into consideration. There was also, further on, a nasty little slope to the left. The thing called for profound thought, and for some reason he found himself unable to give his whole mind to the problem.

Then he saw what the trouble was. Irwin Botts was standing beside him, shouting "Hey!" in his left ear, and Ponsford Botts was standing on the other side, shouting "Hi!" in his right ear. It was this that was affecting his concentration.

He gazed at them, momentarily at a loss. How, he asked himself, would Bobby Jones have handled a situation like this? The answer came in a flash. He would have taken Irwin Botts by the scruff of his neck, led him to the brink of the chasm and kicked him into it. He would then have come back for Ponsford Botts.

Horace did this, and resumed the scrutiny of the line. And at this moment, accompanied by a pretty, soulful-looking girl in whom I recognized Vera Witherby, R. P. Crumbles came on to the green. As his eye fell on Horace, his face darkened. He asked Sir George Copstone how the match stood.

"I should have thought," he said, chewing his cigar ominously, "that it would have been over long before this. I had supposed that you would have won on about the fifteenth or sixteenth."

"It is a point verging very decidedly on the moot," replied Sir George, "if I'm going to win on the eighteenth. He's got this for it, and I expect him to sink it, now that there's nothing to distract his mind. He was being a bit bothered a moment ago," he explained, "by Botts senior, Botts junior and the Botts dog. But he has just kicked them all into the chasm, and can now give his whole attention to the game. Capable young feller, that. Just holed out a two hundred–yard brassie shot. Judged it to a nicety."

I heard Vera Witherby draw in her breath sharply. R. P. Crumbles, switching his cigar from one side of his mouth to the other, strode across to where Horace was bending over his ball, and spoke rapidly and forcefully.

It was a dangerous thing to do, and one against which his best friends would have advised him. There was no "Yes, Mr. Crumbles," "No, Mr. Crumbles" about Horace Bewstridge now. I saw him straighten him with a testy frown. The next moment, he had attached himself to the scruff of the other's neck and was adding him to the contents of the chasm.

This done, he returned, took another look at the hole with his head on one side, and seemed satisfied. He rose, and addressed his ball. He was drawing the club head back, when a sudden scream rent the air. Glancing over his shoulder, exasperated, he saw that their little group had been joined by Mrs. Botts. She was bending over the edge of the chasm, endeavouring to establish communication with its inmates. Muffled voices rose from the depths.

"Ponsford!"

"Wah, wah, wah."

"Mr. Crumbles!"

"Wah, wah, wah."

"Irwin!"

"Wah, wah, wah."

"Alphonse!"

"Woof, woof, woof."

Mrs. Botts bent still further forward, one hand resting on the turf, the other cupped to her ear.

"What? What did you say? I can't hear. What are you doing down there? What? I can't hear. What is Mr. Crumbles doing down there? Why has he got his foot in Irwin's eye? Irwin, take your eye away from Mr. Crumbles's foot immediately. What? I can't hear. Tell whom he is fired, Mr. Crumbles? I can't hear. Why is Alphonse biting Mr. Crumbles in the leg? What? I can't hear. I wish you would speak plainly. Your mouth's full of what? Ham? Oh, sand? Why is your mouth full of sand? Why is Alphonse now biting Irwin? Skin whom, Mr. Crumbles? What? I can't hear. You've swallowed your cigar? Why? What? I can't hear."

It seemed to Horace Bewstridge, that this sort of thing, unless firmly checked at the source, might go on indefinitely. And to attempt to concentrate while it did, was hopeless. Clicking his tongue in annoyance at these incessant interruptions, he stepped across to where Mrs. Botts crouched. There was a sound like a pistol shot. Mrs. Botts joined the others. Horace came back, rubbing his hand, studied the line again and took his stance.

"Mr. Bewstridge!"

The words, spoken in his left ear just as he was shooting, were little more than a whisper, but they affected Horace as if an ammunition dump had exploded beneath him. Until this moment, he had evidently been unaware of the presence of the girl he loved, and this unexpected announcement of it caused him to putt rather strongly.

His club descended with a convulsive jerk, and the ball, as

if feeling that now that all that scientific nonsense was over, it knew where it was, started off for the hole at forty miles an hour in a dead straight line. There were slopes to the right. There were slopes to the left. It ignored them. Sizzling over the turf, it struck the back of the cup, soared into the air like a rocket, came down, soared up again, fell once more, bounced and rebounced and finally, after rattling round and round for perhaps a quarter of a minute, rested safe at journey's end. The struggle for the President's Cup was over.

"Nice work," said Sir George Copstone. "Your match, what?"

Horace was gazing at Vera Witherby.

"You spoke?" he said.

She blushed in pretty confusion.

"It was nothing. I only wanted to thank you."

"Thank me?"

"For what you did to Aunt Lavender."

"Me, too," said Sir George Copstone, who had joined them. "Precisely what the woman needed. Should be a turning point in her life. That'll take her mind off pixies for a bit. *And* beetles."

Horace stared at the girl. He had thought to see her shrink from him in loathing. Instead of which, she was looking at him with something in her eyes which, if he was not very much mistaken, was the love light.

"Vera . . . Do you mean . . . ?"

Her eyes must have given him his answer, for he sprang forward and clasped her to his bosom, using the interlocking grip. She nestled in his arms.

"I misjudged you, Horace," she whispered. "I thought you were a sap. I mistrusted anyone who could be as fond as you seemed to be of Aunt Lavender, Uncle Ponsford, little Irwin and Alphonse. And I had always yearned for one of those engagements where my man, like Romeo, would run fearful risks to come near me, and I would have to communicate with him by means of notes in hollow trees."

"Romantic," explained Sir George. "Many girls are."

Into the ecstasy of Horace Bewstridge's mood there crept a chilling thought. He had won her love. He had won the President's Cup. But, unless he had quite misinterpreted the recent exchange of remarks between Mrs. Botts and R. P. Crumbles at the chasm side, he had lost his job and so far from being able to support a wife, would now presumably have to starve in the gutter.

He explained this, and Sir George Copstone pooh-poohed vehemently.

"Starve in the gutter? Never heard such bally rot. What do you want to go starving in gutters for? Join me, what? Come over to England, I mean to say, and accept a prominent position in my chain of dashed stores. Name your own salary, of course."

Horace reeled.

"You don't mean that?"

"Of course I mean it. What do you think I meant? What other possible construction could you have put on my words?"

"But you don't know what I can do."

Sir George stared.

"Not know what you can do? Why, I've seen you in action, dash it. If what you have just done isn't enough to give a discerning man an idea of your capabilities, I'd like to know what is. Ever since I went to stay at that house, I've wanted to find someone capable of kicking that dog, kicking that boy, kicking old Botts and giving Ma Botts a juicy one right on the good old spot. I'm not merely grateful to you, my dear chap, profoundly grateful, I'm overcome with admiration. Enormously impressed, I am. Never saw anything so adroit. What I need in my business is a man who thinks on his feet and does it now. Ginger up some of my branch managers a bit. Of course, you must join me, dear old thing, and don't forget about making the salary big. And now that's settled, how about trickling off to the bar and having a few? Yoicks!"

"Yoicks!" said Horace.

"Yoicks!" said Vera Witherby.

"Tallo-ho!" said Sir George.

"Tallo-ho!" said Horace.

"Tally-ho!" said Vera Witherby.

"Tally-bally-ho!" said Sir George, driving the thing home beyond any possibility of misunderstanding. "Come on, let's go."

The Long Hole

O

The young man, as he sat filling his pipe in the club-house smoking-room, was inclined to be bitter.

"If there's one thing that gives me a pain squarely in the centre of the gizzard," he burst out, breaking a silence that had lasted for some minutes, "it's a golf-lawyer. They oughtn't to be allowed on the links."

The Oldest Member, who had been meditatively putting himself outside a cup of tea and a slice of seed-cake, raised his white eyebrows.

"The Law," he said, "is an honourable profession. Why should its practitioners be restrained from indulgence in the game of games?"

"I don't mean actual lawyers," said the young man, his acerbity mellowing a trifle under the influence of tobacco. "I mean the blighters whose best club is the book of rules. You know the sort of excrescences. Every time you think you've won a hole, they dig out Rule eight hundred and fifty-three, section two, sub-section four, to prove that you've disqualified yourself by having an ingrowing toe-nail. . . . Well, take my case." The young man's voice was high and plaintive. "I go out with that man Hemmingway to play an ordinary friendly round — nothing depending on it except a measly ball — and on the seventh he pulls me up and claims the hole simply because I happened to drop my niblick in the bunker."

The Sage shook his head.

"Rules are rules, my boy, and must be kept. It is curious

that you should have brought up this subject, for only a moment before you came in I was thinking of a somewhat curious match which ultimately turned upon a question of the rule-book. It is true that, as far as the actual prize was concerned, it made little difference. . . . But perhaps I had better tell you the whole story from the beginning."

The young man shifted uneasily in his chair.

"Well, you know, I've had a pretty rotten time this afternoon already. . . ."

"I will call my story," said the Sage tranquilly, " 'The Long Hole,' for it involved the playing of what I am inclined to think must be the longest hole in the history of golf."

"I half promised to go and see a man. . . ."

"But I will begin at the beginning," said the Sage. "I see that you are all impatient to hear the full details."

Rollo Bingham and Otis Jukes (said the Oldest Member) had never been friends — their rivalry was too keen to admit of that — but it was not till Amelia Trivett came to stay at Manhooset that a smouldering distaste for each other burst out into the flames of actual enmity. It is ever so. One of the poets, whose name I cannot recall, has a passage, which I am unable at the moment to remember, in one of his works, which for the time being has slipped my mind, which hits off admirably this age-old situation. The gist of his remarks is that lovely woman rarely fails to start something. In the weeks that followed her arrival, being in the same room with the two men was like dropping in on a reunion of Capulets and Montagues.

You see, Rollo and Otis were so exactly equal in their skill on the links that life for them had, for some time past, resolved itself into a silent, bitter struggle in which first one, then the other gained some slight advantage. If Rollo won the May medal by a stroke, Otis would be one ahead in the June competition, only to be nosed out again in July. It was

a state of affairs which, had they been men of a more generous stamp, would have bred a mutual respect, esteem, and
even love. But I am sorry to say that, apart from their golf,
which was in a class of its own as far as this neighbourhood
was concerned, Rollo Bingham and Otis Jukes were nothing
less than a couple of unfortunate incidents. A sorry pair —
and yet, mark you, far from lacking in mere superficial good
looks, they were handsome fellows, both of them, and well
aware of the fact; and, when Amelia Trivett came to stay,
they simply straightened their ties, twirled their mustaches,
and expected her to do the rest.

But here they were disappointed. Perfectly friendly
though she was to both of them, the lovelight was conspicu-
ously absent from her beautiful eyes. And it was not long
before each had come independently to a solution of this
mystery. It was plain to them that the whole trouble lay in
the fact that each neutralised the other's attractions. Otis felt
that, if he could only have a clear field, all would be over
except the sending out of the wedding invitations; and Rollo
was of the opinion that, if he could just call on the girl one
evening without finding the place all littered up with Otis,
his natural charms would swiftly bring home the bacon. And,
indeed, it was true that they had no rivals except themselves.
It happened at the moment that Manhooset was extraordinarily short of eligible bachelors. We marry young in this
delightful spot, and all the likely men were already paired
off. It seemed that, if Amelia Trivett intended to get married,
she would have to select either Rollo Bingham or Otis Jukes.
A dreadful choice.

It had not occurred to me at the outset that my position in
the affair would be anything closer than that of a detached
and mildly interested spectator. Yet it was to me that Rollo
came in his hour of need. When I returned home one evening I found that my man had brought him in and laid him
on the mat in my sitting-room.

I offered him a chair and a cigar, and he came to the point with commendable rapidity.

"Manhooset," he said, directly he had lighted his cigar, "is too small for Otis Jukes and myself."

"Ah, you have been talking it over and decided to move?" I said, delighted. "I think you are perfectly right. Manhooset *is* overbuilt. Men like you and Jukes need a lot of space. Where do you think of going?"

"I'm not going."

"But I thought you said. . . ."

"What I meant was that the time has come when one of us must leave."

"Oh, only one of you?" It was something, of course, but I confess I was disappointed, and I think my disappointment must have shown in my voice, for he looked at me, surprised.

"Surely you wouldn't mind Jukes going?" he said.

"Why, certainly not. He really is going, is he?"

A look of saturnine determination came into Rollo's face.

"He is. He thinks he isn't, but he is."

I failed to understand him, and said so. He looked cautiously about the room, as if to reassure himself that he could not be overheard.

"I suppose you've noticed," he said, "the disgusting way that man Jukes has been hanging 'round Miss Trivett, boring her to death?"

"I have seen them together sometimes."

"I love Amelia Trivett!" said Rollo.

"Poor girl!" I sighed.

"I beg your pardon?"

"Poor girl," I said. "I mean to have Otis Jukes hanging 'round her."

"That's just what I think," said Rollo Bingham. "And that's why we're going to play this match."

"What match?"

"This match we've decided to play. I want you to act as one of the judges, to go along with Jukes and see that he doesn't play any of his tricks. You know what he is! And in a vital match like this. . . ."

"How much are you playing for?"

"The whole world!"

"I beg your pardon?"

"The whole world. It amounts to that. The loser is to leave Manhooset for good, and the winner stays on and marries Amelia Trivett. We have arranged all the details. Rupert Bailey will accompany me, acting as the other judge."

"And you want me to go round with Jukes?"

"Not round," said Rollo Bingham. "Along."

"What is the distinction?"

"We are not going to play a round. Only one hole."

"Sudden death, eh?"

"Not so very sudden. It's a longish hole. We start on the first tee here and hole out in the doorway of the Hotel Astor in Times Square. A distance, I imagine, of about sixteen miles."

I was revolted. About that time a perfect epidemic of freak matches had broken out in the club, and I had strongly opposed them from the start. George Willis had begun it by playing a medal round with the pro, George's first nine against the pro's complete eighteen. I was extremely pleased when the pro did a sixty-two, a record for the course, thus getting home by three strokes and putting George back a matter of two hundred and fifty dollars. After that came the contest between Herbert Widgeon and Montague Brown, the latter, a twenty-four handicap man, being entitled to shout "Boo!" three times during the round at moments selected by himself. There had been many more of these degrading travesties on the sacred game, and I had writhed to see them. Playing freak golf matches is to my mind like ragging a great classical melody. But of the whole collection this one, considering the sentimental interest and the magnitude of the stakes, seemed to me the most terrible. My face, I imagine, betrayed my disgust, for Bingham attempted extenuation.

"It's the only way," he said. "You know how Jukes and I are on the links. We are as level as two men can be. This, of course, is due to his extraordinary luck. Everybody knows that he is the world's champion fluker. I, on the other hand, invariably have the worst luck. The consequence is that in an ordinary round it is always a toss-up which of us wins. The test we propose will eliminate luck. After sixteen miles of give-and-take play, I am certain — that is to say, the better man is certain to be ahead. That is what I meant when I said that Otis Jukes would shortly be leaving Manhooset. Well, may I take it that you will consent to act as one of the judges?"

I considered. After all, the match was likely to be historic, and one always feels tempted to hand one's name down to posterity.

"Very well," I said.

"Excellent. You will have to keep a sharp eye on Jukes, I need scarcely remind you. You will, of course, carry a book of the rules in your pocket and refer to them when you wish to refresh your memory. We start at daybreak, for, if we put it off till later, the course at the other end might be somewhat congested when we reached it. We want to avoid publicity as far as possible. If I took a full iron down Broadway and hit a policeman, it would excite remark."

"It would. I can tell you the exact remark which it would excite."

"We shall take bicycles with us, to minimize the fatigue of covering the distance. Well, I am glad that we have your coöperation. At daybreak to-morrow on the first tee, and don't forget to bring your rules book."

The atmosphere brooding over the first tee, when I

reached it on the following morning, somewhat resembled that of a dueling ground in the days when these affairs were settled with rapiers or pistols. Rupert Bailey, an old friend of mine, was the only cheerful member of the party. I am never at my best in the early morning, and the two rivals glared at each other with silent sneers. I had never supposed till that moment that men ever really sneered at one another outside the movies, but these two were indisputably doing so. They were in the mood when men say "Pshaw!"

They tossed for the honour; and Otis Jukes, having won, drove off with a fine ball that landed well down the course. Rollo Bingham, having teed up, turned to Rupert Bailey.

"Go down on to the fairway of the seventeenth," he said. "I want you to mark my ball."

Rupert stared.

"The seventeenth!"

"I am going to take that direction," said Rollo, pointing over the trees.

"But that will land your second or third shot in the Sound."

"I have provided for that. I have a flat-bottomed boat moored close by the sixteenth green. I shall use a mashie-niblick and chip my ball aboard, row across to the other side, ship it ashore, and carry on. I propose to go across country as far as Flushing. I think it will save me a stroke or two."

I gasped. I had never before realised the man's devilish cunning. His tactics gave him a flying start. Otis, who had driven straight down the course, had as his objective the highroad, which adjoins the waste ground beyond the first green. Once there, he would play the orthodox game by driving his ball along till he reached the Fifty-ninth Street Bridge. While Otis was winding along the highroad, Rollo would have cut off practically two sides of a triangle. And it was hopeless for Otis to imitate his enemy's tactics now. From where his ball lay he would have to cross a wide tract of marsh in order to reach the seventeenth fairway, an impossible feat. And, even if it had been feasible, he had no boat to take him across the water.

He uttered a violent protest. He was an unpleasant young man, almost — it seems absurd to say so, but almost as unpleasant as Rollo Bingham; yet at the moment I am bound to say I sympathised with him.

"Where do you get that stuff?" he demanded. "You can't play fast and loose with the rules like that."

"To what rule do you refer?" said Rollo coldly.

"Well, that damned boat of yours is a hazard, isn't it? And you can't row a hazard about all over the place."

"Why not?"

The simple question seemed to take Otis Jukes aback.

"Why not?" he repeated. "Why not? Well, you can't. That's why."

"There is nothing in the rules," said Rollo Bingham, "against moving a hazard. If a hazard can be moved without disturbing the ball, you are at liberty, I gather, to move it wherever you darn please. Besides, what is all this about moving hazards? I have a perfect right to go for a morning row, haven't I? If I were to ask my doctor, he would probably actually recommend it. I am going to row my boat across the Sound. If it happens to have my ball on board, that's not my affair. I'll play it from where it lies. Am I right in saying that the rules enact that the ball shall be played from where it lies?"

"Very well, then," said Rollo, after we admitted that he was. "Don't let us waste any more time. We will wait for you at Flushing."

He addressed his ball, and drove a beauty over the trees. It flashed out of sight in the direction of the seventeenth tee. Otis and I made our way down the hill to play our second.

It is a curious trait of the human mind that, however little personal interest one may have in the result, it is impossible to prevent oneself taking sides in any event of a competitive nature. I had embarked on this affair in a purely neutral spirit, not caring which of the two won, and only sorry that both could not lose. Yet, as the morning wore on, I found myself almost unconsciously becoming distinctly pro-Jukes. I did not like the man. I objected to his face, his manners, and the colour of his tie. Yet there was something in the dogged way in which he struggled against adversity which touched me and won my grudging support. Many men, I felt, having been so outmanœuvred at the start, would have given up the contest in despair; but Otis Jukes, for all his defects, had the soul of a true golfer. He declined to give up. In grim silence he hacked his ball through the rough till he reached the highroad; and then, having played twenty-seven, set himself resolutely to propel it to New York.

It was a lovely morning, and, as I bicycled along keeping a fatherly eye on Otis's activities, I realised for the first time in my life the full meaning of that exquisite phrase of Coleridge:

> Clothing the palpable and familiar
> With golden exhalations of the dawn,

for in the pellucid air everything seemed weirdly beautiful, even Otis Jukes's heather-mixture knickerbockers, of which hitherto I had never approved. The sun gleamed on their seat, as he bent to make his shots, in a cheerful and almost a poetic way. The birds were singing gaily in the hedgerows, and such was my uplifted state that I, too, burst into song, until Otis petulantly desired me to refrain, on the plea that, though he yielded to no man in his enjoyment of farmyard imitations in their proper place, I put him off his stroke. And so we passed through Bayside in silence and started to cover that long stretch of road which ends in the railway bridge and the gentle descent into Flushing.

Otis was not doing badly. He was at least keeping them straight. And in the circumstances straightness was to be preferred to distance. Soon after leaving Little Neck he had become ambitious and had used his brassie with disastrous results, slicing his fifty-third into the rough on the right of the road. It had taken him ten with the niblick to get back to the car tracks, and this had taught him prudence. He was now using his putter for every shot, and, except when he got trapped in the cross-lines at the top of the hill just before reaching Bayside, he had been in no serious difficulties. He had once, so he informed me, had to fulfil an election bet by rolling a peanut down Seventh Avenue with a toothpick, and this stood him now in good stead. He was playing a nice easy game, getting the full face of the putter on to each shot.

At the top of the slope that drops down into Flushing Main Street, he paused.

"I think I might try my brassie again here," he said. "I have a nice lie."

"Is it wise?" I said.

"What I was thinking," he said, "was that with luck I might wing that man Bingham. I see he is standing right out in the middle of the fairway."

I followed his gaze. It was perfectly true. Rollo Bingham was leaning on his bicycle in the roadway, smoking a cigarette. Even at this distance one could detect the man's disgustingly complacent expression. Rupert Bailey was sitting with his back against the door of the Flushing Garage, looking rather used up. He was a man who liked to keep himself clean and tidy, and it was plain that the 'cross-country trip had done him no good. He seemed to be scraping mud off his face. I learned later that he had had the misfortune to fall into a ditch just beyond Bayside.

"No," said Otis. "On second thought, the safe game is the one to play. I'll stick to the putter."

We dropped down the hill, and presently came up with the opposition. I had not been mistaken in thinking that Rollo looked complacent. The man was smirking.

"Playing three hundred and ninety-six," he said, as we drew near. "How are you?"

I consulted my score-card.

"We have shot a snappy seven hundred and eleven," I said. Rollo exulted openly.

Rupert Bailey made no comment. He was too busy with the alluvial deposits on his person.

"Perhaps you would like to give up the match?" said Rollo to Otis.

"Tchah!" said Otis.

"Might just as well."

"Pah!" said Otis.

"You can't win now."

"Pshaw!" said Otis.

I am aware that Otis's dialogue might have been brighter, but he had been through a trying time.

Rupert Bailey sidled up to me.

"I'm going home," he said.

"Nonsense," I replied. "You must stick to your post. Besides, what could be nicer than a pleasant morning ramble?"

"Pleasant morning ramble my number nine foot! I want to get back to civilisation and set an excavating party with pick-axes to work on me."

"You take too gloomy a view of the matter. You are a little dusty. Nothing more."

"And it's not only the being buried alive that I mind. I cannot stick Rollo Bingham much longer."

"You have found him trying?"

"Trying! Why, after I had fallen into that ditch and was coming up for the third time all the man did was simply to call to me to admire an infernal iron shot he had just made. No sympathy, mind you! Wrapped up in himself. Why don't you make your man give up the match? He can't win."

"I refuse to admit it. Much may happen between here and Times Square."

I have seldom known a prophecy more swiftly fulfilled. At this moment the doors of the Flushing Garage opened and a small car rolled out with a grimy young man in a sweater at the wheel. He brought the machine out into the road, and alighted and went back into the garage, where we heard him shouting unintelligibly to some one in the rear premises. The car remained puffing and panting against the curb.

Engaged in conversation with Rupert Bailey, I was paying little attention to this evidence of an awakening world, when suddenly I heard a hoarse, triumphant cry from Otis Jukes, and turning, I perceived his ball dropping neatly into the car's interior. Otis himself, brandishing a niblick, was dancing about the fairway.

"Now what about your moving hazards?" he cried.

That moment the man in the sweater returned, carrying a spanner. Otis sprang forward.

"I'll give you twenty dollars to drive me to Times Square," he said.

I do not know what the sweater-clad young man's engagements for the morning had been originally, but nothing could have been more obliging than the ready way in which he consented to revise them at a moment's notice. I daresay you have noticed that the sturdy peasantry of our beloved land respond to an offer of twenty dollars as to a bugle-call.

"You're on," said the youth.

"Good!" said Otis Jukes.

"You think you're darned clever," said Rollo Bingham.

"I know it," said Otis.

"Well, then," said Rollo, "perhaps you will tell us how you propose to get the ball out of the car when you reach Times Square?"

"Certainly," replied Otis. "You will observe on the side of the vehicle a convenient handle which, when turned, opens the door. The door thus opened, I shall chip my ball out!"

"I see," said Rollo. "Yes, I never thought of that."

There was something in the way the man spoke that I did not like. His mildness seemed to me suspicious. He had the air of a man who has something up his sleeve. I was still musing on this when Otis called to me impatiently to get in. I did so, and we drove off. Otis was in great spirits. He had ascertained from the young man at the wheel that there was no chance of the opposition being able to hire another car at the garage. This machine was his own property, and the only other one at present in the shop was suffering from complicated trouble of the oiling system and would not be able to be moved for at least another day.

I, however, shook my head when he pointed out the advantages of his position. I was still wondering about Rollo.

"I don't like it," I said.

"Don't like what?"

"Rollo Bingham's manner."

"Of course not," said Otis. "Nobody does. There have been complaints on all sides."

"I mean, when you told him how you intended to get the ball out of the car."

"What was the matter with him?"

"He was too — ha!"

"How do you mean he was too ha?"

"I have it!"

"What?"

"I see the trap he was laying for you. It has just dawned on me. No wonder he didn't object to your opening the door and chipping the ball out. By doing so you would forfeit the match."

"Nonsense. Why?"

"Because," I said, "it is against the rules to tamper with a hazard. If you had got into a sand-trap, would you smooth away the sand? If you had put your shot under a tree, could your caddy hold up the branches to give you a clear shot? Obviously you would disqualify yourself if you touched that door."

Otis's jaw dropped.

"What! Then how the deuce am I to get it out?"

"That," I said gravely, "is a question between you and your Maker."

It was here that Otis Jukes forfeited the sympathy which I had begun to feel for him. A crafty, sinister look came into his eyes.

"Say, listen," he said. "It'll take them an hour to catch up with us. Suppose, during that time, that door happened to open accidentally, as it were, and close again? You wouldn't think it necessary to mention the fact, eh? You would be a good fellow and keep your mouth shut, yes? You might even see your way to go so far as to back me up in a statement to the effect that I hooked it out with my . . . ?"

I was revolted.

"I am a golfer," I said coldly, "and I obey the rules."

"Yes, but . . ."

"Those rules were drawn up by" — I bared my head reverently — "by the Committee of the Royal and Ancient at St. Andrew's. I have always respected them, and I shall not deviate on this occasion from the policy of a lifetime."

Otis Jukes relapsed into a moody silence. He broke it once, crossing the Fifty-ninth Street Bridge, to observe that he would like to know if I called myself a friend of his, — a question which I was able to answer with a whole-hearted negative. After that he did not speak till the car drew up in front of the Astor Hotel in Times Square.

Early as the hour was, a certain bustle and animation already prevailed in that centre of the great city, and the spectacle of a man in a golf-coat and plus-four knickerbockers hacking with a niblick at the floor of an automobile was not long in collecting a crowd of some dimensions. Three messenger-boys, four stenographers, and a gentleman in full evening-dress who obviously possessed or was friendly with someone who possessed a large private stock formed the nucleus of it; and they were joined about the time when Otis addressed the ball in order to play his nine hundred and fifteenth by six newsboys, eleven charladies, and perhaps a dozen assorted loafers, all speculating with the liveliest interest as to which particular asylum had had the honour of sheltering Otis before he had contrived to elude the vigilance of his custodians.

Otis had prepared for some such contingency. He suspended his activities with the niblick, and calmly proceeded to draw from his pocket a large poster which he proceeded to hang over the side of the car. It read:

COME

TO

McCLURG

and MacDONALD

18 West 49th Street

for

ALL GOLFING

SUPPLIES

His knowledge of psychology had not misled him. Directly they gathered that he was advertising something, the crowd declined to look at it; they melted away, and Otis returned to his work in solitude.

He was taking a well-earned rest after playing his eleven hundred and fifth, a nice niblick-shot with lots of wrist behind it, when out of Forty-fifth Street there trickled a weary-looking golf-ball, followed in the order named by Rollo Bingham, resolute but giving a trifle at the knees, and Rupert Bailey on a bicycle. The latter, on whose face and limbs the mud had dried, made an arresting spectacle.

"What are you playing?" I inquired.

FORE!

"Eleven hundred," said Rupert. "We got into a casual dog."

"A casual dog?"

"Yes, just before the bridge. We were coming along nicely, when a stray dog grabbed our nine hundred and ninety-eighth and took it nearly back to Flushing, and we had to start all over again. How are you making out?"

"We have just played our eleven hundred and fifth. A nice even game." I looked at Rollo's ball, which was lying close to the curb. "You are away, I think. Your shot, Bingham."

Rupert Bailey suggested breakfast. He was a man who was altogether too fond of creature comforts. He had not the true golfing spirit.

"Breakfast!" I exclaimed.

"Breakfast," said Rupert firmly. "If you don't know what it is, I can teach you in half a minute. You play it with a pot of coffee, a knife and fork, and about a hundredweight of scrambled eggs. Try it. It's a pastime that grows on you."

I was surprised when Rollo Bingham supported the suggestion. He was so near holing out that I should have supposed that nothing would have kept him from finishing the match. But he agreed heartily.

"Breakfast," he said, "is an excellent idea. You go along in. I'll follow in a moment. I want to buy a paper."

We went into the hotel, and a few minutes later he joined us. Now that we were actually seated at the table, I frankly confess the idea of breakfast was by no means repugnant to me. The keen air and the exercise had given me an appetite, and it was some little time before I was able to assure the waiter definitely that he could cease bringing orders of scrambled eggs. The others having finished also, I suggested a move.

We filed out of the hotel, Otis Jukes leading. When I had passed through the swing-doors, I found him gazing perplexedly up and down the street.

"What is the matter?" I asked.

"It's gone!"

"What has gone?"

"The car!"

"Oh, the car?" said Rollo Bingham. "That's all right. Didn't I tell you about that? I bought it just now and engaged the driver as my chauffeur. I've been meaning to buy a car for a long time."

"Where is it?" said Otis blankly. The man seemed dazed.

"I couldn't tell you to a mile or two," replied Rollo. "I told the man to drive to Boston. Why? Had you any message for him?"

"But my ball was inside it!"

"Now that," said Rollo, "is really unfortunate! Do you mean to tell me you hadn't managed to get it out yet? Yes, that *is* a little awkward for you. It means that you lose the match."

"Lose the match?"

"Certainly. The rules are perfectly definite on that point. A period of five minutes is allowed for each stroke. The player who fails to make his stroke within that time loses the hole. Unfortunate, but there it is!"

Otis Jukes sank down on the sidewalk and buried his face in his hands. He had the look of a broken man.

"Playing eleven hundred and one," said Rollo Bingham in his odiously self-satisfied voice, as he addressed his ball. He laughed jovially. A messenger-boy had paused close by and was watching the proceedings gravely. Rollo Bingham patted him on the head.

"Well, sonny," he said, "what club would *you* use here?"

"I claim the match!" cried Otis Jukes, springing up. Rollo Bingham regarded him coldly.

"I beg your pardon?"

"I claim the match!" repeated Otis Jukes. "The rules say

that a player who asks advice from any person other than his caddy shall lose the hole."

"This is absurd!" said Rollo, but I noticed that he had turned pale.

"I appeal to the judges."

"We sustain the appeal," I said, after a brief consultation with Rupert Bailey. "The rule is perfectly clear."

"But you had lost the match already by not playing within five minutes," said Rollo vehemently.

"It was not my turn to play. You were away."

"Well, play now. Go on! Let's see you make your shot."

"There is no necessity," said Otis frigidly. "Why should I play when you have already disqualified yourself?"

"I claim a draw!"

"I deny the claim."

"I appeal to the judges."

"Very well. We will leave it to the judges."

I consulted with Rupert Bailey. It seemed to me that Otis Jukes was entitled to the verdict. Rupert, who, though an amiable and delightful companion, had always been one of Nature's fat-heads, could not see it. We had to go back to our principals and announce that we had been unable to agree.

"This is ridiculous," said Rollo Bingham. "We ought to have had a third judge."

At this moment, who should come out of the hotel but Amelia Trivett. A veritable goddess from the machine.

"It seems to me," I said, "that you would both be well advised to leave the decision to Miss Trivett. You could have no better referee."

"I'm game," said Otis Jukes.

"Suits *me*," said Rollo Bingham.

"Why, whatever are you all doing here with your golf-clubs?" asked the girl wonderingly.

"These two gentlemen," I explained, "have been playing a match, and a point has arisen on which the judges do not find themselves in agreement. We need an unbiased outside opinion, and we should like to put it up to you. The facts are as follows."

Amelia Trivett listened attentively, but, when I had finished, she shook her head.

"I'm afraid I don't know enough about the game to be able to decide a question like that," she said.

"Then we must consult the National Committee," said Rupert Bailey. "They are the fellows to give judgment."

"I'll tell you who might know," said Amelia Trivett after a moment's thought.

"Who is that?" I asked.

"My *fiancé*. He has just come back from England. That's why I'm in town this morning. I've been down to the dock to meet his boat. He is very good at golf. He won a medal at Little-Mudbury-In-The-Wold the day before he sailed."

There was a tense silence. I had the delicacy not to look at Rollo or Otis. Then the silence was broken by a sharp crack. Rollo Bingham had broken his mashie-niblick across his knee. From the direction where Otis Jukes was standing there came a muffled gulp.

"Shall I ask him?" said Amelia Trivett.

"Don't bother," said Rollo Bingham.

"It doesn't matter," said Otis Jukes.